HANDY *at* HOME

HANDY *at* HOME

Tips on Improving Your Home
from America's Favorite Handyman

RICHARD KARN *and*
GEORGE MAIR

St. Martin's Griffin
New York

HANDY AT HOME. Copyright © 2002 by Richard Karn and George Mair. All rights reserved. Printed in the United States of America. No part of this book may be used or reproduced in any manner whatsoever without written permission except in the case of brief quotations embodied in critical articles or reviews. For information, address St. Martin's Press, 175 Fifth Avenue, New York, N.Y. 10010.

www.stmartins.com

Library of Congress Cataloging-in-Publication Data

Karn, Richard.
    Handy at home : tips on improving your home from America's favorite handyman / Richard Karn and George Mair.
       p. cm.
Includes bibliographical references (p. 283) and index.
    ISBN 0-312-30606-7
    1. Dwellings—Maintenance and repair—Amateurs' manuals.
    2. Dwellings—Remodeling—Amateurs' manuals.   I. Mair, George, 1929–
II. Title.
    TH4817.3 / .K37 / 2002
    643'.7—dc21   2002003648

First Edition: October 2002

10 9 8 7 6 5 4 3 2 1

CONTENTS

Introduction   ix

1. An Ounce of Prevention   1

Easy things to do to keep your home in good shape so you don't have to do the hard things—like repairing and replacing—later

2. Making Repairs   10

A guide to making some of the simple repairs you have to do around the house from time to time

3. Shopping and Saving Money   21

Tips to make your shopping easier and help you save money in the process

4. Keeping Safe   48

How to protect yourself and your family from injury, crime, and other bad things

5. Hiring Help   78

You can't do it all yourself. Here are some tips on hiring the right people to help you.

6. Cooking and Kitchen Tips   89

The kitchen can be warm and friendly or a frustrating mess. Here are hints on making it warm and friendly.

7. Cleaning   98

Helpful hints to make cleaning as quick and easy as possible

8. Gardening   142

Guidance on how to make the outside of your home as nice as the inside

9. Making Storage Space Count   152

Ideas for how to put things away, keep them in good shape, and find them again when you need them

10. Decorating   163

Some inexpensive decorating tips to make your home even more beautiful

11. Maintaining Your Car   171

You depend on your car for transportation and here are some ideas to make sure it is dependable transportation.

12. Caring for Pets and the Homes They Live In   185

Hints on caring for the pet members of the family to make their lives and yours easier

13. Maintaining Your Wardrobe   193

Hints for keeping your clothing neat and clean without a lot of work

14. When Your House is Not Just a Home   203

Tips on "alternative" home uses—the party site and the home office

15. Plumbing   216

Is there anything worse than plumbing out of control? Here are some ideas on easing the pain and the problem.

16. Building and Remodeling 230

Ideas for changing things around and rebuilding for a better place to live

17. Personal Care 254

Hints on all aspects of caring for your family and yourself

18. Odds at the End 275

A variety of hints and tidbits to make you life better with some nifty ideas that just defy categorization

Richard's Guide to Home Improvement Books 283

Index 289

INTRODUCTION

It seems funny, but I am like multibillionaire Bill Gates in a way.

We were both born and raised in Seattle. We both had great parents. He made a lot of money with Windows 95 and I spent a lot of money on the 95 windows. I needed money for the remodel of my house. Okay that's where the similarities end. His house on Lake Washington, which cost $80 million and uses 4.7 million gallons of water every year. The figures that apply to my home are somewhat more modest.

Along the way, however, I learned a lot about home building and care. Part of my knowledge came from my father and grandfather, both of whom were homebuilders. Another part my knowledge came from my pioneer relatives. One of my favorite tips is my grandmother's trick of holding a piece of bread in her mouth when peeling onions. The bread served to protect her from the tear-producing fumes. My grandmother had other special tips.

In this book, I have gathered together hundreds of tips that I have learned over the years on caring for and repairing your home, as well as the stuff you keep in it.

This special knowledge has kept me in good stead as I got involved

GRAMMA KARN'S TOP HOUSEHOLD HINTS

To eliminate garbage disposal odors: Sprinkle baking soda into the disposal, along with a few drops of dishwashing liquid. Turn on the water and disposal and flush thoroughly. For a fresh citrus scent, throw in a few cut-up lemons or limes and run them through the disposal.

To get candle wax drippings out of the carpet: Let the wax harden. You can help by putting ice cubes on it. Then, scrape up what you can. Next, heat with a hair dryer and blot—do not rub—with paper towels. Repeat as necessary.

To get rid of roaches: Mix equal parts boric acid powder and sugar or flour. Sprinkle the mixture in shelves, cabinets, and cracks around the kitchen or place in jar lids set in the kitchen. **Warning!** This mixture is toxic! Keep it away from children and pets.

To clean crayon marks off painted walls: Carefully spray the wall with multipurpose lubricating oil—be careful! Don't let it drip on the floor! Then gently wipe, using a paper towel or clean white cloth.

To remove ink from clothing: If the label says, "dry-clean only," you zip over to the dry cleaner immediately and have him or her do it. If the label says "washable," then, you can clean it yourself. Try cleaning fluid or spot remover. Test in an inconspicuous area to be sure it's safe for the fabric. Then place the fabric stain side down on paper towels and dab cleaner on the stain using a paper or terry-cloth towel. Check the paper towels underneath, changing them frequently, so there's always a clean area under the stain to absorb the ink. Keep at it until the ink is gone.

in the care and repair of assorted apartments and homes in various parts of the country. It has even helped in my acting career—I spent eight years playing Al Borland, the go-to guy on the top-rated sitcom *Home Improvement*.

My home-care background also landed me a wonderful wife. Actress Tudi Roche and I were dating for a year and a half when I decided to pop the question. I wanted to ask her on her birthday, at or near the time of her birth. Luckily it was at noon; I don't know what I would have done if it was three in the morning. However, I waited until noon and just as I was about to propose, the thought occurred that it was New York City time instead of Texas time. So by waiting another hour, we ended up in the housewares section of Zabar's on Manhattan's Upper Westside.

She began crying and said, "You know I hate to cook."

I assumed that was a "yes."

Since that fateful moment in Zabar's kitchenware section, we have been keeping house in various homes, including the kitchens. During this time, we've had our share of household problems. For example, there were three months between the Zabar's proposal and the wedding date. Because we were going to have a lot of people in town, we decided we had to get our little tiny bathroom a facelift. It was a typical New York apartment bathroom: so small you had to back into it.

With a wedding a few months away you don't have enough things to do, so it's always a good idea to start remodeling your bathroom. This project involved scraping off seventeen layers of paint from a prewar building, without, of course, the right tools. I was using a screwdriver and a three-inch paint scraper. Later I found out that there are actual tools designed to do stripping that get into corners and all that.

Meanwhile, Tudi decided to wallpaper one of our walls. As she said afterward, "I got it done, but I cursed the whole way and ended up saying 'I will never do this again. We don't need wallpaper.'"

The prewar tub in the place was bare down to the metal, and we found out you have to paint over that with porcelain paint and let it dry for at least three days during which there are no baths or showers. We did all they said to do, let it dry for three days while we showered at friends', and then it bubbled up anyway.

The kitchen was an old ratty New York apartment kitchen and it had this gross, old linoleum on the floor that I peeled up one day to discover a hardwood floor. Wonderful, we'll revert to the lovely hardwood floor. Trouble was, the linoleum came up, but not all the glue that had been holding it down. We ended up getting some professionals to come in and sand the floors down. Finally, even they had to stop for fear of sanding away all the wood. Then, we started to scrape twelve layers of paint off the kitchen cabinet doors and discovered, after much chipping and scraping, that the panels were glass. In the end, we gave up and broke the old glass out and replaced it.

We moved to California in 1989 and I took a job managing a thirty-unit apartment building in West Hollywood. Once again my years of experience paid off. I spent a lot of time keeping things in repair even though I would make the occasional mistake. When I started managing this big apartment building, I didn't have all that much experience in some of the repair trades such a plumbing. One day, a tenant complained about a leak under her kitchen sink and I went to check it out. It turned out that the pipes were plastic, so I was able to crawl under the sink and tighten them with my bare hands—without using any tools! Man oh man, I was suddenly a plumbing expert. As I proudly left that apartment, I decided to practice on some of the plumbing in the apartment in which my wife, Tudi, and I lived to sharpen my new-found skill.

Back in our apartment I began fiddling with valves and pipes in our bathroom when, all of a sudden, something slipped and a geyser erupted. I yelled and did the only thing I could think of, ran outside to where the building's main valves were and began turning off everything in sight. The second step was calling a plumber, and the third was answering all the irate tenants whose showers and other water-related activities were suddenly interrupted. I told them all it was "a building emergency," which luckily they seemed to accept without further explanation. The plumber showed me the valve I didn't turn off that caused the problem, and soon everything was soon all right. But what an adrenaline-surging experience!

During this time, I was also looking for work as an actor and ultimately got the role of Al Borland doing home improvement things on TV.

In spite of getting the part, I kept my regular job and worked honing my skills as an apartment manager as well as as an actor. I wasn't sure which I would end up doing, and I wanted to be prepared. (I also didn't want to leave the building's owner in the lurch.)

In time, I quit the apartment manager's job. But my role on *Home Improvement* has not only taught me even more about home care, it has connected me with home-improvement professionals at their stores, factories, and conventions all around the country. You've probably seen me in some TV commercials for home improvement products, and I continue to learn from the experts in the home-improvement and home-care field. For example, did you know that the only comfortable new toilets being sold in America are smuggled in from Canada?

In my experience, your relationship with where you live is much like your relationship with whom you live. You fall in love with a home or another person and the first thing you want to do is change it—or them—you want to remodel!

Also, I notice that actors in particular always seem to be involved in a remodeling or do-it-yourself project, even if they aren't inspired by working on a show like *Home Improvement*. This interest undoubtedly stems from our artistic sensibility (unless it's just that we have too much spare time). In any event, during my years on *Home Improvement*, it seemed everybody on the show was involved in some kind of remodeling, including the star, Tim Allen. If it's any consolation, even famous entertainers suffer from the indignities that occur with home-care jobs. For example, after Tim had his house rewired, the TV reception was fuzzy. Seems they put the cable and electric too close together under two feet of cement. In another instance, he spent an enormous amount of money for a special spotlight system to illuminate his classic-car collection. The lights, however, got so hot that they were dangerous, and they were unusable much of the time. Crazy.

My wife and I are friends with actors Shelly and Mike Farrell. You may remember Mike from the hit show *M.A.S.H.* The Farrells bought what we call the "horse house," a house previously owned by Alan Young, who owned the horse Mr. Ed, star of the TV show with the same name. They too were into housekeeping and remodeling and we learned a lot from their experiences with the horse house.

The first house we bought in California was owned by two of the writers for *Cheers*. It was expensive and too big. Thus, it was in perfect keeping with the first rule of home ownership in California, namely, no one is allowed to buy a house they can afford. You may not find this rule in the California statutes, but if West Coast residents didn't follow it, they wouldn't have come up with movies about its veracity. Way back in 1948, Cary Grant starred in a very funny movie called *Mr. Blandings Builds His Dream House*, in which virtually everything about his home construction project goes awry. It seems that the cost of the house goes up every minute. The movie was remade nearly forty years later as *The Money Pit* with Tom Hanks and Shelley Long. As you can see, the rule has withstood the test of time.

THE HOLISTIC HANDYMAN

Your house is really its own little ecosystem, in which very few things function in isolation. So, if you change something in one place, the odds are that the change will affect something else. Suppose you change the grade of your lawn. You may have also inadvertently altered the way that rainwater drains from your property and end up with a flooded basement. Or, you might want to add or remove a window, in turn throwing your heating system out of balance. If you use a chlorine-based scouring powder to clean your wooden cutting board in the kitchen, the chlorine may seep into the wood grain and get absorbed by the next food you cut on that board.

So, the idea is to contemplate the ultimate reach—the ramifications—of every care, repair, and remodeling job. On some of the buildings we remodeled, we worked with a designer who applied the "total home" concept. He used the theatrical device of running the home-improvement movie backward before beginning. That is, he thought at length about the end result before he began. Ironically, the designer we used was a professional actor for twenty-five years before going into home design full-time.

KNOW WHEN TO SAY "WHEN"

Even if you find that you just don't know enough to envision the many effects of a project, you can nonetheless resist being seduced by the *what if?* factor. The *what if?* factor arises when you contemplate enlarging a closet or changing some windows and then say, "That's nice but *what if?*" and add another change.

In our latest home remodeling venture, we planned on changing the kitchen tile. By the time we were through, the *"what if"*'s that sprang from the kitchen tiles resulted in the installation of all new appliances, including two microwaves; staining the cabinets (twice because of error); the addition of antique glass cabinet doors and hard-to-find special pull knobs, a wine rack, and spice rack (both put up improperly); and a tumbled marble floor. All of that started with *what if?*

The same thing happened in the rest of the house. We were going to make some minor changes in one bedroom and ended up raising the ceilings in the dining room, the kitchen, the master bedroom, the living room, and the entryway.

The lesson: when you feel the *what ifs?* coming on, pause and reflect a bit. If this house is so badly in need of so many alterations, why did you buy it in the first place?

EXPECT TO DISAGREE

Another truth about home remodeling is that everybody has his or her own view of what should be done. For example, what got us to decide on replacing the entire kitchen tile was the cow. Yes, the existing tile had a cow pattern with a moo-moo motif throughout. The immediate reaction of my wife was, "The cow must go." This may have been in rebellion against her St. Angelo, Texas, upbringing. Anyhow, that was the decision.

Then, my mother-in-law came visiting and toured through our new house. As she stepped into the kitchen, she exclaimed, "Oh, what a cute cow! You're not going to get rid of the cow are you?"

My wife retorted, "Mom, the cow is history. We are getting rid of this kitchen. I want new tile."

My mother-in-law couldn't understand why we were getting rid of the cow. So I had the contractor take it out and put it in the garage to give to her for Christmas. Fortunately, this provided a happy ending to what could have been a contentious situation.

THE FORMAT OF THIS BOOK

From my family and through my own experiences, I've learned lots of home maintenance and housekeeping tips. I've also learned many things that I think are important to know, but that don't fit into one or two sentences. I struggled with whether to include information that was too extensive to qualify as a "hint" per se. Ultimately, I decided that homeowners were better off with more information than with less. So, when you see the occasional tip that goes on for a few paragraphs, it just means that I couldn't resist letting it all be known.

HANDY *at* HOME

1

AN OUNCE
OF PREVENTION

*Easy things to do to keep your home in good shape so you don't have to do
the hard things—like repairing and replacing—later*

The phrase "preventive maintenance" is widely used and widely confused.
Actually, it means to prevent repairs. It means doing little things now that
are relatively easy and inexpensive to avoid doing big things later that are
harder and costly. Examples are regular attention to keeping hair and guck
from going down the plumbing pipes to avoid an expensive plumbing clean-
out later, and regular painting of wood siding to keep it from blistering or
rotting and having to have it be replaced. So, it comes down to simple, low-
cost activities now to avoid complicated, expensive things later.

RICHARD'S INSPECTION CHECKLIST
Little Checks to Save Big Checks

There are routine examinations you should make regularly around your
home to spot little problems that could turn into major repair jobs (and big
checks drawn on your bank account). To make it easy, here is a home-
happiness checklist of inspections you should make and how frequently you
should make them.

Smoke detectors should be checked every month to make sure they are working. Most smoke detectors have a button you can push for this purpose. You should have smoke detectors all over your house. Be sure you have one in each bedroom because that's where you and your family are most vulnerable—fires that break out when people are sleeping are particularly dangerous. Smoke detectors are either hardwired, which means they are connected directly into your home electrical system or battery operated with a 9-volt battery power source. Some are both—that is, they are hard wired and have a battery as a backup in case the house power fails. In either case, batteries should be changed regularly. An increasingly popular way of remembering to change smoke detector batteries is to install new batteries the day you change to or from daylight saving time.

Check your hot water heater for leaking water. A hot water heater is usually pretty durable (lasting up to ten or fifteen years), but on occasion a defect will allow corrosion to set in, eating a hole in the tank and causing it to leak. This leak usually starts small and expands over time; these leaks are often too hard to fix and a new hot water heater is the best solution. Looking under the heater for puddles of water is a good way to catch this problem before it gets out of control. It's a lot better than standing naked in the shower and finding out there is no hot water.

Check your forced-air furnace filter. If it's dirty, replace it. This is very easy to do since most filters are designed to simply slip in and out of place. Actually, a good idea is to buy several filters at one time at the hardware store. Save the extras in the furnace closet for later use. The dimensions of most filters are written right on the filter's side. For example, if you see a number like 14-24-1, the filter is 14 inches wide, 24 inches long and one inch thick.

In most places, appliances that generate carbon monoxide gas, such as furnaces, hot water heaters, and dryers, are legally required to have venting pipes that expel the gas outside. However, these venting pipes are useless if they have holes, are rusted out, are not properly connected and sealed, or clogged with lint or dirt. So, check them out monthly for wear and tear.

Most modern appliances that we have scattered throughout the house have built-in circuit breakers. This is a kind of fuse that will interrupt the electrical current if there is a ground or electrical short in the appliance that could shock you. Circuit breakers can be found in new models of major appliances such as dishwashers and washers and dryers, as well as smaller items such as blenders. The circuit breakers are generally located inside the appliance, often behind a square or rectangular piece of metal. (The idea is to make the circuit breaker accessible to the owner without having it exposed to the workings of the appliance itself.) Every month you should check that these circuit breakers are still working to protect you and your family. To test them, you will usually find a test button on the appliance to push (just as you do when testing your smoke alarms). Once a month, make a circuit breaker tour of your home and wander around, pushing those test buttons. If you find an appliance with a circuit breaker that doesn't work, disconnect it immediately and either have it repaired or replaced.

EVERY THREE MONTHS

Drain a bucketful of water from your hot water heater. This helps to flush out sediment and reduces the chances of corrosion.

Check all your roof gutters and downspouts to make sure they are all properly connected and firmly fastened in place. Also, clean out leaves and debris so rain can run off freely (we'll talk more about gutters and downspouts in the following pages).

EVERY SIX MONTHS

Check your chimneys and furnace flues to make sure they are open and clear. Look for signs of deterioration such as crumbling mortar, loose bricks, and clogged or poorly fastened flues.

Make a slow circuit of your house on the outside—include a visit to your roof—peeking, poking, and pondering to see where maintenance work might be needed. Consider activities such as trimming bushes and trees, needed paint touch-ups, and the like. This may sound silly to you, but people often just forget about parts of the house that they don't often see. Any number of small problems could be slowly growing into a serious, expensive repair job.

ANNUALLY

With the arrival of spring, make a walking/climbing inspection of the outside of your house to see if the winter weather has caused any problems. Carefully inspect all the outside walls for holes, damage, or deterioration. If you have brick or stone walls, examine the mortar between the bricks or stone. Mortar may begin to crumble from extremes in temperature during the winter and may need tuck pointing (tamping new mortar in to replace any that has crumbled or is missing). If you have wood siding, how does it look? Are any boards pulled away from the house frame? Is it in need of repainting? Check around the doors and windows to see if joints need to be recaulked or if weather stripping needs to be replaced.

Finally, get up on the roof—be careful—to check for holes or missing shingles or tiles. Replacing them now is easy and inexpensive. If you wait until winter comes again, you'll be like the traveler who stayed overnight at a wayside cabin with a leaky roof. When the traveler asked the owner about the leak, the owner said it was a real problem because, when it was raining, he couldn't get up on the roof to fix it and, when it wasn't raining, it wasn't leaking.

It's good to have a professional inspector check out all the major mechanical units in your home, such as the water heater, the furnace, the air-conditioning units, and the like. Also, examine the areas where vents, pipes, and chimneys go through an outside wall. There may be loose bricks or shingles that need resealing or cracks and holes that need to be closed up. It is important to check that the flashing—the metal used for waterproofing, often placed in areas such as where the chimney meets the roof—is intact and secure. You may want to get a professional in to have your chimney swept clean and clear. If your home operates with a septic tank, get it examined in case it needs to be pumped out.

MISCELLANEOUS MAINTENANCE TIPS

Now that you've mastered the critical inspections for home maintenance, here are some tips that cover a wide variety of issues.

ANTS, REPELLING

Use a spray bottle or mister filled with a solution of equal parts vinegar and water around doorjambs, windowsills, water pipes, and foundation cracks to keep ants out.

BATHROOM FIXTURES

In the bathroom, store heavy items underneath the sink. Placing them on shelves is courting disaster. If they fall (which may even bring the entire shelf down), you could need an expensive replacement for a damaged toilet or sink.

Another way to keep your toilet running smoothly is to simply not jam the drain with things that don't belong there. For example, don't throw Q-Tips, disposable diapers or tampons into the toilet. Don't put dirty diapers in the toilet to soak. Soak dirty diapers in a bucket of water and, then throw them into the washing machine. The water remaining in the bucket can be tossed into the toilet.

Another great way to keep your toilet unclogged is to keep the lid down. Experienced plumbers tell me that they have pulled everything from hair curlers to wallets out of toilet lines. The "lid down rule" is particularly helpful anytime kids are in the bathroom. When in the tub, children often play with small toys that could flip into the toilet. Moreover, kids are fascinated by the things that swirl down and disappear!

CARPET STATIC

Zap! Do you get a static shock when you walk on your wall-to-wall carpeting? Some people think this is kind of fun, but many of us don't agree. One solution is a solution. Mix up a solution of fabric softener liquid and water, with a ratio of 1 part softener to to 5 parts water, put it in a plastic spray bottle, and move across the carpeting applying a light mist.

DRAINS

To keep drains open and running smoothly, pour one-half box of old baking soda down the drain followed by one cup white vinegar. When the bubbling stops, run the hot water.

GARAGE DOORS

I strongly recommend that you trim your garage door with weather stripping insulation. This is a heavy rubber strip an inch or so wide, which you can buy at most hardware or home-improvement stores. Normally, you just nail it on the edge of the garage door using galvanized nails with a wide head. Weather-strip *all* edges of the door—it will keep cold wind out of your garage and it will also help you keep mice, rodents, and other vermin out. (As I'll mention later, rodents, cats, and other critters have been known to crawl into the hoods of cars to curl up on the warm engine. Both you and the animal will have a nasty surprise when you start the car in the morning.)

GLASSWARE

Put a metal spoon into a glass before you fill it will hot liquid. The spoon will absorb some of the heat so the glass won't crack from expanding too fast.

When you have nested glasses one inside the other and they're stuck together, put some cold water in the top glass and dip the bottom glass in warm water. The cold will make the top glass contract and warm will make the bottom glass expand and presto magic! The two are unstuck.

PAINTING

A new paint job can significantly improve the durability of the outside of your home as well as the appearance. As with all kinds of improvement tasks, you need to have all the preliminary, base work done before you start on what appears to bēbe the main job. This preparatory work is crucial to a successful final result.

For example, you may buy an excellent exterior paint for your home, but if it doesn't have a clean, dry surface in good repair to cling to when you roll or brush it on, you are not going to have a lasting paint job. So, first inspect the outside surface on which you plan to paint. If your house has shingle siding, test and check each shingle to make sure it isn't loose, broken, or uneven. If the exterior is aluminum or masonry, look for cracks, holes, and missing pieces. Patch, repair, and replace any part of the shingles, siding, masonry, and so on that is broken. A beer-can opener can be handy for scraping open and widening cracks so you can smooth grout into them in preparation for painting. Then, use a wire brush to get off all the loose old paint. It is important that the surface be as clean and as smooth as possible. If old paint simply won't come off the wall, let it be, but be sure to sand paper around the edges to make them smooth.

Picking the color and type of paint is a big part of the fun. A paint store's or hardware store's paint department has a jillion color chips or swatches that are available to help you find the perfect shade. If you have narrowed your choice down to just a few, ask a knowledgeable staff member if anyone else has picked that color for his or her house. If so, maybe you and the family can go by and see how it looks in real life on a real house instead of a 1-inch-square chip. If you have a sample color from some other source that you like, ask a staff member to match it. With all the colors available, it's likely that he or she will be able to do so. In any case, take your time picking the color. You're going to live with it for a long time and another day or three in choosing isn't going to hurt. When you finally make your paint choice, record the manufacturer's name, the paint name, and batch code along with the date and where you bought it. Put that information in a safe place where you can find it in several years when you'll want it.

What type of paint should you use? (Remember what we just said— you're going to live with it for ten or fifteen years, so make sure it is a good investment.) Explain what your project and objectives are to a store staff member, including what kind of surface you're painting on, and get his or her advice. The right paint for a particular surface will vary depending on the climate in which you live. Latex-based paint has become one of the most popular choices because 1) it's easy to work with; 2) it's easy to clean up; and 3) it lasts a long time.

Next, mask any hardware you don't want painted over, like the window and door trim, light fixtures, and so on. Masking tape and vaseline will both work to prevent paint from dripping onto fixtures. Put drop cloths over plants, walks, drives, or any other areas you don't want splattered with paint. If you don't tape or weigh down the drop cloths, you're bound to have paint drippings in the wrong places, and your result will look terribly amateurish. As you're beginning to see, painting the exterior of a building is actually about 75 percent preparation, 15 percent perspiration, and 10 percent painting.

When it comes time to paint, here are some suggestions. Paint the shady side of the house first because the paint won't dry as fast and you'll have more time to get familiar with the characteristics of the paint before you make any major mistakes. I suggest you paint on a warm, nonhumid day when the temperature is between 60 and 85 degrees. Don't start too early when there is still dew on the walls, and take breaks at logical points in the painting job, such as when you have come to the end of a wall section. Before you start painting, take a moment to write the paint brand and color code on the bottom outside of the can for future reference. If you write it on the side, paint drippings will cover it up. Also be sure to scoop a little paint out of the can to diminish spillage. Finally, be a big spender and buy an extra gallon or two of the same paint and color that you won't need for this paint job. You'll be happy you did in months or years to come when you want the same color paint for touch-ups.

PIPES, WINTERIZING

If you live where the temperatures drop below freezing, you need to protect your plumbing (and your bank account!) when you are not there.

Keep the heat on when you are gone for a short time during cold weather. It doesn't have to be as warm as you want it when you are there and it need only be in rooms where you have plumbing pipes with water in them. If you don't keep some heat in these rooms, the water in the pipes will freeze, expand, and burst the pipes. This is not a happy event to discover when you get home. You might also install so-called heat tape or heat cable. This is a tape you can connect to an electricity source (usually with a thermostat) and then wrap around your pipes to keep the water in them warm enough to stay fluid. Don't forget the room where the hot water heater is!

If you are going away for an extended period (like closing up a house for the season), turn off the water at the street and drain all the pipes. Don't forget to drain the hot water heater and the toilet tanks. Leave all your faucets open.

If you find out that you have a frozen pipe, *be careful!* If you heat the frozen pipe too quickly, it can explode in your face and then they will rush you to a nice warm room in the hospital! The best solution is to let the pipe thaw out naturally. If you are too impatient for that, try using a hair dryer to *slowly* heat the pipe. Start at a faucet and gently apply hot air back toward the frozen part of the pipe. With a little time and patience, things will be flowing again.

TRASH BARRELS

Keep stray dogs and other animals from upsetting your trash barrels and making a mess rummaging through your garbage. Obviously, tight lids on your barrels are the first defense. If the lids don't fit just right, try strapping a bungee cord or rope from one side handle, over the lid and through the lid handle, to the barrel handle on the other side. You can also spray ammonia on and around the barrels every few days or soak a rag in ammonia or turpentine and tie it on to the trash-barrel handles. The smell usually discourages animals from coming near. Another method some have suggested is to turn on an old radio and leave it by the trash barrels. The idea presumably is that the marauding animals will think there are people by the barrels and will stay away. I have been unable to learn whether the radio should be tuned to all news, talk, rock-and-roll, or classical for the best results. . . .

2

MAKING REPAIRS

A guide to making some of the simple repairs you have to do
around the house from time to time

The objective of repairing is to restore something—a window, floor, wall, chair—to good, working condition. In this book, I have making repairs follow preventive maintenance, because that is often the sequence of events in real life. Those things we don't properly maintain end up being the things we have to repair. A common home repair involves sealing up cracks and gaps through which we lose heat in the winter and cool air in the summer. This type of work can't really be summed up in a sentence or two, so I've devoted the beginning of the chapter to putting a tight seal on the gaps that occur in most people's homes. The remainder of the chapter is full of simple repair tips.

SEALING WINDOWS, DOORS, AND ASSORTED CRACKS

Cold air from outside can have an amazing chilling effect on your home. It is estimated that unsealed gaps or cracks in the foundation of your home or around windows and doors can really affect inside temperature. Experts believe that a crack only $1/8$ of an inch wide is the equivalent of leaving a window open all winter. Everybody with an opinion on the subject seems to agree that the money you spend on caulking or weather stripping is paid back in one heating season or less by the reduced cost of heating oil, coal, or natural gas you save.

So, sealing up those cracks can pay off in saving heat (and in turn, money).

WEATHER STRIPPING

Weather stripping (rather than caulk) is used around doors that lead to the outside. Weather stripping is relatively easy to apply. It comes in convenient rolls and you just unroll as much as you need for each door bottom, top, or side and tack it on snugly.

CAULKING

A claylike substance you should get to know well is technically called "caulk," and it has been used by mankind (seemingly forever) to tightly seal walls, windows, and roofs. In pioneer days, when cabins were built out of logs, it was impossible to get each log to fit into the next log in a way that was air- and watertight. So, pioneers stuffed mud or sod into the cracks to seal the cabin up against bad weather. The same technique was used with tar or comparable substances to make boats and bridges watertight. We do the same thing today to seal cracks in our walls, around windows and doors, in floors and ceilings, but we have better choices now than just sod or mud or tar. You may use a variety of caulks and different ways of applying them. For household use, we commonly apply caulk with our fingers, a putty knife, a "caulk gun," or a combination of these methods. The caulk gun is like a giant tube of toothpaste with a plunger that forces the caulk into the cracks. The method of application that you use will depend on your own inclination and the nature of the job.

Kinds of Caulk

Of course, you'll need to purchase some caulk before you begin. The following list of some varieties of caulk will get you started, but you may want to discuss your selection with a member of the staff at your local home-improvement store.

- **Silicone Caulk:** Silicone caulk is usually the best stuff. It sticks better than other kinds, lasts longer than others (up to thirty years), and can be used on almost any surface. Silicone caulk should usually be used only on cracks or wall gaps that are one-quarter inch or less in width. The biggest disadvantage to silicone caulk is that it may not take painting, so it remains the color it is—usually white.
- **Butyl Caulk:** Butyl caulk is of good quality and can be used like silicone caulk, but it will last about one-third as long (ten years). One appealing aspect of butyl caulk is that it is available in a lot of different colors.
- **Acrylic Latex Silicone Caulk:** This combination caulk has many of the same characteristics as silicone and butyl caulk, and lasts about twenty years. It is the easiest of all the caulks to manipulate, but it often will not take painting.
- **Acrylic Caulk:** Acrylic caulk is fairly easy to use, has no odor, and cleans up with water. It lasts about ten years.
- **Latex Caulk:** Latex caulk lasts about the same length of time as acrylic caulk and has many of its advantages (it cleans up with water, for example). It comes in many colors and can also be painted.
- **Oil-Based Asphalt Caulk:** Oil-based asphalt caulk lasts a much shorter time than most of the other caulks (about four years), is harder to clean up, and sometimes cracks. So, why use it? It hardens quickly and some experts recommend it as a good caulk to use around chimneys and exhaust pipes that lead through exterior walls.
- **Caulking Variations:** There are two related caulking substances you should also know about for special uses. They are caulking cord and oakum.

Caulking cord, as the name implies, is a form of caulk in a rolled-up rope or cord. It is designed for quick-fix jobs and only lasts a year or two. To use, you simply peel off however much caulking cord you need, cut it, and stuff it in place around windows, air-conditioning units, or whatever. Save whatever you don't use for the next job.

Oakum is a sealing substance that's been around for centuries. To me the word brings back memories of old Prince Valiant cartoons about warrior life in ancient times and Vikings building sailing ships. Specifically, oakum is old, untwisted ropes, often impregnated with tar, used to caulk ship seams. It is forced into cracks with a chisel and a mallet. Ship builders have long stuffed oakum into the seams and spaces between the ship's planks to seal them up watertight. In fact, untwisting old rope to make oakum used to be daily work in medieval prisons and poorhouses. Oakum is still widely used today, but I expect that it's created in a more genteel manner.

How to Caulk

So, now you're ready to apply whatever caulk you decide to use for the holes, gaps, and cracks in your foundation, walls, window and door frames. I urge you to use a caulk gun—a handy device loaded with a cartridge full of caulk. This tool is the easiest, neatest, and most effective way to apply caulk. Essentially it is a device with a chamber for a caulk cartridge and a squeeze handle that allows you to squirt the caulk evenly into spaces where it is needed. Areas that are likely caulking candidates are around window- and doorjambs, faucets, vents, pipes, and electrical outlets as well as where walls meet foundations, other walls, or the roof. Other places to check as possible caulking spots include dryer vents, where porches attach to the house, seams between masonry and siding, chimneys, and inside corners.

- **Step One:** Scrape and brush the crack, seam, or hole clean. If you squirt caulk on a loose piece of wall, the caulk will stick to the loose piece and fall out shortly. You want the caulk to adhere to clean parts of the wall, not old caulk and loose paint or dirt.
- **Step Two:** Check the places to be caulked. Most caulk delivered by a caulk gun is designed to seal up cracks and seams no greater than $1/4$ inch in width. If the space you are looking at is wider than that,

you should narrow the crack or seams by first jamming caulking cord or oakum into the space.

- **Step Three:** Snip off the tip of a caulk cartridge at a 45-degree angle. Puncture the tip by shoving a nail or screwdriver into it. Now, the cartridge is open and ready to use.
- **Step Four:** Insert the cartridge into the caulking gun and begin squeezing the caulk into place in slow, smooth strokes. Let it set and dry.

Repairing Large Plaster Cracks

When you have a large crack in one of your plaster walls, it is not always possible to repair it by filling with wet plaster. You need to get a roll of what is appropriately called "plaster patching tape" at a paint store. With this perforated tape and some wet plaster, you can then do the job with a putty knife.

First, scrape off all loose plaster and then apply wet plaster to the crack. After you have filled it with the wet plaster, press the perforated tape into the wet plaster with a wide putty knife. Scrape and trim any excess plaster off so the patch is nice and smooth and no excess is hanging out of the crack. Let this dry until it is hard. Finish the job off by sanding it smooth so it is the same level as the wall around the crack. Paint to match the wall.

REPAIR TIPS

All the tender loving care you give your home and what's in it will undoubtedly prevent a lot of repairs. But things go bust nonetheless. The following tips tell you how to cope when they do.

APPLIANCES, OLD

Is it possible to fall in love with an appliance? Oddly enough, I think so. I've known people who are truly enamored of their blender, microwave, or toaster oven—a reliable appliance that's been with them over the years. One problem with good appliances is that they last too long. They are like the

Energizer Bunny and keep going and going and going *until* . . . one day they stop. That's when you learn the horrible truth, namely, they don't make that model anymore and your appliance can't be fixed because nobody stocks parts for those old models. Well, almost nobody.

The happy news is called Culinary Parts Unlimited. It is a company that is devoted to stocking those impossible-to-find parts for those impossibly old countertop appliances. It is a mail-order house that claims to stock 500,000 parts for more than 40 brands, including Krups, Cuisinart, KitchenAid, Sunbeam, Hamilton Beach and Braun. Of course, you don't care about those 500,000 parts—all you want is that one particular part. To order your missing piece by phone, call Culinary Parts Unlimited, 800-543-7549, or go to www.culinaryparts.com on the Internet. The company policy is to ship within 24 hours and air shipping is available for "emergency cooking or entertaining situations." That, we assume, is when either your mother-in-law or boyfriend is coming for dinner.

BED SLATS, SLIPPING

If the slats that hold up your mattress slip around, try placing a large rubber band around each end where the slat is in contact with the bedframe. An alternative is to tape them in place with duct tape.

CERAMIC FLOOR TILES, LOOSE

Loose tiles are not only unsightly, they're a serious safety hazard. They also tend to become cracked or broken tiles, requiring that you replace them altogether. Often a tile pulls up and becomes loose because it wasn't laid right in the first place. For example, tile installers should scrape off all the paint from the subfloor before gluing down the new tile. The glue normally seeps into both the under side of the porous tile and the top of the porous subfloor. This creates a strong bond that, when dry, holds the tile firmly in place. However, if there is still paint covering the subfloor, this bonding cannot take place and, soon, the tiles begin to loosen. If the installation was done poorly, chances are you either have more than one loose tile, or you're about to. A particularly bad sign is when you see "tenting"—the tiles begin to tilt upward, having lost all bond with the subfloor, and they look like rows of itty-bitty army tents. When your tile floor starts tenting, you are in *mucho* trouble. The best solution is to rip up all the tiles, scrape or sand the subfloor raw, and retile the whole room. It is the best solution, but it is very costly and annoying. You have to move everything out of the room and it is unusable for several days. Not fun.

If tiles start pulling loose, it's something you want to catch as early as possible. Regularly get on your hands and knees and carefully inspect your tile floor both visually and by trying to move the tiles around with your hands. Pay particular attention to the grout between tiles, because cracks in the grout are an early sign of trouble. Another test is to gently tap the tiles with the handle of a broom or other tool, or with a wooden rod. Tiles that are not well bonded to the subfloor will sound hollow compared with tiles that are firmly in place. If some tiles seem to be coming loose, you may be able to benefit from a relatively new repair method. Some flooring companies have developed a way to inject fresh glue under tiles without pulling them up. The method seems to be pretty effective and is only about half the price of a new floor.

CRYSTAL, CHIPPED

If your crystal has a rough or chipped edge, try smoothing it down with a piece of emery cloth or emery board.

DOORBELL, BROKEN

Let's face it, you probably don't give your doorbell much thought as you go about your day. This simple little amenity is easy to take for granted until it stops working. Luckily, it is one of the easiest things in the home to fix. But although fixing a doorbell is not really a big job, you can't do it if you don't know how it works. And so I offer the following brief explanation.

Two wires connect a doorbell's button to the bell or chimes that announce someone is at the door. A low-voltage electric current runs in the wires and, when somebody pushes the button, it brings the two separated ends of the wires together, completing the electrical circuit and making the bell ring or the chimes chime.

Usually, when the doorbell doesn't work, it is because the button is not making contact with the two wires. So, you should start by opening up the doorbell button mechanism. Unscrew the two screws in the faceplate of the button mechanism and examine the two wires. You don't have to turn the power off because the doorbell system is run on very low voltage, usually less than 24 volts.

Test the system by pushing the button. If there is no ring or chime, disconnect both wires and touch them together. If you now hear the bell ring, you simply have a worn out button that you need to replace.

If neither pushing the button nor touching the bare wires together works, scrape or sand the ends of each wire to make sure you are getting a good connection and touch them together again. If you now hear the bell ring, you just had a dirty electrical connection. Reassemble everything and the bell should now function properly.

If that doesn't work, the problem may be with the bell or chimes. Inspect them and make sure all the connections are tight and clean. If the system doesn't work after checking the bell or chimes, you have a more extensive problem.

Try cleaning the connections of your power transformer. As I said before, the doorbell system uses fairly low-voltage electricity. But that power comes from the high-voltage electrical current of the main house and it can give you a nasty shock! The high-voltage power passes through an electrical box called a transformer and is "transformed" into low-voltage power. The electricity level is something like 110–120 volts going into the transformer box and 18–24 volts coming out of the transformer and into the doorbell system. So, you don't want to mess around with the transformer while the regular household power is on. Turn it off at the fuse box before you inspect the transformer and clean all the connections. When you are done, you can turn the power back on and try everything again.

If cleaned transformer connections didn't get the doorbell working again, try replacing the transformer altogether (with the power switch off, of course). Finally, if none of the above work, you'll want to replace the thin copper wires that run from the button through the walls to the chimes or bell. Buy a roll of ordinary insulated copper wire. Twine the new wire around the end of the old wire and use the old wire to carefully pull the new wire through the wall or conduit pipe until you have replaced all of the old with all new wire.

If you have to go through all of this, you'll start to appreciate your doorbell in a whole new way.

EYEGLASS FRAMES, BROKEN

When those pesky tiny screws get loose and you don't have a tiny screwdriver handy, tighten the screw by pressing down and turning the screw head with the eraser end of a pencil. You might want to put a drop of nail polish or super glue on the screw head to seal it tight. If you have lost the screw entirely, take one of those plastic ties used to seal packages and peel the plastic off of it. This will reveal a thin wire that you can thread through your glasses to hold them together. This looks better than using the old paper clip method. *But do this carefully!* Be sure to clip off any excess wire so you don't poke yourself in the eye! Dental floss is also a good way to tie your glasses back together again.

GARAGE FLOORS, OILY

Kitty litter works and absorbs all kinds of leaks. Spread it over the part of the garage floor where your car engine sits when the car is parked and it will soak up oil drips. To remove drips from places unprotected by kitty litter, cover the oil drip with a generous layer of litter and work it in back and forth with your foot. Then, sweep up the litter and dispose of in the trash. For stubborn stains, spray on detergent and then use the kitty litter.

To clean your garage floor of oil and grease, put layers of newspapers down over the stained spots and soak the papers with water. Press down or trample on the newspapers, then let them dry. When you pull up the dried newspapers, you should be also pulling up a lot of the oil and grease stains.

Another approach is to slosh paint thinner or cola on the grease and oil and cover it with kitty litter or baking soda. Let it sit overnight and you should be able to sweep it clean the next day. (Paint thinner is flammable, and so I would recommend using the cola. If you do use the paint-thinner method, don't park your car in the garage until after you have cleaned the mess up. A hot engine near the flammable paint thinner is a dangerous combination.)

LID HANDLES, MISSING

If the little knob that serves as the handle to your pot and pan lids breaks off, try sticking an old cork on to the remaining screw.

LOCKS, STICKING

To get a smoother turning lock, run a pencil heavily over your key and turn it in the lock several times. The pencil "lead" is actually graphite, which is an excellent dry lubricant.

SLIDING DOORS AND WINDOWS, STICKING

To make sliding doors and windows slide easier, lubricate the tracks with a bar of soap or candle or furniture wax.

VINYL FLOOR TILES, CURLING

Curling vinyl floor tiles are a safety hazard and are just plain ugly. Tiles curl up when the glue under the tile has dried out; perhaps it was poorly glued in the first place. The glue may also fail to stick in rooms where the temperature or humidity gets high. Here's an idea: Take a hair dryer, hand-held vacuum cleaner, vinyl-tile glue, and a heavy stack of books or whatever. Heat the tile and the space beneath it (where the glue is) with the hair dryer. Not too hot! Then, carefully grasp the turned-up edge of the tile (wear work gloves so you don't get your fingers burned) and pull the tile up a tiny bit. Now, quickly vacuum out any dirt or guck that's under there, smear in some vinyl glue, and press the tile back into place. Immediately put a pile of heavy books on top and let it set there for an hour or more. That should get the wayward tile cemented back where it belongs.

WINDOW SHADES, WON'T ROLL UP

If your window shade is stuck, remove the shade and the connected round rod. Roll the shade up tightly by hand and replace the rod in the brackets at the top of the window. Usually, it will roll up as it's supposed to do.

WOODEN FURNITURE, LOOSE LEGS

As it ages, wooden furniture sometimes dries out and shrinks so that table and chair legs become loose. Of course, you will want to ask why, if the legs shrink, doesn't the rest of the table or chair also shrink and keep the legs tight? Well, I don't know, it just happens.

To fix the problem, you want to make the loose leg a teeny bit fatter. To do so, drape a strip of cloth or a piece of duct tape over the inserted end and screw it into the table or chair hole. Some people like to put a few drops of super glue or some other adhesive cement in the hole to help bind the leg to the table or chair.

By the way, if the old glue makes it tough to get the loose leg separated from the body of the furniture, try dripping or squirting some nail-polish remover into the joint. This should let you pull it apart cleanly and fix it the way you want it.

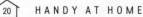

3

SHOPPING AND
SAVING MONEY

Tips to make your shopping easier and help you
save money in the process

I have a friend who says that having a dog is better than having a girlfriend, because a dog never asks why you didn't call and, more important, a dog is born without a shopping gene. While the former statement may be true, the latter is an unfair canard about women. From our perspective, both men and women have shopping genes. They are just attuned to different products. I've found that, traditionally, women tend to shop for things to make other people happy and items that are mostly used inside the house. Men tend to shop for things that make themselves happy and are mostly used outside the house. Of course, with today's great variety of lifestyles, these dividing lines have become increasingly blurred.

Regardless of your gender (or your inclinations), this chapter is designed to make you a better shopper and better at getting the most out of what you buy. There are oodles of ways to save household money that can add up to big bucks. Too often we buy things, use only part of them and throw away the rest. When we reuse, recycle, and retain goods thoughtfully, we avoid just throwing money in the trash. I've been lucky enough to learn more than just "hints" about shopping for (and saving on) some purchases, and so have included a bit of discussion about those things. Here are some tips and some advice for saving money on all sorts of items.

MAJOR SAVINGS

I'll be discussing smart saving practices for buying cars, on your electric and heating bills, and similar topics in the next few pages.

BATTERY SAVINGS

We live in a world of electric power and one of the most useful aspects of it is that it's portable, in the form of batteries. Although electricity has been known since the time of the ancient Greeks (didn't know that, did you?), we've only recently come to rely on the electricity in batteries in the past fifty years. Batteries operate our cars, and some of our telephones, radios, TVs, and recorders. In fact, 75 million rechargeable batteries are sold every year in the United States. By properly charging and recharging your batteries (rather than just replacing them), you can save a lot of money.

So, I am glad to be an official spokesperson for the nonprofit organization dedicated to telling us how to best use our rechargeable batteries. Called the Rechargeable Battery Recycling Corporation (RBRC), the organization identifies the batteries handled by its member companies by the RBRC symbol on a circular sticker.

Rechargeable batteries include nickel cadmium, nickel metal, lithium ion, and small sealed lead varieties. They are mostly used to power cell phones, cordless phones, laptop computers, cordless power tools, camcorders, two-way radios, emergency lighting, and other wireless electronic equipment.

Here are some tips on using and recharging these batteries:

- Read the charging instructions that come with the battery. Each charging unit and battery has a particular way of charging and recharging. They are not all the same.
- Charge your new battery overnight for 14 to 16 hours before you

use it for the first time. This is called "initializing" and will give you maximum battery capacity.

- Let a discharged battery cool to room temperature before recharging. A warm battery prematurely sends a signal to the thermal cut-off switch to stop charging, so your battery will not get a full charge.
- Recharge batteries only when they are near to fully discharged. You can tell that a sharp drop in speed or power discharges your battery. Do not put your battery back into the charger when it is fully charged for an "extra boost" because this will overcharge it and shorten its life.
- Don't leave your cell phone, camcorder, or other appliance in the charger when not charging unless the manufacturer's instructions direct you to do so. Continuous charging shortens battery life.
- Store batteries in a cool, dry place away from flammable materials and heat sources.

When your battery no longer holds a proper charge, recycle it. Many batteries can be recharged up to 1,000 times and, when they are of no more use, they can be recycled. In fact, they should be recycled. Don't throw batteries in the trash. If the trash is incinerated, the battery can explode and cause injuries. There are over 30,000 recycle centers in the United States. To find the one nearest you, call toll free 1-800-8-BATTERY or check the Web site of the RBRC—www.RBRC.org. In fact, if you call this 800 number, you will hear my voice.

SMART CAR SHOPPING

Probably the second most expensive item most of us buys is a car. In some cases, in fact, people are paying more for a car than my building contractor father and grandfather used to sell homes for in Seattle.

Curiously, owning a car is a wonderful experience for many of us, but buying one can be a real pain in the pattootie. Sometimes I think of car shopping like a love affair—the courting is often painful and annoying but the end result is exhilarating. The following advice will help make the ride to owning a car a smoother journey. Let's start with two of the biggest causes of unhappiness with a new car: buying one that ultimately doesn't fit your family needs and buying one that has little resale value.

Don't Get Taken for a Ride

Before you even think of making an offer on a new car, take the time to organize your thoughts and shop around. Consider the following issues and take the following steps.

- Be honest with yourself. Start out by deciding what kind of a car you *need,* not what is the sportiest or best looking. How much space do you need? If you have a long commute to work, you'll want a car that is really comfortable. Everyone wants a car that's safe and reliable, so these factors are mandatory on the list.

- Be realistic about money. This means being realistic privately, *with yourself.* What can you *really* afford in monthly payments? Car payments are usually one of the biggest expenses in a person's budget. Figure out your realistic budget and decide what you can actually afford to pay.

- Don't forget additional costs. Include into your monthly car payment an estimate of the other costs of car ownership. The sticker price is *just the beginning.* You'll also have to pay the sales tax and finance charges. You'll need to pay for insurance, the cost of registering the car, and in many states, for yearly inspections. Finally, operating and maintaining a car obviously requires you to pay for gas, oil, and repairs.

- Calculate the costs of "extras." When you buy a new car, there is the "basic price" plus the cost of extra features you may want. Be aware that car dealers are notorious for ballooning the basic price by including "extras" like special wax jobs, deluxe visors, and designer colors. For comfort, you will probably want an air conditioner, power steering, and power brakes. All of these are extras, so be prepared and figure them in your budget.

- Shop, shop, shop. If you are smart, you'll be prepared to spend some days or weeks visiting various dealers, comparing their cars and prices and taking notes. (Interestingly, studies show that men tend to get the better discounts on car purchases because car salesmen view women as ignorant and vulnerable. But even men get taken because they have to put on the bravado of knowing all about cars when most of them don't. This makes them suckers for the buddy salesman who says, "Naturally, you'll want the hypercharged diddle-do-wah-diddy even though most uninformed shoppers don't know about that." Chances are you don't know about it either because there is no such thing, but it costs $375 extra anyhow. Come shopping armed with notebook and pad in which you take notes—this intimidates many salesmen. Ask knowledgeable questions. How do you do that? Easy. Go to the next points on the list.

• Learn about the car you're interested in. Go to the library and check the history of the make and model car you are interested in buying. There are numerous motor magazines and consumer reports that evaluate cars. What is the car's reputation among mechanics? Has it had a lot of recalls? FIAT, for example, is said to stand for "Fix It Again, Tony" because they're constantly in need of repairs. When you find a specific car to buy, you can now look up its history on the Internet. Whether you know it or not, a "new" car may secretly be a refurbished car the dealer is selling as "new." You can do this by getting the car's I.D. number and checking it on the Internet at www.carfax.com. (I'll talk about this Web site in the section on buying a used car.)

• Shop for a dealer. Understand one important fact about buying a new car. When you do it, you are also buying a new car dealer because you will be returning repeatedly to the dealer for servicing under the warranty gimmick designed to hold on to you as a customer. So, ideally, it is wise to buy from a dealer who has a good service department. You can use many of the same tests for his service department that you also use when looking for an independent repair shop (see Chapter 5). There is also a good reason to buy from a dealer close to where you live—if the dealer provides loaner cars when doing repair work is being done, you won't be stranded in case of a major service job.

- Beware the booster salesman. In the car trade, the insiders often refer to one specialist salesman in the dealership as the "booster." His job is to promote extras on the car you buy because it means a bigger commission for him and the dealer. Use the Nancy Reagan approach with these types, Just Say No—and keep saying it!

- Haggling is the name of the game. One of the most unsettling things about buying a car is that it is too much like being in a bazaar haggling over a camel. Many of us aren't very experienced or very comfortable engaging in this type of bargaining. Whether you feel good about it or not, you must force yourself (and the dealer) to negotiate. Remember, it's okay to walk away and it's okay to go to other dealers. Experts say it is a fact that if you hold out a little, you'll go home with a lot.

- Don't focus on the wrong things. A well-kept secret about buying a car is that the majority of new car buyers focus on the *wrong things*. They waste most of their time skipping from one dealer to the next comparing paint jobs, air-conditioner prices, and upholstery. In fact, the available cars are much the same from dealer to dealer and you can haggle over a $100 here and $100 there. What really is important is the difference in financing you can get from one dealer to another. It could be a difference of *thousands* of dollars. What most new car buyers don't know is that the dealer makes most of his profit off the financing of the car and not on the sale of the car. Therefore, obtaining your financing through the dealer is often the worst choice you can make. If you belong to a credit union or are a member of Triple A, consider starting with these groups. Whatever you do, shop, shop, shop—*financing!*

- Don't be a "first on the block" sucker. If you tell yourself that you must have the first doo-wah-diddy 17 cylinder, purple-colored, convertible roadster on your block, don't bother shopping for a new car. Just send your check in by mail. You are already considered a sucker sale—in more ways than one. Not only will you walk out the door with a lousy deal (for you), you may also get a lousy car. New model cars often have a lot of bugs to be worked out and it can take a year or three for the manufacturer to get it right. Best to wait until at least the third-year model.

The Truth About Car Dealers

The first thing you must understand about a new-car dealer is not what he or she is but what he or she isn't. A new-car dealer is not the Community Chest, a chapter of the Boy Scouts, or the Red Cross. A car dealership is not a charity. It is a capitalist venture. The car dealer is out to make a profit off you, or he or she will go out of business.

No matter what you hear about how sweet and wonderful a dealer is, he and his staff have only one objective: to make a commission for the salesperson and a profit for the dealer. Once you have this principle clearly in mind, you will be a happier buyer. The best you can do is to keep the commission and the profit to a reasonable level.

It doesn't take Einstein to figure out how this is done. The dealer has to sell you a car for more than he paid for it or give you less for your trade-in than it is worth, or both. In addition to getting a profit on the purchase of the car, the dealer will try to get you to buy as many extras as possible, because the profit margin on the extras is often much bigger than the profit on the basic car. The dealer will make it as easy as possible for you to buy the car that same day and he'll use various gimmicks to entice you, even bribing you with money. He might offer to sell the car for *nothing down* and even *give you a cash bonus* for buying it. This is when you need to run outside and remind yourself that the car dealership is not a charity. So, how does he work this? The cash bonus is tacked on to the cost of the car and you end up with a bigger loan with interest to pay off. In other words, *the dealer is bribing you with your own money.*

You should understand something else when you finance a new car through a dealer: You are not borrowing the money from the dealership. Before the ink is dry on the contract, the dealer has sent the papers to his friendly banker with whom he has a line of credit. The dealer sells the banker the loan at a discount. For example, if you borrow money to buy the car, you will pay several thousands of dollars in interest to the bank during the next three to five years. The bank loves these loans because they are secured by the value of the car, your credit, and the dealer's credit (although strong dealers can get out from under any liability on some car loans) and it costs the bank almost nothing to generate the loan.

All this financial finagling will sometimes result in what is known as an "upside down" loan, in which you owe more against the car than it is worth. If you have the credit, the bank will go along with this because it wants the dealer to be happy and it knows you will eventually get the loan paid down. So, the inside dope is that most dealers make more profit on selling your car loan to the bank than on selling you the car. This is why most dealers don't want cash buyers.

The Dance of the Trade-in

In theory, the value of the car you are trading in for the new car is a big factor in the deal you make. In fact, however, dealers have several financial variables to fiddle with to create the illusion of a great deal for you. Using the price of the new car, the financing available on the new car, and the net worth of your old car as variables, the dealer will dance around until you're really confused. At the same time, the salesperson will try to psych you into a deal. No matter what the deal is, however, remember the sign out front—this is not a charity hall.

Remember, under normal circumstances, the dealer is never going to pay you more than the wholesale price for your old car. If you believe anything else, you are dreaming. The two biggest things the dealer has going for him on the trade-in are your ignorance and his well-rehearsed dancing.

On the ignorance thing, admit it. You didn't go to the library and research the wholesale market price of your car in the *Kelley Blue Book*. It is hundreds—maybe thousands—less than it will sell at retail. That figure is part of the dealer's profit margin and he will play with it in making you a deal. Therefore, you have to know what your trade-in is actually worth, minus the "pay-off" cost of the existing loan (whatever it costs to clear financial obligations secured by the car, which would include loan principal, interest, penalties, etc.). Simply call whoever is financing your car and find out what this "pay-off" cost is. It is not just the total of all outstanding payments, because you will be charged less interest if you pay the loan off early. (Unless, of course, you signed a loan agreement—which, of course, you never read—that calls for an early pay-off penalty.)

Okay. Now you know what the net wholesale value of your trade-in is. Keep it a secret. Don't drive the car you plan to trade in to the dealership so the dealer's "appraiser" can look at it. Don't even discuss it with the salesperson. Keep the trade-in out of the picture until you get price quotes on the new car deal. This way you keep the dealer from using the trade-in as a lever in making the initial deal.

When you enter into conversations with the salesperson, don't forget his motive is to make money selling you a car. The salesperson will try to seem like your friend and will try to get you to make a decision immediately. A purchase decision postponed is too often a sale lost and the salesperson knows that. For example, he might tell you the dealer or manufacturer is having a contest and, if you buy today—right now—you can share in a special discount. Or the salesperson will brazenly show you the cost estimate his appraiser made of your trade-in, believing that such openness will inspire your trust. He may, however, have the evaluation written in code. A common code used in the car business is to substitute the first ten letters of the alphabet for the numerals 1 through 0, with A = 1, B = 2, and so on to J = 0. If it says on your appraisal sheet "CEJJ," that means $3,500, which may or may not be the same number given to you by the salesperson.

Some of the most confusing gimmicks are connected to the various names given the price of the car in which you are interested. You'll hear terms such as sticker price, dealer's price, factory invoice, invoice price, and on and on. The many terms are deliberately confusing. If you begin to feel that you can't really understand what's being said, the hope is that you'll stop trying and trust in your salesperson's integrity.

Suppose, for example, the salesperson shows you the "dealer's invoice" or the "factory invoice." This is supposed to convince you that this is what the dealer had to pay the factory for this car. That's why advertisements yelling "$100 OVER INVOICE" are essentially meaningless. In truth, that amount may be altered by special discounts, manufacturer incentives or a variety of other arrangements the dealer has with the factory. There is a lot of "back-door" money between the manufacture and dealer, but nobody wants you to know that. This is why it is important for you to check an independent source such as the *Kelley Blue Book* and go into the dealership *knowing* the wholesale and retail price of the car you want.

Closing the deal

Buying a new car is an exciting experience. The smell of the new car, the feel of the leather and dreams of the vagabond life on the open road are all secret support for the car dealer. And once you have concluded the haggling and made the deal, it's all over, right? *Wrong!* This is when the dealer makes his "real money."

You're sucker enough to think the deal is closed and you're about to slip behind the wheel and drive your new car straight to the beach or the mountains or to your best friend's house. But, wait, the salesperson is saying something, "Oh, sure, just a few odds and ends and the darn paperwork is finished up." So, what can that matter? You want to rush through it and get out of here! You are in yes-yes-yes mode and the salesperson knows it.

This is the time the seller is smiling and rubbing his hands together. This is where he gets the extra profits with all the "back end" stuff and that's where you are getting stuck—in the back end. You are now turned over to the tender mercies of what they often call the F & I Department. That ostensibly means the Finance and Insurance Department, which sounds appropriately innocuous. Actually, F & I should stand for Finagle and Inveigle Department.

Here is where the dealership gets the financing, insurance, extended warranties, and whatever other add-ons the staff can think of into the deal, starting with the financing. In this, the dealer will be working with a banker who never heard of you. The dealer will check with the banker, who will loan you the money to buy the car at 9 percent interest, but the dealer will present the loan to you at an interest rate of 14 percent. You don't know any better because you never get to talk to the nameless, faceless banker. It's all done through the dealer, which means you'll pay the dealer $1,500 to $2,000 more than you need to. That's a lot more than he makes on the mark-up from the price of the car. You can avoid this if you shop for financing *before* you start the negotiations. Unfortunately for most car buyers, they don't.

At least two other gimmicks for dealer back-end profits are the "extended warranty" and car insurance. The extended warranty means the dealership will give you, for example, a three-year warranty instead of one year. This is convenient and you are right there ready to sign, but the chances are you can shop around and get it cheaper elsewhere. Keep in mind that warranties are designed to protect the dealer and the car manufacturer, so you might not want to spend a lot for one.

Reread this last paragraph and substitute the word "insurance" for "warranty" and you have our view on that. By shopping you should be able to get a better deal.

These are just some of the potholes of buying a new car.

Refurbishing as an Alternative

A simple alternative to buying a snazzy, stylish, stratospherically expensive new car is to make-over your existing car. In fact, if you look around you'll discover that keeping cars for a long time is trendy, so your savings strategy has the extra benefit of being stylish. The average car on the road today is nine years old, which means that half the cars in America are ten years old or older.

Yes, there are disadvantages to giving your car a make-over, but you should be smart enough to at least consider it. Make a *realistic* estimate of what a new car will cost, remembering that a new car loses 25 percent of its value the minute you drive it out of the lot. With a remodeled car, there are no big monthly payments to make, no sales tax to pay, and lower insurance premiums. Another advantage is that you know the car's idiosyncrasies and don't have to deal with a completely new set of quirks. Of course, you don't want to refurbish a car if the cost of the make-over is greater than the car's value. If you want to explore refurbishing, you might request an interesting pamphlet on the subject by sending a self-addressed, stamped envelope to Car Care Council, Dept. R, One Grande Lake Drive, Port

Clinton, OH 43452. Ask for "Renew vs. Replace (Rx for Making a Decision)."

THE SECRETS TO BUYING A GOOD USED CAR

Many people buy used cars and usually from a smart dealer such as the new car dealer I have already described or from a not-so-smart private party selling direct. Either way, you are on you own and have to be very careful to avoid getting cheated either on purpose or by accident.

Realistically, most of us haven't got a clue about what to look for and what to be careful of when buying *any* kind of car. Used-car salesmen have a reputation for being less than candid about the condition of the cars they sell and, in honesty, the same is true of private car owners, too. So, here are some secrets you should know when buying a used car from anybody.

- The very first thing to do when you find a used car you think you want to buy is to go to www.carfax.com on the Internet and order a report on the car's history. This is a commercial site from which you can access the information on accidents the car has been in, whether the odometer has been tampered with, as well as possible lemon history, flood history, junked titles, state emissions test results, lien activity, and uses such as a lease car or taxi. The cost of using the site is minimal and the information it provides is invaluable for making a sound buy.
- Insist that you have the vehicle inspected by your mechanic.
- Private sales are not usually covered by the "implied warranties" of most state laws. That means a private sale probably will be on an "as is" basis, unless your purchase agreement with the seller warrants that the car is in good condition.
- Some sellers will say the car is still covered by the manufacturer's warranty or some service contract. However, warranties and service contracts may not be transferable or have restrictions that prevent them from applying to you.
- Many states don't require sellers to guarantee the car will pass state

inspections before it is sold. Check your state's consumer protection agency on this.

- Evaluate the car yourself using an inspection checklist. You can find a checklist in many of the magazine articles, books, and Internet sites that discuss buying a used car.
- Test-drive the car under varied road conditions—on hills, highways, and in stop-and-go traffic.
- Ask for the car's maintenance record. If the owner doesn't have copies, contact the dealership or shop where most of the work was done. They may share their files with you.
- If there was an owner prior to the seller, track that person down and speak with him or her about the car's history.
- If, after the sale, you find out you were misled (intentionally or not), ask the seller to correct the problem. If he won't, send him a certified letter, return receipt requested, spelling out the problem and demanding he correct it. If that doesn't work, you can seek relief from the motor vehicles department or consumer-protection agency in your city, county or state.
- If none of the above steps are successful, you may have to sue the seller in small claims court. The clerk of your local small claims court can tell you how to file a suit and whether the amount of money you seek is within the small claims court's jurisdiction.

Car Insurance Savings

You may not realize it, but the insurance rates you pay for your car can vary dramatically depending on the insurance company, agent, or broker you choose, the coverage you request and the kind of car you drive. Listed below are a number of things you can do right now to lower your insurance costs.

- Comparison shop for best rates. Prices for the same coverage can vary by hundreds of dollars, so it pays to shop around. Ask your friends, check the local yellow pages and consumer guides, or call your state insurance department. These resources will give you an idea of price ranges and tell you which companies or agents have the lowest prices. But don't shop only for a good price.

The insurer you select should offer both fair prices and excellent service. Good-quality personal service may cost a bit more, but you'll appreciate the personal attention. Referrals from friends can be helpful in finding an agency and a broker that you like. In addition, check the financial ratings of the agencies under consideration. Then, when you've narrowed the field to three insurers, get price quotes.

- Ask for higher deductibles. Deductibles represent the amount of money you pay before you make a claim. By requesting higher deductibles on collision and comprehensive (fire and theft) coverage, you can lower your costs substantially. For example, increasing your deductible from $200 to $500 could reduce your collision cost by 15 to 30 percent.

- Don't buy collision and comprehensive insurance for older cars. It may not be cost-effective to have collision or comprehensive coverage on cars worth less than $2,000 because any claim you make would not substantially exceed the annual cost and deductible amounts. The famous *Kelley Bluebook* that lists the value of cars can be found in most local libraries and on the Internet.

- Eliminate duplicate medical coverages. If you have adequate health insurance, you may be paying for unnecessary medical coverage in your auto policy. In some states, eliminating this coverage could lower your personal-injury-protection cost by up to 40 percent.

- Buy a "low profile" car. Cars that are expensive to repair or that are favorite targets for thieves have much higher insurance costs than your everyday sedan. Write to the Insurance Institute for Highway Safety, 1005 North Glebe Road, Arlington, VA 22201, and ask for the Highway Loss Data Chart for details.

- Take advantage of low-mileage discounts. Some companies offer discounts to motorists who drive fewer than a predetermined number of miles each year.

- Explore the variety of discounts that may be available to you. Some insurers offer discounts if you insure more than one car, have had no accidents in three years, are over 50 years of age, have taken driver-training courses, have antitheft devices, or antilock brakes. Some insurers even offer discounts to students with good grades. Make sure you don't bypass any discounts for which you qualify.

ELECTRICITY

Saving on electricity is one of our big goals these days. Here are some easy, money-saving methods.

MANAGING YOUR POWER BILL

A simple, smart way to do so is to learn how to read your meter. It's easy. You probably know there is a meter outside your house that measures the amount of electricity that flows in. But, I'll bet what you didn't know is that the meter is wrong on occasion and often the reading on the meter is not even checked by a member of the power company's staff. In fact, it is common that somebody back at the electric company office is sitting at a desk guessing what the reading is. And that guess is what goes on your account and in the bill they send you to pay!

One way to combat this absurdity is to read the meter yourself and check it against the bill the company sends you. Getting into this practice will also educate you about how much electricity you use at different times of the day and different days of the week. Here's how to do it.

First, find your electric meter. This should be fairly easy. It is usually outside your house in a round, glass casing. Inside and visible from the outside through the glass cover are five dials with arrows over a circle of numbers.

Now, this is the only tricky part. The five dials each have an arrow and the arrows do not all rotate or turn in the same direction. Why this is, I can't tell you, and it really doesn't matter as long as you understand which way each one turns so you can read it and write down the figures. I recommend that you check the meter and write down the numbers every day.

On the extreme left and right meters the arrows rotate clockwise. The same applies to the arrow on the middle dial. The second from the left and second from the right arrows rotate counterclockwise.

Write down the number that each arrow is pointing to and this will give you a five-digit number. That is your base number for today. Repeat this process at the same time tomorrow. Subtract yesterday's number from today's, and that will tell you the number of what are called "kilowatts hours" you have used in that 24-hour period. You can continue this day after day, week after week, and so on, which will give you an exact reading of how much electricity you are using. The charge per kilowatt hour should be printed on your bill and you will, thus, be able to figure the cost. In the year 2000, the national average was 9 cents per kilowatt hour, according to California electric power company statistics. You will also be able to compare your reading with the electric company's estimate.

Reading your meter regularly will also give you an incentive to adjust your power use or to reschedule it if, for example, there is a lower kilowatt hour charge at certain times of the day, such as late at night or early in the morning. In any event, you will at least be on an equal footing with the power company because you will actually know how much power you're using at any given time.

ENERGY, SAVING

Another way to take control of your power bill is to take control of the temperature inside your home. Our highest energy costs are often those incurred in heating and cooling our homes. In Chapter 2, I describe how to repair the cracks and holes through which we lose some of our heated and cooled air. Keeping your house well sealed is critical to keeping your power bills down. In addition to the advice in Chapter 2, be sure to:

- Monitor vents. Check deliberate "leaks" in your home, such as your fireplace and the exhaust outlets for your stoves and laundry dryer. You obviously don't want to seal these up permanently but you do want them closed when not in use. The normal way to do this is to mount so-called flap vents on the outlets. These are hinged vent covers that only open when exhaust air is being pushed out through them. Otherwise, they stay closed. Of course, you don't need a flap vent on the fireplace because it has a damper. Just make a point of keeping the damper vent closed except when there is a fire going. You may want to mount a clip or a little flag or symbol on the fireplace screen every time you close off the chimney damper as a reminder that the damper needs to be opened before you start a fire in the fireplace.

- Fix leaky faucets. Leaky faucets often drain hot-water, which means your hot-water heater is going on and off uselessly and wasting electric or gas power.

- Insulate your hot-water heater. Your hot-water heater has a thermostat designed to keep the water at a certain temperature all the time so you have the luxury of hot water on demand. And, yes, most hot water heaters have some insulation, but you can buy a hot-water-heater insulating "blanket" at most plumbing or home-improvement stories to wrap around the outside of the water heater. This will keep the heat inside from radiating out. When the water stays hot longer, less gas or electric power is needed, cutting costs and saving energy. Also, check the thermostat on your hot-water heater. Try adjusting it a few degrees lower than it is, and see if that lower setting keeps the water hot enough for your needs. A few degrees lower can save a lot of that expensive energy. Most hot-water heater thermostats are normally set at 140 degrees when 120 degrees is comfortable for most people.

- Install temperature control timers. Put your air-heater or air-conditioner thermostat on a timer so it is off when no one is home or when everyone is asleep. According to the U.S. Department of Energy, you can cut your energy costs by at least 10 percent a year if you just turn your thermostat down 10 percent for a third of the day. They recommend a setting of 68 degrees during the day and 55 degrees at night.

- Install motion switches. Motion sensors will turn lights on and off automatically depending on whether anyone is in the room. If you have kids, for example, it can be hard to get them to turn lights on and off when they are going into or leaving a room. It's not something kids think about. Having the lights on a motion sensor means they will go on when somebody is in the room and off when they leave.

- Let nature help out. Finally, let nature help cool and heat your home. Plant shade trees and shrubs along the west and south sides of your house to cut down on direct sun, and thin the plantings on the north and east sides to take advantage of the warmth of the sun. Naturally, open your shades and drapes when you want it warm and close them when you want it cool.

SAVING ON LIGHTBULBS

Most of us are in the dark when it comes to buying lightbulbs but the modern concern about electrical shortages makes it worthwhile for us to learn some of the basics. About one-sixth of all the electricity we use at home goes to these little bulbs, so they are important.

The two most common types of lighting used in most homes are fluorescent and incandescent. The fluorescent bulb or tube normally will throw off more illumination than an incandescent bulb of the same size. Politicians say this saves energy and in some parts of the country, the law states that in certain rooms, the first light that the switch turns on must be a fluorescent light. Notably, these laws also help the fluorescent-light industry. In any event, these laws ignore the reality that most women hate putting on makeup under a fluorescent light because it is too pale or too flat or too something. So, builders and homeowners installing new lights or remodeling have been forced to install fluorescent lights that nobody wants to use. The result is that homeowners frequently rip out the fluorescent lights.

You should know that the wattage marked on a lightbulb or on its package is sometimes misleading. For example, two bulbs with the identical number of watts marked on them don't necessarily give off the same amount of light. The secret is to look for a second number on the package or the bulb—the one that tells you the number of lumens the bulb produces. Watts indicate how much electricity the bulb uses, but lumens measure how much light it throws out and this will vary according to the bulb's design. So, the smart way to buy lightbulbs is to get the highest lumens with the lowest wattage—they're the most efficient bulbs. You may also want to take notice of the number of hours the bulb is expected to last, which is another quality the manufacturer notes on the package. This could be particularly convenient to know when you're installing a bulb in a location that is inconvenient to reach.

So, to make the best choice of a bulb, start with one that gives you the kind of light you want. Then, compare the cost of the bulb per lumen and per watt so you can compare the illumination costs among the various bulbs. A fluorescent bulb will normally throw off three or four times the light of an incandescent bulb at the same watt and cost, but it may not be a kind of light you like. Similarly, two incandescent bulbs may give the same number of lumens of light but require vastly different wattage to do it, which means one of them is going to require a lot more electricity. It comes down to comparison shopping for the lowest price per lumen.

AVOIDING HOME IMPROVEMENT SCAMS

One way you can get cheated is to fall for one of the many home-improvement scams. Two prevalent types involve roof problems or driveway paving. Often these scam artists roam well-to-do, middle-class neighborhoods during the day in what looks to be an authentic building contractor's truck. Generally, they strike their targets on impulse, deal in home improvements the homeowner doesn't understand, and appeal to the homeowner's inclination to save a buck.

A typical scenario may look like this: one or more individuals will come to your door and say they were "just in the neighborhood finishing up another job when they happened—by accident—to notice your home seems to have a something-something problem. They say something like they just repaved the driveway of a lady in the next block and have some leftover paving material and noticed your driveway needed some work. If you could pay them $150 (cash only), they would give your driveway a cutrate repaving. If you go along with it, they will fiddle around your driveway, spray it with five dollars' worth of some adhering oil to make it look new and fresh, and be on their way leaving you $150 poorer with a sticky, messy driveway.

Another favorite scam is to recommend roof repair. One member of the con team will come to your door to say they "were just driving by after finishing a job nearby and noted the sorry condition of your roof." Clearly, this scam artist will say, your roof must be so bad that it had to be leaking through your ceiling. Then, he sends a fellow scam artist through the house "checking" while the first hustler is distracting the homeowner. What the second scammer is actually doing is going from room to room spraying cola in spots on the ceilings. When called to the homeowner's attention, he or she sometimes agrees to the quickie cutrate roofing job that has the scam artists crawling around on the roof for a little while, making noise and doing nothing. The homeowner, of course, isn't going to go up there to watch them. Then, they come down, get their money, and take off.

Another common method of initiating a scam is to offer a "free test" for termites, roaches, lead or radon poisoning, or some other problem. Surprise! Surprise! These "free test" inspectors always find something wrong that they can fix for you on the spot for cash—only cash.

According to the Federal Trade Commission, the following clues should alert you that you're being hustled:

An individual or team appears at your door without warning to solicit you.

You're told that:
- They "just happened to be in the neighborhood doing another job for one of your neighbors." This statement is to assure you of the hustlers' respectability. The theory is, if your neighbor hired him, he must be okay. Of course, your neighbor has never heard of him.
- They "just happened to have material left over from the neighbor's job."
- Cash is the only acceptable form of payment.
- An immediate decision is required (the worker is booked for the next two months, or the work is urgent to avoid some catastrophe).

- The work is guaranteed for a long time (which, of course, means nothing since the scam artists leave town the next day).
- Payment for the entire job must be up front, or a part payment (of a lot of money) is acceptable, because they'll be back to collect the rest of the fee later—wrong.

Usually, new owners are inundated by calls from people selling all kinds of services and products from credit to life insurance to hot-water heater inspections. In warm climates the infamous air-conditioner scam chills a lot of homeowners, particularly new homeowners who have only been in their houses a short time. Here is how this scam works.

An individual on the phone or at the door will try to convince you that a busted air conditioner will cost you hundreds of dollars to repair, and since they always break down during a heat wave, you may not be able to get it repaired for months. So you let him come over for a "free inspection."

The drill varies among swindlers. Some may break a tube or fitting on your air conditioner while you're not looking. Then, they show how the unit is malfunctioning or leaking or whatever. Or, they will point to rust on the coil that, incidentally, is normal. Very quickly you are being alarmed into an expensive repair or replacement of the entire unit.

Your best protection is to insist on seeing a state contractor's license, to have two contractors inspect your unit, and to insist on a written report. Then check the state licensing board to make sure the contractor is legitimate.

For your own peace of mind, check your air-conditioner filters monthly and change them when the old ones gets dirty. Meanwhile, keep cool.

TIPS ON SAVING ON ALL SORTS OF STUFF

Over the years, I've picked up many ways to save money (and to avoid wasting it). I hope that these ideas put pennies in your piggy bank.

BULK BUYING

It's tempting to believe that purchasing items in bulk is a good way to save money, and it can be. So what if we have to take home a 55-gallon barrel of salt? We'll use it up eventually and it only cost $20. But buying oversized packages is not always cost effective. Researchers from Purdue University have taken a close look at the idea and have found that most consumers have been so sold on the "bigger is cheaper" pitch that they never compare prices on an ounce-by-ounce basis. So, relying on this principle, some manufacturers take advantage of the consumer by charging *more* per ounce when packaging their product in a big size box. Technically, this is called "surcharging." Interestingly, the researchers also found that the people most commonly conned by surcharging were the well to do. Surprising as that may seem at first, it does have a logic about it. Well-to-do people put a premium on their time and don't want to spend all day in the grocery store aisle reading labels and comparing ounce-by-ounce prices. For those on tighter budgets, the money is more important than the time.

CLEANING PRODUCTS

Instead of paying for expensive commercial cleaning products, save money by using some of the following: clean the toilet by pouring a can of cola or cup of vinegar into the toilet bowl and letting it soak for an hour or two. Wash windows with a paper towel dipped in warm water to which you have added one-quarter to one-half cup of vinegar. Wipe with crumbled newspaper. Toothpaste will remove those crayon markings children have put on the wall.

COFFEE, SAVING

Coffee, tea, and other beverages can be expensive and it's a shame to waste them just because we make more at one time than we drink. A money saver is to keep the surplus beverage in a Thermos or frozen in ice cubes for later use.

COUPON SAVING, CUSTOMIZED

Not many people are familiar with the services of Savings in Your Pocket, a company that I think is great. This is how is works: you start by sending in a self-addressed, stamped envelope along with $2. The company sends you a list of hundreds of products. You choose from this list the coupons you want and send it in. After a few weeks, your customized coupon book will arrive with savings on those products you selected. Each book will typically be worth over $100 in savings. You can reorder more of your customized coupon savings book for $15 each. Contact: Savings in Your Pocket, 121-C Leonard Street, Columbus, GA 31905.

DATED FOODS

Many food containers, such as milk cartons and eggs, are dated to tell you how long you can comfortably use the contents. To get the freshest product available, take the container that is stacked farthest back on the shelf. Retailers always push the oldest product to the front in order to sell it before it goes stale. If you have any doubt about this, check the container dates from the front row to the back row at your local store.

DOG DAMAGE

If you have a dog that likes to chew things up, rub the things he goes after with a bar of ordinary laundry soap (any soap with a strong odor should do). Most dogs hate the smell and the taste and will avoid those things.

GIFT WRAP

Instead of expensive gift wrap bought at the store, make your own personalized gift wrap from newspapers and magazines, with help from marker pens or crayons. Write memorable times or places on the paper in bold, bright letters. Cut and paste photos together with funny remarks. It becomes a personalized gift wrapping and is more meaningful than the commercial kind.

GROCERIES

Many retailers, such as grocery stores, liquor stores, and bookstores rent their most valuable shelves and locations to particular producers. For example, eye-level shelves are the most desirable in the grocery store and many food producers pay a premium to the grocery store to display their products on these shelves. Naturally, the food producer may recoup some of that cost by charging a bit more. So, you can often save big simply by bending over—the place to look for bargains is on the lower and less convenient shelves.

LUMBER

The rule "measure twice, cut once" is used by professional carpenters to prevent making mistakes and wasting material. It is self-explanatory and you can improve upon it by having another person measure twice too and then agree on what the measurement is before cutting. This rule is also applicable to fabrics you use in sewing and for cutting wrapping paper.

ORGANIZING YOUR SHOPPING

To many of us, saving time is as important as saving money. One way to do so is to make one trip to the store, post office, and other destinations. How many times do you return home *without* the dry cleaning, the prescription, or whatever you meant to take care of? When you're home and remember an errand to run, write it down, and put it in your "to go" box. Put a modest-sized box or bag by the door by which you usually leave the house. In time you will get used to checking the "to go" box every time you leave the house and you'll come home with your errands completed.

OUTDOOR PARTY LIGHTS

You can make your own inexpensive, festive outdoor party lights that won't attract bugs. Get some medium-sized paper bags, fill them one-third to one-half full with sand, and folding the sides of the bags to the level of the sand, and insert a lit candle. Line, the driveway or walks or patio with the bag-lights, and put at strategic places around where people gather for a party mood.

PAINTBRUSHES, USED

If you forget or don't have time to clean paintbrushes, they can become hard and yucky. But don't throw them away. Try soaking them overnight in water if the paint was water-soluble or turpentine if the paint was oil based. They may be salvageable. Also, some experts recommend hot vinegar as a solvent.

PANTYHOSE

I can't explain why, but if you keep pantyhose in the freezer, they will last longer. If they do develop runs, don't throw them away. They make good polishers for shoes, silverware, furniture, and cars.

PHONE CARDS

There are all kinds of phone cards available today and the benefits of one over the other can be confusing. I've found that the best value seems to be the prepaid cards that specifically provide the amount of time you get on that card and for what price. These are often sold in discount stores such as Wal-Mart and Costco. From what I understand, the most expensive cards are those issued by AT&T, Sprint, and other phone companies. The charge per minute is not indicated and the user can receive a very high bill—sometimes over $100. Be wary of any card that doesn't give you all the information up front.

PHOTO ALBUMS, MAINTAINING

When the pages of a family photo album get damp or start to stick together, save them by fanning the pages and sprinkling them with baby powder or talc. Remove spots by gently rubbing them with a piece of bread. Repair tears by coating the torn part with egg white and letting the page air-dry.

PLASTIC CONTAINERS, SAVING

The plastic containers we use to store food can take on odors from what has been stored in them, prompting you to throw them out. Don't discard them! Instead, ball up a newspaper page and store it in the container. This will often absorb the unwanted odors and make the container like new.

POSSESSIONS, PROVING OWNERSHIP

Ownership of a bike, scooter, skateboard, or baseball mitt can become the subject of debate at parks and playgrounds. To easily identify your things, write your name and address on a small piece of paper, insert it in a little baggie to protect it from moisture and slip it into the item's handle or frame. Or, write name and address directly on the equipment in an obscure spot and coat it with clear nail polish to protect against the weather.

REPAIR JOBS

Every do-it-yourselfer knows any particular "five-minute job" around the house takes three hours and three trips to the hardware store. You can save time, money, and gasoline by carefully measuring the item you need and by noting the make and serial number of every part you are trying to replace. Better yet, take the part with you to the hardware store or, at least, a Polaroid photo of it—especially if the color match is important. If you do this, you may cut the five-minute job rule to one hour and one trip. When you come home with a part in a plastic bag, don't become a maniac and rip it open in a burst of enthusiasm. Before opening the bag, make sure that the part name, model, and number matches the old part. Even then, open the package very carefully with a razor blade or by undoing the staples or gently pulling the top. Why the fuss? So that you can reseal the package and get your money back if the part isn't right after all.

SCISSORS, SHARPENING

Don't throw away those dull scissors or knives. By cutting through sandpaper several times, they'll become sharp again.

SOUP, SAVING

Make a big pot of soup and pour into bowl-sized snap-top plastic containers, but don't fill them too full. Remember, liquids expand as they freeze, so leave room for the soup to expand in the container. Round containers are best. Store in the freezer. When you want a fast bowl of soup, take off the lid and pop into the microwave for 4 or 5 minutes and there you are. The container will be very hot, so be careful when removing it from the microwave.

STAMPS

Don't throw away stamps or labels that get stuck together. Freeze them instead. After some time in the freezer, they should be okay.

TOOLS, MAINTAINING

To prevent your tools from getting rusty (and the need to replace them), keep them in a toolbox or other sealed compartment along with something that absorbs moisture, such as rice, mothballs, or baking soda.

WAX LINERS

Save the wax liners of cereal boxes to wrap sandwiches for the kids' lunch boxes and for other foods.

4

KEEPING SAFE

How to protect yourself and your family from injury,
crime, and other bad things

How we keep our families safe has changed over time. I recall how my grandmother saved her family from being attacked by Native Americans as they traveled by covered wagon from the Midwest to Seattle, Washington. To attain the friendship of the women in the tribes, she gave them gifts and, particularly, highly prized coffee grounds. Once, when some rogue men decided to attack, the Native American women warned my grandmother so her family and the others travelers were not taken off-guard. In the same way, we want to protect ourselves and those we love from the dangers we face today, such as criminals, poisons, hazardous chemicals and materials, and fires. We may be living in the modern age of TV, cell phones, and pizza, but life is just as dangerous as it was in Grandma's time.

IN-HOME PRECAUTIONS

It doesn't take a lot of work to diminish or remove the hazards in the home. The following ideas are designed to do just that.

APPLIANCES

Keep appliances unplugged until you want to use them. No doubt because it's dangerous, flipping switches off and on and fiddling with gadgets is inexplicably entertaining to children. When you unplug or plug in an appliance, be sure your hands are dry. Wet hands—common in the bathroom and the kitchen—can lead to a bad electrical shock. When plugging and unplugging an appliance, push or pull the plug straight out, not at an angle that can bend or break the plug's tines. Also, always push in or pull out holding on to the plastic of the plug itself. Don't unplug by yanking on the cord. This can pull the wire out of the plug and leave you holding a hot, bare wire. It also means you'll have the annoyance of reconnecting the wire to the plug.

BATHROOM SAFETY TIPS

The bathroom can be full of hazards, but it doesn't have to be. Use the following tips to prevent accidents in the bathroom.

Electric Appliances

First of all, water and electricity are a dangerous mixture. You should not use electric appliances such as hair dryers, curlers, or radios in the bathroom. If you absolutely must have a radio so you can listen to the news and traffic reports while you get ready to leave for work, use a battery-operated radio only. If you have an electric radio going while you bathe and listen to the news, you may end up on the news.

Preventing Falls

Of course, water and slippery surfaces in the bathroom and shower can result in falls. Have rubber mats in the shower and bath and rubber-backed throw rugs on the floor. If you don't, what may get thrown is you. Liquid soaps have become popular for use in kitchens and bathrooms, but be careful when you use them. Some liquid soaps are especially slick and, when used to wash your legs and feet, may make your feet especially slippery.

Handgrips and grab bars are always a good idea around the shower or tub. These are strong bars that you can either mount on the wall or, with some U-shaped styles, over the side of the bathtub. If you think these safety bars are really for nursing homes, think again. They can prevent serious injury to children and ablebodied adults, too.

For a grab bar to work, it has to withstand a sudden jerk by an adult who is slipping and falling. So, it has to remain in place as a 125- to 200-pound weight is suddenly yanking on it. This is why grab bars must be anchored into wall studs by bolts that enter the stud at least two inches or more. The angle of their placement depends on what you think is most convenient. Often they are installed horizontally about three feet up but this may depend on whether you mostly take a shower or a bath. Some people find them more convenient to be installed either diagonally or vertically.

Finding a stud can be particularly tricky when it's behind a tile wall. For a number of methods for how to locate a stud, see Chapter 10. Suffice to say, the easiest method is to invest in a stud-finder device from the store.

You want to attach the grab bar with a strong bolt such as a two- or three-inch lag bolt or expansion shield bolt. You are also probably going to have to drill through some tile to properly and securely hang your grab bar. Drilling through ceramic tile requires an electric drill and a carbide-tip drill bit that you can get at the hardware store. It also requires some brains about safety. When you touch that ceramic tile with that high-speed whirling drill bit, it is going to churn up tiny pieces of very hard and sharp ceramic tile and spin them out in all directions. So, you must be wearing a face mask with eye protection or goggles, hat or cap, and protective long-sleeved, long-legged clothing. You must not have any friends, children, pets or visiting Australians standing in the bathroom watching unless they also have such safety gear on. A grab bar isn't worth a punctured eyeball!

CARBON MONOXIDE, PREVENTING POISONING

In addition to having a smoke alarm, you should also have a carbon monoxide alarm in your home. Carbon monoxide, which is odorless, can be emitted through leaks in anything in the home that burns fuel, including furnaces, stoves, fireplaces, clothes dryers, water heaters, and space heaters.

Carbon monoxide can be deadly. To prevent it from entering your home, have your chimneys, flues, and vents checked by a professional for leakage and blockage by creosote and debris. Black stains on the outside of the chimney or flue may be a sign that pollutants are leaking into the house. Also be sure to have all vents to furnaces, water heaters, boilers, and the like inspected. You want to be certain that these vents are not loose or disconnected.

CHRISTMAS TREES

Most of us know that Christmas trees are highly flammable. The trees contain natural saps and oils that burn hot and quickly once the tree dries out. When you bring the tree inside your home, be sure to set it in a dish or bucket of water. You can purchase a tree stand that has a built-in water reservoir or put the tree in a large bucket of rocks and sand. Refill any container daily. It is also important that you make new cuts diagonally on the lower parts of the truck that will be immersed in water. The water will be absorbed into the cuts and move throughout the tree to reduce chances of it catching fire.

DOOR SECURITY

Have a shelf or small tabletop near the door you normally use when you come home from shopping. When you return from the store laden with bags, you'll have a convenient place for them while you open the door (the keys for which, of course, are in your hand, and not somewhere at the bottom of your purse).

FIREPLACES

Don't burn colored newspapers, magazines, pamphlets, or other paper products with colored ink in your fireplace. Colored ink contains lead and, when you burn it, the lead gets in the air of your home and is dangerous to everybody, but especially to the children.

FIRE EXTINGUISHERS

Fire is a serious threat to your safety at home and to protect against it, you need to have the right fire extinguisher in the right place.

Most people don't know that there are three kinds of fire extinguishers for three different kinds of fires. It's important to make the distinction and choose the right kind, as you may not be able to put out the flames (and may even spread the fire!) with the wrong one. I would refrain from saying all of this is as easy as ABC, except fires are classified as being one of those three types: an A fire or a B fire or a C fire. Be aware that a fire could start out as one kind and spread to include another kind of fire, as we shall see.

The A fire is the simplest and involves the burning of wood, paper, or cloth. The B fire is the type you will most likely encounter in your kitchen or garage. It involves cooking oil, fat, grease, paint, solvents, or gasoline. Finally, the C fire is an electrical fire that can start wherever there is electric power such as a light switch, electric plug, or lighting fixture.

Fire extinguishers for the home are marked with both a letter and a symbol for the type of fire they're designed to put out. A fire extinguishers are marked with an "A" and a triangle, B fire extinguishers with a "B" and a square, and C fire extinguishers with a "C" and a circle. Be sure any extinguisher is also marked as being approved by the Underwriter's Laboratory. If you use an "A" extinguisher, which is designed for wood and paper on a grease fire, the blazing grease will probably float on top of the extinguisher liquid and spread. In the same way, the liquid in an "A" extinguisher may carry electrical current from a "C" fire and also spread the fire. So, have the right extinguisher in the right place.

Speaking of the right place, my father had some good advice about where to keep a fire extinguisher. Naturally, it should be mounted near the stove where a fire is most likely to break out, but not so that it protrudes into walking space. If the extinguisher is knocked on to the floor, it will likely spray stuff all over the kitchen and make a terrible mess. Also—and you'd be surprised at how many people never think about this—you should not have to reach through or over a fire to get the extinguisher. Mount it away from the logical place for a fire so you can get to it quickly without burning yourself.

If you don't have a fire extinguisher in the kitchen and a grease fire occurs, cover it with loads of baking soda. A word of caution—*never* try to put out a grease fire with flour or with water.

FLASHLIGHTS

Flashlights and eyeglasses have something in common; you need one to find one. Sometimes we can't find our glasses without having our glasses on to see. In the same way, what good is a flashlight for seeing in the dark if you can't find the flashlight because it is dark? Give your flashlight a distinct appearance by pasting on a piece of luminous tape or one of the luminous stickers that kids put on their ceilings.

FUSES

As with flashlights, you often need to locate fuses in the dark. Tape extra fuses inside or alongside the fuse box with luminous tape.

GARAGE DOORS

Until a little while ago, I didn't know all that much about garage doors. But since becoming a spokesperson for the Wayne-Dalton Corporation, a garage-door manufacturer, I have learned a great deal about them. The following is valuable information from the experts at Wayne-Dalton about garage-door safety.

Your garage door is the biggest piece of moving equipment in your house. With a properly designed garage-door system, regular maintenance, and— this is important—safety instruction for everyone in your family, your garage door and door opener can give you years of safe, trouble-free operation.

One thing you should do is have a garage-door professional inspect your garage door regularly. (The Wayne-Dalton staff will do that for you free if you call their toll-free line, 1-800-827-DOOR.) In the meantime, they have given us this checklist that will help you evaluate how safe your garage door is.

- Do your garage door sections have a "pinch resistant" design? This type of design can prevent finger and hand injuries when fingers or hands are accidentally put between the garage-door panels as they close.
- Are the springs that lift the door enclosed in a metal tube? If not, a spring that breaks could snap out and cause a serious injury.

- Does your opener have a properly working reversing mechanism attached to the bottom of the door? If the door comes down and hits an object such as a person or a car, it should automatically reverse before causing severe injury or damage. Openers installed after 1991 are required to have this feature.
- Are the cables that attach from the spring system to the bottom brackets on both sides of the door in good condition? If there are frayed or worn stands hanging loose, the cables are in danger of breaking and should be inspected by a professional immediately. Don't try to do this yourself because it is very dangerous and, if any of the springs under tension do snap, you could be badly hurt.
- Does your door go up and down smoothly when you open and close it by hand? If it doesn't, the door may be out of balance and, again, should be inspected by a professional.
- If your door has extension springs, is there a spring-restraint cable running through the spring and anchored to the wall or ceiling at each end? When your garage door is down or closed, the extension springs are under their highest tension. If they are not enclosed in a metal tube and break, they could fly across the garage and seriously hurt someone. A safety cable running through the spring can keep it from doing this. It is even better, of course, to have the spring inside a metal tube.
- Do the bottom brackets on the door use tamper-resistant screws? The bottom brackets are under a lot of tension and should only be adjusted or loosened by a trained service person using special tools. Tamper-resistant screws and bolts prevent accidentally loosening these brackets with ordinary household tools.
- Does your opener have a properly working photoelectric eye connected to the bottom of the track that will automatically reverse the door when its invisible beam is broken? Unlike the reversing mechanism attached to the door, nothing has to physically touch the door to make it reverse. Openers installed after 1993 are required to have photoelectric eyes.
- Is the wall control panel for your opener mounted at least five feet

above the floor so that children cannot easily reach it? Accidents can happen when a child begins playing with opening and closing that heavy door. Teach all the children in your household about the danger of playing with the garage-door control panel.

- Are the remote controls for your openers kept where children cannot play with them? Just as with the wall-control-panel admonition above, children playing with the remote-control unit can cause serious accidents.

- Does your opener have a rolling access-code technology? Some thieves have access to universal control codes that can be used to open your door by reading the access code on the opener or remote control. Prospective thieves might see these when, for example, you park your car unlocked in a public place. Then, they can use it to open your garage door when you're not home and burglarize your house. Rolling code technology changes the code on your opener system after every use.

- Does your garage door have a step plate or lift handle attached to the inside and outside of the bottom section that can be used to lift and close the door manually? A step plate or lift handle is the only safe way to open or close the door manually. You must never—as in *never*—put your hand in between the garage door sections to open or close it. It is a guaranteed way to lose a hand or some fingers.

- Has your garage door been serviced within the last year? While there is some light maintenance you can do yourself, it should be checked, inspected, and serviced by a professional once a year. This may sound like an extreme measure, but for such a huge, dangerous appliance, it is only good sense.

- Do you keep your owner's manual where you can find it and you can check out questions as needed?

- Have you taught everyone in the household about the dangers of the garage door? This is the most basic safety protection you can take. Children, in particular, should know that they should not play around the garage door; to always use handles to open and close manually; to never stand or play under the door; and, to never race under the door as it closes. This last stunt looks glamorous in the movies but it is deadly dangerous in your garage.

GLASS, BROKEN

You undoubtedly know not to pick up broken glass with your bare hands. Pick shards of glass up using soft slices of bread, raw vegetables, leather work gloves, or sweep it up in a dustpan. Throw the glass away immediately in a sealed garbage can where pets can't get to it.

HOUSE KEY, HIDDEN

Many people like to have a key to their front door hidden someplace outside in case they lose their key or to accommodate a friend or family member who needs access to your home when you're not there. Too often these "hidden house keys" are not hidden at all because the entire world plus three other people know where they are. Common "hiding" spots include under the front doormat, over the door, and on a ledge near the door, so don't use these areas.

I've got some ideas for other hiding places that may not be totally safe, but are less conventional. For example, you can buy plastic containers that look like rocks into which you can secret a key, and then place the "rock" in the garden. The real estate industry has another approach that works for them. It is a lock box (shades of Al Gore!) with a combination lock that is hung on the front door knob. Only the real estate agents who have access to the house know the combination. The box is too unsightly to hang on the door for most people, but the idea of a lock box is one good idea. Using a magnetic box and attaching it to something metal in an out-of-sight location is another approach often used.

In my experience, here are some of the things you should do if you are going to have a house key that safely hidden.

- Do not "hide" it in the tired old "usual" places such as under the doormat or on the ledge over the door.
- An ideal spot is some place not related to your house, such as with

the neighbor across the street. Even if somebody finds the key, they won't automatically connect it with your home.

- When you hide or retrieve it, don't do it when or where everybody in the neighborhood can watch you. Put it in a place where you are preferably out of public view and, when you emerge from that out-of-sight spot, don't brandish the key. This is a good time to be paranoid and assume that people are watching you.

  Suppose, for example, that you live in an apartment building with a parking garage. A good approach would be to hide your key some-place in the garage away from your normal parking space. Then, you can drive in and be out of sight while you retrieve the key (of course, you'll want to be sure that no one is watching). Once you have the key—and this is an important point—put it in your pocket or purse as if it had been there all along and take it out the same way. Of course, you want to have the key in your hand so you can immediately open your door and get inside before anyone bothers you.

- Change hiding spots regularly. If you routinely walk back to the rubbish bins, turn over one and pull out a key, they'll catch on.

HOME SECURITY TIPS

There are lots of ways to make your house a safer place to be. Start now by taking advantage of the following methods.

- Bushes that screen doors and windows from the street also screen burglars. Don't allow your shrubbery to become a wall for burglars to hide behind.
- Remove inside crank handles of casement windows to help keep intruders out.
- All exterior doors should have locks that require a key to open from the inside.
- Install motion alarms on all windows and doors.
- You can also install interior, movable motion alarms in the living room, kitchen, or hallway. These have remote controls that you can keep at your bedside, so you can turn them on or off at will.

- To prevent easy access through a sliding door, put a wooden rod in the track.
- If there is too much "play" in a sliding window or door, a burglar can simply lift it out. To reduce the play, put sheet metal screws in halfway in the upper frame, next to the door.
- Mount the hinges on all exterior doors on the inside of the house to prevent removal.
- Door chains are usually held in with short screws that are easy to pop out. Install them with long, heavy screws and install a dead bolt on the inside of the door as well.
- Have a peephole in your front door and install an outside light over the door.
- Keep mace or ammonia spray by the door for defensive purposes. Also keep a whistle by the door or install a scream alarm.
- All outside doors should have a heavy, solid core. Replace any doors with a hollow core with a more substantial door.
- Keep valuables hidden. Place them in a fake heating vent, hollow books, or secret compartments in stairs, plumbing, or other unlikely places.
- Have nightlights plugged in by every exit door.
- Have both battery-operated smoke alarms and carbon monoxide alarms around the house. Also, have rechargeable emergency lights that go on automatically when the power fails placed around the house.
- Trick potential burglars into thinking you have a dog by putting a dog's water dish by the back door and by leaving a dog leash hanging over the doorknob.
- Have one or two inside lights on a timer that will turn them on during the time you might ordinarily be home. Also, set them to go on briefly in the middle of the night as if someone were home and getting up at night. Change the time settings regularly. A smart burglar will catch on if the same lights go on and off at the same time night after night.

- When you are away from home, ask neighbors to pick up your mail and newspapers. Having their delivery stopped is insufficient because other services such as FedEx and UPS may leave items at your door—these packages are dead giveaways that nobody is home. Also, on trash collection day, ask a neighbor to put one of his full trash barrels in front of your house for collection. When you are away from home, it is smart to put your TV on a time clock so it goes on and off. This is more convincing to potential burglars than just a living room light.

KITCHEN SAFETY

While the kitchen is often the most popular room in the house, it is also one of the most hazardous. Use these tips for a cozy kitchen.

Childproofing

Children are naturally curious, and you probably know how they like to explore and fiddle with things. This curiosity can be disastrous in the kitchen. My advice is to simply make it impossible for them to do things such as open cabinets, fiddle with stove and appliance controls, and so on when adults are not looking. There are easy-to-install cabinet latches that kids can't readily undo and those should be on *all* kitchen cabinets. I say *all* because kids can (and will) get up on the counters and try opening upper cabinets—not just lower ones. A temporary cabinet latch can simply be a strong rubber band strung over two adjacent knobs. Put latches on major appliance doors such as refrigerators, freezers, dishwashers, and compactors so the tykes can't open them and crawl inside. Compactors and dishwashers can be particularly dangerous since they are at floor level and often contain silverware, glass, sharp can lids, and other hazards.

All electrical outlets should have tight-fitting safety plugs inserted so the little ones cannot stick fingers, tongues, or pieces of toys into them. Taping over plugs is a good temporary solution, but the kids will soon figure out how to peel off the tape, so only rely on this for the short-term.

Countertop appliances should be anchored down in some way and electric cords wound up and out of reach. Kids have been known to pull appliances off the counter, injuring themselves and others. For more tips on keeping kids safe in the home, see Chapter 17.

Food safety

One food expert says we are potentially exposed to five times as much bacteria as our grandparents were. This is probably due, in part, to the fact that we are eating a greater variety of foods in America from a greater variety of places on the planet than ever before. Food inspection services are overtaxed and can't catch everything, so there may be some things you or your family will catch. Here are some food safety tips for protecting yourself and your family. Some of these tips are obvious but it is surprising how we often forget them.

At the store:

- Shop at reputable stores where things are kept clean and neat. Don't buy fruits or vegetables with bruises or dents.
- Don't buy anything in a dented can.
- Don't buy anything in a package that is not completely sealed.
- Check expiration dates on perishables. Remember the goods with the latest date are at the back of the shelf.
- Make grocery shopping your last stop before going home. Don't let perishable groceries sit in your car too long before getting them home and into your refrigerator.

At home:

- Keep your hands and your kitchen clean. Keep countertops, work areas, and cutting boards washed down with cleanser, soap, or disinfectant.
- Wash your hands in soap and hot water after handling raw meat or poultry. *Do not* use a dishtowel to dry your hands. Use paper towels and throw them away after one use. If you have been handling meat

or fish, you may transfer bacteria to the dishtowel and, then in turn, to your dishes on which you are serving food.

- To kill any possible *E. coli* bacteria, cook meat and poultry well. Rare meat may be a treat in your household, but it is also an invitation to a deadly disease. Refrain. Well done is a much better choice.
- Wash fresh fruit and vegetables thoroughly, even the kinds that come in plastic bags with the notation "Ready To Use." Some food analysts believe that vegetables that come washed and sealed in plastic are probably cleaner than those you wash yourself, but why take chances?
- Don't eat raw cookie dough tasty as it may be.
- Open and carefully inspect packages of flour and grains for mites and little critters. If clear, keep them in well-sealed cans or jars.
- Promptly refrigerate foods that need it. Clean out your refrigerator from time to time and throw away old food.
- Refrigerate or freeze leftovers right away. If something has been left standing in the kitchen for more than two hours, dump it. If it has been outside for a barbecue, a tailgate party, or picnic in warm weather for over an hour, dump it.
- Store your staple goods in a dry place and in sealed containers. Rotate them periodically; turn them upside down regularly.
- Clean up the kitchen promptly after a meal. Dirty dishes are an open invitation to germs that can get into other food or on your hands or in your mouth and nose.
- Wash your kitchen sponges and pot scrubbers in the dishwasher every time you use them. They are germ magnets.
- Wash stirring spoons, knives, ladles, cutting boards, and other utensils before you use them.
- Keep anyone who is ill (including yourself) away from areas where you prepare food. We all love your bratwurst or tacos, but we don't want your microbes.
- Certain foods have parts that are poisonous. Don't eat avocado leaves, apple seeds, rhubarb leaves, tomato leaves, or the pits of apricots, cherries, peaches, and plums.

- The value and safety of "natural" and "health" foods are controversial topics that can't be addressed fully in these pages. Nonetheless, there are a few common misunderstandings that I'd like to clarify. For one, it is unwise, according to some medical experts, to use raw milk, raw milk products, or juices that have not been pasteurized. Cases of food poisoning connected with these products have been reported. Second, be apprised that products called "power," "energy," or "sports" candy bars and "power drinks" are not what they are advertised to be. They are usually low-fat concentrations of carbohydrates, sugar, caffeine, and protein, all of which you can get from other, less expensive sources such as fruit and yogurt.

LIGHTBULBS

Before you change a light bulb, *turn off the electricity!* To remove the remains of a broken lightbulb from the socket, impale the sliced end of a potato on the broken bulb and unscrew. *Turn off the electricity first!*

MICROWAVES

Never heat a cup of water in the microwave without something (non-metal) in the water such as a tea bag, stirring stick, coffee, cocoa. A cup of only water can explode in your face when you take it out of the microwave and stick a spoon in it. This sounds crazy but a researcher at the Los Alamos National Laboratory confirms it. The scientific explanation is this: The cup with only water in it has no points to focus on to start the boiling action. So, the complete cup of water becomes super hot and when disturbed by inserting a spoon, for example, all the stored up energy is released at once and propels the scalding hot water a significant distance.

PLANTS, POISONOUS

Be aware that some houseplants can be poisonous if eaten. For example, azaleas, chrysanthemums, creeping Charlie, mistletoe, morning glories, and oleander should be kept away from children and pets. Also keep children and animals away from the water in which these plants sit.

REFRIGERATOR AND FREEZER SAFETY

Your refrigerator and freezer are two of the most important (and most dangerous) appliances you have in your home and here are some tips about getting the best and safest use out of them.

Safe Usage

First, it is helpful if you understand that both refrigerators and freezers cool or freeze food by pumping blasts of cold air into the compartment where the food is stored. So, you want to be sure that, when loading up either unit, you don't accidentally cover up the cold intake air vents. Second, you want to have some space among the various items in either unit so the cold air can circulate. If you cram either unit too full, you risk diminishing the units' functionality and, ultimately, the safety of eating your food.

Most modern refrigerators and freezers have the temperature controls inside the storage box along with a thermostat that measures the air temperature (not the food temperature) and turns on the pump when more cold air is needed or turns it off when it isn't. The air being pumped into these units comes from outside initially. Then, it is compressed, chilled, and pumped into the units. Experts say the optimum temperature for your freezer is about zero degrees F and your refrigerator between thirty-five and forty degrees F. So, keep your refrigerator and freezer nice and cold and not too full.

Safe Disposal

Refrigerators and freezers can be deadly. Tragically, too often people move their old units into their garage or basement where children play unsupervised. And too often, children climb into the unit and have the airtight door seal them in. The smartest thing to do with an old refrigerator or freezer is to get rid of it immediately! Don't have a tragedy occur where you live.

In spite of the known dangers, some people will advise you to just tape the door closed or put a rope around it. I think you might just as well put a rope around a small child's neck. I've even heard it suggested that you put a wad of paper or cloth or a block to hold the door ajar so the inside won't mildew and, then, tape the door. This, of course, is all the more inviting to little kids and makes it easier for them to open the door wide enough to crawl inside. If, for some insane reason, you keep an empty, used refrigerator or freezer around your place, *remove the door!*

(This, of course, is all part of a long argument about the hazards of one-way doors. For years, people would get trapped in walk-in coolers because the doors only had one-way door handles and locks. Now most units have two-way locks so you can't get trapped inside. Unfortunately, car manufacturers are still debating whether to put handles inside car trunks. I can't explain why. . . . To my knowledge, no one has lobbied refrigerator and freezer makers to install two-way locks on their products. So, it's up to you. In some cities, incidentally, the electric utility company will haul away your used refrigerator or freezer at no charge as a public service.)

THROW RUGS

If you have throw rugs on slippery floors that make people slip and slide, try one of the following ways to anchor them. Sew some kind of non-slip item on the underside, such as the rubber seals from mason jars, nonslip bathtub decals or even double-sided tape. This tape is available in most home improvement or stationery stores. Another handy product is double-backed Velcro strips. These are tape strips that are adhesive on one side and have Velcro on the other side. Tape a strip on the rug and another on the floor—both with the Velcro side facing out—and push them together. This approach also works for sofa and chair cushions that find their way off the furniture.

WATER, SAFE

Everybody understands the importance of clean water and these days almost all of us buy bottled water for drinking. Of course you will want to have some bottled water in your home in case of an emergency. But for everyday use, bottled water can be expensive and is not always dependable. Sadly, there have been cases reported of "bottled water" companies simply filling up bottles out of the local taps and selling it as especially pure spring water. A popular alternative to buying bottled water is to filter your water at home.

There are several types of at-home water filtering or purifying systems, and you should be familiar with the options before you buy. One type of system will process all the water coming into your house and another system will just process water coming out of a particular tap such as at the kitchen sink.

To decide what you want in a water processing system, you first have to decide what you *don't* want in your water. In general, there are four substances that we want to keep out of the water we use.

Lead

Because exposure to lead is dangerous, particularly to children, we don't want lead in our morning coffee or in the water we use to cook dinner. Unfortunately, lead has been widely used in many construction projects. For example, if your house was constructed before 1986, the chances are good—or, rather, bad—that it was built with lead plumbing and lead solder was used. This is probably true of the community water system where you live, too. Lead poisoning is particularly troubling for several reasons. For one, it is hard to detect lead in the water because it is tasteless and odorless. A special test must be conducted to reveal its presence. In addition, even if your public water system is lead-free and pure water is delivered to your home or you have a water filter outside the house, the water will pick up lead from running through your own plumbing system. I'll come back to this.

Chemicals

In some locales, the water may taste bad or smell bad even though it is perfectly safe. This is often true of systems that depend on well water or on community systems where a lot of chemicals such as chlorine are used to kill parasites in the water. It is like drinking water out of a chlorine-laced swimming pool. In this situation, you are less concerned about the purity of the water than its cosmetic qualities. You don't want your breakfast orange juice to smell and taste of chlorine.

Rust and mud

Although we want some iron in our daily diet, we don't want to see iron particles floating in our drinking water nor do we want rust in the sink and toilet bowl. A simple sieve filter that strains out large particles can prevent this, and the aerator at the nozzle of most faucets will do so. However, it may not be fine enough to strain out the small specks you will still see in a clear glass of water.

Bugs

Finally, there is the icky case of having actual bacteria and parasites in the water you drink and use for cooking. This is a common problem for houses that rely on well water. It can be a difficult issue to solve since certain parasites such as cysts (officially called *Crystosporidium* and *Giardia*) are difficult to kill or get rid of even with such treatments as chlorine. A good water filter system using particular cartridge filters for these pesky parasites will usually eliminate this risk.

FILTER SYSTEMS

As I mentioned before, there are a number of water filter systems available. Many of them can be installed by the homeowner and others require installation and maintenance by a contractor. Some systems have one filter cartridge and some have more than one to deal with multiple water purity problems.

Filter systems are basically identified by geography—by where they are located in your house. The whole-house filter is designed to treat the water for—guess what?—the whole house. Usually, these filters are a large tank that you connect to the incoming water line outside your house. Some people don't see much sense in filtering all their water since a lot of it is for bathing, washing the car and the dog, watering the lawn, and hosing down the patio or deck. Moreover, these filters do not address the contamination that comes from the house plumbing itself, such as the lead in many older pipes. Thus, a whole house filter is best for new homes where the local water supply is suspect.

Another system is the under-the-sink filter that treats the water going to one faucet. That can solve the problem of contamination from in-house lead pipes and solder, but it limits the source of drinkable water to one faucet unless you want to mount several filter systems under several faucets.

Faucet filters, as the name says, are attached to the faucet. They need no plumbing connections as do the whole house or under-the-sink systems. You just follow the instructions and screw them on to the end of the faucet and there you are. The kind of results you get from these depends (as it does with all the other systems) on the brand you buy. Generally, you will get less from faucet filters because they are much smaller and less sophisticated than the whole house or under-the-sink kind. The smaller filter means you will have to change it more frequently than the larger systems. Also, some householders don't like the bulky appearance of faucet filters.

Finally, the countertop filter is the easiest and simplest system of all. You just pour the water into it, wait a minute or two as it seeps through the filter, and pour clean, treated water out. The disadvantages are obvious: you can only purify or treat a little water at a time and it sits on the counter for all to see (you could keep it in the refrigerator, of course). The advantages are that they are relatively inexpensive and you can buy one at the store today. They also, like the under-the-sink filter and the faucet filter, handle all types of contamination problems.

WATER, SCALDING

One of the more serious safety hazards around the home—particularly for young kids or seniors—is scalding hot water. I have mentioned elsewhere that many hot-water heater thermostats are set at 140 degrees F and I recommend that setting be lower, at about 120 degrees. One hundred forty degrees is supposed to be for optimum operation of your dishwasher but it will work just fine at 120 degrees, according to some dishwasher manufacturers. In addition, many dishwashers have a built-in temperature booster that will heat the water coming into it to an even high level. So, set your hot-water heater at 120 degrees. If you want to double-check that the thermostatic thermometer on your hot-water heater is accurate, try running the hot-water over a meat thermometer.

Water at 140 degrees can scald and with kids in a bathtub this can be a disaster. There are thousands of kids scalded by too-hot water ever year—at least five times as many as are hurt in fireworks accidents. Toddlers under the age of four are particularly at risk because their skin has not finished developing and it is less protective than that of older people.

To protect your child from getting burned in the tub, put your hand in the bath water to test the temperature or test it with a meat thermometer. As a rule, the water should be absolutely no hotter than 100 degrees F.

When you put your child in the tub for a bath, face him or her away from the faucets and as far down toward the other end of the tub as possible. Kids are always fooling around and exploring and part of their learning process is to imitate everything adults do. So, when your child sees you fiddling with the faucet handles, he or she wants to do it too. The minute you're not looking or have turned your back to get a towel or something, the child will be playing with the faucets and may accidentally turn on the scalding hot water.

Never, leave your child alone in the tub for any reason. Not to answer the phone or the door or to turn on the TV—*never*.

DANGERS OUTSIDE THE HOME

When you're in public or traveling (or even in your own backyard), you face all sorts of potential problems. Use the following tips to prevent them.

CREDIT CARD SECURITY

Photocopy all the important cards that you keep in your wallet such as your credit cards, driver's license, medical insurance, work identification, and so on. Write any important contact addresses or phone numbers alongside each card. Make several copies and keep one in a different safe place, including with relatives or trusted friends. If you lose your wallet or if it gets stolen, you'll be able to resolve the ensuing credit card/identification problems quickly and easily.

INSECTS, PROTECTION AGAINST

We attract insects through our smell—and it isn't that our deodorant has failed. It's just that it's in the wrong place. So we smear another deodorant we call pesticide on our exposed body parts and that is supposed to work. Sometimes it does and sometimes it doesn't.

The hazards of being bitten can be more severe than just the irritation of our skin. In the process, some insects transfer diseases from their bodies to ours. Here are some examples: the bite of deer ticks in the woods of the Northeastern states can cause Lyme disease, and the bite of dog ticks in the Rocky Mountains can give us Rocky Mountain spotted fever. In the New York City region mosquitoes are carrying what is called West Nile virus, which can be serious enough to make people very sick and, in some cases, die.

What to do to protect yourself and your family and friends? Well, consider yourself the lunch. What would you do if you didn't want flies to eat food you have on the table? You would cover it up among other things. So, that's the easiest, most effective way. Wear long-sleeved shirts or blouses, pants you tuck into your shoes, headgear, and so on. If the critters can't get to your naked body, they can't feast on it. To make your clothing itself repulsive to insects, you should spray some appropriate repellent on your clothes too.

What kind of repellent is best? (I'm now talking about repellent, something that drives bugs away, and not insecticide, something that kills bugs.) Well, there are a variety of commercial repellent products, most of them based on the same chemical. You need to read the instructions and see what chemical is in the repellent you are considering buying. Yes, I know that reading the instructions is un-American and violates some sacred code of our society, but I urge you to read them anyhow and I promise not to tell anybody.

The chemical you are most likely to find listed is N,N-diethyltoluamide that, also in keeping with a great American tradition, no one tries to pronounce and so has been shortened to "DEET." DEET works because it is powerful, and because it is powerful you want to keep it away from your face, cuts, or any breaks in your skin. You also don't want to use any product that contains more than 30 percent DEET. DEET in high concentrations (greater than 35 percent) provides no additional protection. There is no need to apply a repellent made with DEET under your clothing—just on your exposed skin. Put it on once and then leave it alone. When you come back inside, wash it off. Commercial repellents containing DEET can be used to keep ticks, mosquitoes, and other insects away.

Tick bite Prevention

To protect yourself against ticks:

- Avoid tick-infested areas, especially in May, June, and July.
- Wear light-colored clothing so that ticks can be spotted more easily.
- Tuck your pants into your boots or socks and tape the area where they meet. Be sure to tuck your shirt into your pants.
- Spray insect repellent containing DEET on clothes and on exposed skin (other than the face), or treat clothes (especially pants, socks, and shoes) with permethrin, which kills ticks on contact.
- Walk in the center of trails to avoid overhanging grass and brush.

After being outdoors, remove your clothing and wash and dry it at a high temperature and inspect your body carefully. If you find a tick, remove it with tweezers, grasping the tick as close to the skin surface as possible and pulling straight back with a slow steady force; avoid crushing the tick's body. In some areas, ticks (saved in a sealed container) can be submitted to the local health department for identification.

To reduce the number of ticks in your yard, remove leaves and clear brush and tall grass from around your home and garden. This is particularly important in the eastern United States, where Lyme disease is most prevalent.

Mosquito Bite Prevention

- Stay indoors at dawn, dusk, and in the early evening when mosquitoes are most active.
- Wear long-sleeved shirts and long pants whenever you are outdoors.
- Spray clothing with repellents containing permethrin or DEET since mosquitoes may bite through thin clothing.
- Apply insect repellent containing DEET sparingly to exposed skin. Repellents may irritate the eyes and mouth, so avoid applying repellent to the hands of children.
- Whenever you use an insecticide or insect repellent, be sure to read and follow the manufacturer's directions as printed on the product.
- If you want to try natural repellents, carry oranges, onions, or basil in your pockets. (Mosquitoes hate these smells.) You can also try dabbing some vanilla extract on exposed parts of your body.
- Try also to keep dry, because they like damp clothing.
- Note: Vitamin B and "ultrasonic" devices are *not* effective in preventing mosquito bites.

Of course, there is still the chance you'll get bitten. Some of the things that normally will take the zing out of the sting if you get bitten by an insect include vinegar, meat tenderizer, bleach, and lemon juice.

Keeping Insects Away from Your Property

If you want to drive insects away from your garden, patio, or deck, try spraying a solution of dishwasher liquid or nicotine solution from soaking cigarette butts or sprinkle coffee grounds in your garden.

Whether you use the inexpensive, "natural" pesticides I suggest above or the commercial kind you buy at the store, there are some basic rules about handling them. The principle rule is that you want to poison insects and bad critters, not yourself, your family, or your pets. Here are some recommendations:

- Read the instructions. You are dealing with poisons that can do serious damage to you and the people around you. Keep the pesticides in their original container with the instructions printed on it.
- Protect yourself. Wear protective gear and clothing when you are using pesticides: rubber gloves, a facemask, long-sleeved shirts, long pants, and closed-toe shoes. You don't want any of the poison spray or fumes to get into your lungs or nose, nor do you want them seeping into the pores of your body.
- Keep pesticides locked up. Store pesticides in locked compartments and on high shelves where children and pets cannot get at them. Do not store them near heat, such as by furnaces or hot-water heaters. Insecticide sprays in aerosol cans will explode when overheated.
- Discard containers carefully. Wrap "empty" containers of pesticide (which are actually never really completely empty) in paper and seal them in a plastic bag. Discard them directly in a secure trash container. You can use a neighborhood dumpster if the contents are not accessible to passersby. Discarding them into your household trash barrel isn't a great idea because kids and pets might still get at them.
- Clear the area before using. Make sure there is nothing around the area that you *don't* want to put poison on. For example, open food, drink, dishes, pots and pans, utensils, clothing, shoes, or anything else that might transfer pesticide from its surface onto anyone's skin, mouth, or nose.
- Stay away from the area after using. If the pesticide is in a spray form, keep your family, your pets, and yourself out of the area sprayed for an hour or more. When you go back in, double-check to make sure there is nothing such as was described above (food, drink, utensils, clothing, etc.) accidentally left behind, which now needs to be removed and discarded or washed. Certainly, don't go into the area and expose yourself by doing something like walking around barefoot.

LUGGAGE TRICK

Airlines recommend that you put a name tag on the outside of your luggage so they can more efficiently route it to Brazil while you're traveling to Chicago. But, how do you prove it's your luggage if the tag is ripped off? It's a good idea to place an identification card somewhere inside your luggage giving your name and phone number.

PICKPOCKETS

Use double-backed Velcro strips inside your pants pocket to deter pickpockets.

DEALING WITH DISASTER

This is a subject that I was a little uncertain about including. Sometimes I think it is human nature to avoid thinking about our mortality. A disaster can't possibly happen to us, so why bother preparing for one? In fact, some people think that doing so will bring on bad luck. The truth is that it is indicative of good sense because every year thousands of people are hit by and often forced out of their homes by hurricanes, earthquakes, floods, slides, fires, tornadoes, and other disasters. So make yourself read and act on the following advice.

GENERAL PREPAREDNESS

This list of ideas gives you the basics of what you need to do to be ready for a crisis.

- Have emergency kits ready with fresh water, a flashlight, a portable radio, extra batteries, a signal mirror, a hand ax, matches, and manual can opener. (I'll talk more about the various emergency kits you should prepare in the upcoming pages.)
- Train everyone in your household about how to respond in an emergency. During an earthquake, for example, take refuge in an inside doorway. Keep away from windows where you could be cut by break-

ing glass and don't run out of the building because pieces of the roof can fall on you.

- Place items like pictures, bookcases, or shelves far away from your bed so they can't fall on you while you're sleeping.
- Turn off your gas supply at the meter in case the disaster causes a pipe to rupture and gas to leak out.
- Make sure everyone in the household knows your phone number and your address and how to call for help on 911. The safety of an entire family can rest with a very young child who calls for help.

EMERGENCY KITS

I recommend that you prepare at least three types of emergency survival kits. You and your family may only have a few minutes to prepare and if you follow the steps below, your survival and comfort rate will be immeasurably higher. These kits are to supplement the emergency kit you have already in your car to handle car problems such as flats and getting stuck in the mud.

Home Survival

A home survival kit is designed to sustain you and your family in your home for three days until help arrives. Have it in a central, easy-to-reach place in your home. The kit should contain a portable radio, flashlight, candles, matches, extra batteries, and the always-handy roll of duct tape. A key kitchen utensil that you never thought you would need again in the world of modern appliances is the hand-operated can opener. When the power goes off, you might have hundreds of cans of food you can't get to unless you have a manual can opener. Of course, you should have a supply of food and water in the house, as well as tools for turning valves, breaking into or out of places, and heavy-duty work gloves.

Other preparations include keeping a broom in a central location so you can sweep up any broken glass or other debris. Know how to shut off your electricity because electrical shorts can cause disastrous fires. Turn off both the gas lines and the water lines until you are sure it is safe to turn them on again. Broken water lines can soak your living quarters, spread electrical shocks, and ruin foodstuff. Gas is doubly dangerous, since a spark from an electrical short, a lighted candle, or a match can make it explode. Interestingly, gas is not poisonous by and of itself. It is lethal because it drives out all the breathable air in an enclosed room or house. Just for the record, that horrible gas smell is not natural. The utility company adds the smell to alert you when gas is on the loose. To take care of the above responsibilities and other needs that may arise, prepare at least one emergency tool kit that includes pliers and wrenches, a small combination hatchet/hammer, and a slot screwdriver and a Phillips-head screwdriver.

Another way to prepare for a crisis is to have all your immunizations up-to-date. It is assumed that you've had the standard childhood vaccinations, such as those for polio, measles, and the like. You should, however, get a tetanus/diphtheria booster shot every ten years. In addition to these shots, you should probably be immunized against cholera and typhoid. This may seem extreme, but in times of disaster, sewers overflow, fresh water is scarce, and a lot of other normal services fail. When they do, diseases like cholera and typhoid can be a very serious problem. So, you and everybody in your family should have those shots, too.

Fresh water is often a problem in major disasters, so it's a good idea to have a minimum of two quarts of bottled water for every person in the household. As I mentioned earlier, turn off the water intake lines coming into your house from outside. That outside water could easily be contaminated and you should wait until authorities report that the water supply is safe before you use it. Which brings me to the secret water reservoirs in your house—the ones you don't think of right away: your hot water heater and the toilet tank. Yes, you can drink the water in the hot-water heater and there is a faucet at the bottom of the tank for you to drain it out as needed. There is also a faucet at the top of the tank that you might want to shut off as extra insurance that no contaminated water comes in from outside. That brings us to the touchy subject of the toilet tank water. Yes, the water in the tank is drinkable. You probably don't want to drink the water in the bowl. In emergency times, you may want to limit the use of the toilet and forbid flushing until safe water is available. It may be somewhat tacky, but it may be necessary. An obvious solution is to have a supply of plastic bags that you can seal and use for human waste without using the toilet.

EVACUATION SURVIVAL

Create an evacuation survival kit for each person in your household. Each should contain the basic supplies to last for three days away from home. It's a good idea to have this all packed in a backpack and ready for instant departure. The kit should include a passport, a cell phone with an extra battery, three days' supply of cash, credit cards, a driver's license, a medical insurance card, and a key to your safe deposit box, if you have one. The kit should also contain a photocopy of all the aforementioned identification and credit cards held by every adult in the family. Every adult should have a copy. Send a copy to a trustworthy person in a far away place. The kit should include prepaid telephone cards for every adult and older child in your group along with phone numbers of a trustworthy contact some distance away who can act as a message center.

In addition, each kit should have a three-day supply of food and water. Pack up basic necessities such as medicines, first aid and sanitary supplies, candles, matches, a flashlight, a portable radio, extra batteries, a signaling mirror, a change of underwear, toilet paper, razor blades, and a small combination tool (there are some very compact gadgets that are many tools in one, available at discount and hardware stores), tea or coffee bags.

Personal Survival

Finally, you should have a personal survival kit for each person in your household. This third kit is a small one that you can carry on your person in a pocket or two. You can create one with a small plastic container or a used tin candy box. This is in addition to what you are able to carry in your wallet in terms of cards and money.

In the kit, place matches, several birthday candles, aspirin, band aids, safety pins, a needle threaded with strong nylon thread, small knife or single-edged razor blade, tea, coffee, or bouillon bags and some cotton pads for injuries. Wrap the box with duct tape and rubber bands.

CLOTHING

In any emergency, you should have on the proper clothing. Remember, you may be faced with wet or cold weather, winds, no bedding, and rough walking conditions through mud, water, rocks, broken glass, snakes, bugs, and the like. Therefore, you should have a waterproof hooded parka, sturdy hiking shoes or boots, and rugged pants that you can live and sleep in for several days. Have some heavy work gloves because you want to protect your hands and you may have to handle some unpleasant and yucky stuff.

If you follow these hints, your chances of survival will go up sharply.

ASSISTING EMERGENCY WORKERS

In case of an emergency, policemen or firemen may be in your home. You may be gone or unconscious and unable to assist them. So, list the names, ages, and descriptions of every member of the household including your pets. Provide their usual nighttime location in the house (for example, "upstairs back bedroom") and any special medical information about them (for example, "diabetic") and medication they require. Also, list the names and phone numbers of people to contact in an emergency. Put all of this on one sheet with a prominent heading—*emergency information*—and tape it securely to the refrigerator door. This tells firemen and police who needs to be rescued and where they are in seconds when every minute is critical.

Finally, everyone in your household should have an identification bracelet or plastic card stating his name, address, and phone, an emergency contact person, his doctor's name and phone and any important medical information. Have the cards laminated and a hole punched in them (you can usually do this at office supply stories or mailbox stations). Have everyone in the family carry the card in their wallet, purse, or on a cord around their neck. This information could literally save a life in an emergency situation.

5

HIRING HELP

You can't do it all yourself. Here are some tips on hiring
the right people to help you.

There are so many things we could do for ourselves if we had limitless time, but we don't. To look after our home and our family, we need to hire baby-sitters, gardeners, mechanics, repairmen, painters, and so on. Here we give you tips on how to make the best choices and get the best results for your money.

AUTO MECHANICS

Even if you are a master of the mechanics of your car, it doesn't mean you want to do all the repair and maintenance work yourself, so it's important to have a trustworthy repair garage. Ideally, you will want a place that lets you take your car for a ride without them taking you for a ride, too.

When finding a mechanic, you need to decide whether you want one who is affiliated with a dealership or who is independent. If you have purchased your car from a car dealer and it's under warranty, you will initially go to the dealer's shop because you have already paid for repair services when you bought the car with the warranty.

Let's pause here for a little truth about car and other warranties that it is helpful to understand. Most people think that the purpose of a warranty is to protect the car buyer. As I mentioned in Chapter 3, the warranty is to protect the car manufacturer and car dealer by limiting their liability in what they are selling you. This is particularly true with "express" or "specific" warranties that spell out the post-sale responsibilities of the car maker and dealer. Without a signed agreement to such warranties, the courts might rule that there is an "implied" warranty that is much broader in its coverage of the buyer. Just to nail it down for the manufacturer and dealer, the warranty you sign often has language saying that this express or specific warranty supercedes any other guarantee of any kind, "stated or implied."

Back to deciding whether you want to continue with the dealer's repair shop or look for an independent shop. Consider the following factors when making your decision.

- **Attitude:** What is the attitude of the mechanics toward you and toward your car? Are all the staff members friendly and willing to be helpful, or do they treat you like a dummy? Some mechanics have been known to deliberately overwhelm car owners with technical jargon, a.k.a. garage gibberish. (While women are likely targets, it can be even worse if you're a man. Men are *supposed* to know all about cars, but many men don't and have to fake it. Don't think mechanics don't catch on when a man is faking his mechanical knowledge.) Remember, everybody is stupid—just about different things. Insist that everything be explained to you in plain English and with respect.

- **Automotive Service Excellence Program:** Auto mechanics have created a certification program of education and training called the Automotive Service Excellence Program. Those who complete the program are awarded certificates of competence in up to eight specialty areas. Any mechanic who has finished all eight and who has at least two years' experience is qualified as a Master Automobile Technician. The program requires mechanics to get recertified every five years so they can keep up on advances in the field. ASE and

MAT certificates are usually proudly on display in the repair shop. Look for them.

- **Evaluating the problem:** It helps a lot if you know your car. Read the owner's manual so you have a good idea of how it works. If you take the time to help the mechanic figure out what is wrong with your car, it will help him correct the problem in a timely and less costly way. Be prepared to describe the symptoms of the problem in detail to the mechanic. Note how the problem presents itself to all of your senses—the sounds, feels, smell, and visuals, too.

- **Written estimates:** Every good repair shop will give you a written estimate of what needs to be done and the cost. The estimate protects both you and the mechanic. The estimate should state that no additional work will be done without your authorization, that replaced parts will be given to you and that only brand-name parts will be used. This is when you should also find out if there is a warranty on the work and parts. If, after you've checked over the written estimate, you're not satisfied, simply say you want to get a second opinion and take your car to another shop. *Do not sign anything that you do not agree to or that you don't understand.* If you don't get a written estimate, walk away. You'll want nothing to do with this shop.

- **Specialty shops vs. general repair shops:** Some repair shops specialize in a particular kind of work such as muffler and exhaust systems, heating and air conditioning, transmission, brakes, and the like. You're probably familiar with franchised specialty shops such as AAMCO, Midas, and Jiffy Lube. You can get fine work done at these shops, but I advise you to approach them with care. Consider them using the same factors that you use to evaluate dealers' repair shops and independent mechanics. I've found that specialty shops are often staffed by people who are specialists who know how to open and close two or three valves, squirt something here and grease something there, and *boom!* out the door you go. They don't have the expertise to spot other important problems or to alert you to them.

- **Price:** If you really want to protect yourself and your budget, go to the library or the Internet and locate a Flat Rate Manual. This is a

POST–CAR REPAIR TIPS

After you get your car fixed, follow these tips: First, read the bill. Check it carefully and make sure you understand every charge. Verify that the math is right. If the warranty is applicable, make sure that it is properly referenced. Test-drive your car before you finish up with the visit to the shop. If there is still a problem, this is the time to point it out. A good repair shop will want repeat business and will make an effort to get the job done right. Pay your bill with a credit card. Should you discover that the work isn't satisfactory, notify the credit card company. It will not pay the shop until the dispute is settled. Keep all the paperwork on everything done. Ideally, you should keep a vehicle log or diary noting everything that has been done to the car.

generic guide to how much time it takes a competent mechanic to do various jobs. Check this time against the hourly mechanic's rate that should be posted on a sign in the repair shop and you'll have your own estimate of what cost of the *labor* for the job should cost. You can find out what the *parts* will cost by checking with your local auto-parts store. Put the labor and parts costs together and you'll have a good idea of what your repair job ought to cost.

On the other hand, don't just shop for the lowest price. Somebody once said the most expensive help you buy is the one that doesn't do the job right. You are not only paying for the price of a part and some of the mechanic's time, you are paying for professional experience and judgment. One joke concerns the man whose car wasn't running right and he turned it over to his mechanic. He quickly tightened one bolt and it was fixed. The bill read, "Labor: Tightening one bolt in less than a minute . . . 35 cents. 20 Years Experience: Knowing what bolt to tighten . . . $50."

• **Do a background check:** Ask your friends and neighbors about where they take their car. In my experience, personal recommendations are very valuable. You should also call the Better Business Bureau and other local consumer protection agencies about the reputation of shops suggested to you. Finally, ask a staff member to give you the names of some of their regular customers to use as references.

- **Inside the garage:** There are certain qualities you should look for in a garage. Do the mechanics seem well organized? Does the shop have modern testing equipment? Are their policies and prices posted openly? Are diplomas, awards, or other indicators of professional competence displayed?

BABY-SITTERS

Parents today are very selective about who they hire to look after their kids, and I'm all for close scrutiny when it comes to picking a baby-sitter. Here are some pointers I've picked up from experts such as the American Red Cross and the U.S. Department of Occupational Safety.

Ideally, pick someone you know and who has sat with other members of your family or friends. A baby-sitter should be 14 years old or older. The American Red Cross advises that you never entrust your children to anyone under 11 years of age. When considering your rate of pay, I recommend paying a bit more than the "going rate." Pay for an early arrival so you have time to brief the sitter. A few extra dollars tells the sitter that you are serious about this job and that she is expected to act accordingly.

BEFORE THE SITTER'S ARRIVAL

Prepare an information sheet and put one by every phone in the house. It should include:

The address and phone number of your home
The name, address, and phone number of your destination
The name, address, and phone number of a neighbor
The name, address, and phone number of your children's doctor

Emergency phone numbers for the police, fire department, and poison-control center

Take a tour of your house. Lock all windows and doors that should be locked. Remove all potential dangers such as toys on stairs and unlocked cellar doors.

Prepare a package of essentials for the baby-sitter, including written instructions and information (I'll cover the details in the following pages), a set of keys, and the location of emergency equipment, such as fire extinguishers and alarm systems.

UPON THE SITTER'S ARRIVAL

Ask the sitter to arrive at least 30 minutes before you are leaving so there is time to brief her, review your rules for the children, the house, and her. Take her on a slow and careful tour of the house. During the walk-through, check for hazards and things that the children can get into, such as matches, electric cords, plastic bags, medication, or anything else that may be dangerous. Remember she is a stranger to your home and can't absorb all she should know in just two minutes. Don't give her the "nice to meet you, see you later" treatment. She may have to get your kids out of the house in case of fire or call for help if there is an accident.

Basic Instructions

Tell her the following information and leave it in writing as part of the baby-sitter kit:

- The names of your children and any special information about each one. Introduce them and let her visit with them for a little while *before* you leave.
- The names of dogs and other pets.
- The time you expect to return.
- How you want incoming phone calls handled. She should never tell a caller she is home alone with the children. Have her say you are there but can't come to the phone.

- Your typical nighttime routine such as which lights should be left on and the like.
- What to do about strange noises, prowlers, or odd phone calls.

Emergency Information

Instruct the sitter on how to prevent an emergency situation and what to do should an emergency occur. For example, in case of a fire, make sure she knows to get the children out of the house immediately. Don't try to put out the fire! Just get everybody out immediately. Keep the children all together at all times. She should know to stay close to the floor to avoid deadly smoke and fumes. She should know to feel doors to see if they're hot before opening them. There may be fire on the other side. When everyone is out, she should go to a neighbor's house and call the Fire Department.

- Tell the sitter the location of medicines, cleaning supplies, and electrical outlets, and tell her to keep children away from them.
- Tell her to check on the children should the house suddenly become quiet—they could be up to something!
- If there is an emergency alarm system, show her how to use it.
- Show the sitter how to secure the house by locking any unlocked windows and doors and how to turn on the outside light.
- Show her where smoke alarms and fire extinguishers are and how to use them. If you are in an apartment, point out the emergency exits.
- Tell her to keep stairs and passageways free of toys or other objects.

Finally, before you leave the house, make sure that the baby-sitter has notified her parents where she is, that you have her full name and the name of her parents, her home address, and phone number. Ask her about any special medical needs she may have.

House Rules

Rather than expect the babysitter to guess, let her know your expectations.

- Tell her what she is allowed to eat and use in the house.
- Let her know that she should not have any visitors without your approval. Generally, male visitors should not be allowed in any case.
- Inform her of your rules about strangers at the door, on the premises, or on the phone. Generally, a baby-sitter should never open the door for a stranger.
- Clarify your preferences about using the telephone. Normally, she should not make any calls of more than a few minutes in length. Long phone calls may prevent you from getting through and keep her attention away from the children.
- Tell her what the children should eat and when. Let her know about any special diets or idiosyncrasies.
- Give her guidelines about where, what, and for how long the children are allowed to play, watch TV, and the like.
- Make sure she knows when bedtime is, and of any special bedtime rituals.
- If any of the children are on medications, let her know about them and when they should be taken.
- Be explicit about what kind of discipline is to be used and when.
- Let her know whether the children may leave the house or have friends visit.
- Also inform the baby-sitter about how you want the children to be monitored. For example, you might tell her that when the children are asleep, she should check on them about every 15 minutes and that when they're up, she must know their location at all times and never leave them alone too long.
- Be sure to let her know about anything special or unusual about your children.

UPON YOUR RETURN

Inquire about any problems the baby-sitter may have had. Check on any messages or visitors. Be sure that the sitter is comfortable with whoever is escorting her home. She may prefer someone from her home to come get her.

SPECIAL CONCERNS FOR DAYTIME BABY-SITTERS

When someone is watching your children in the daytime, there are different issues to consider in addition to those I discussed in the preceding pages. For example, the sitter should know that if the children are out in the backyard, she should make sure the front door and outside gates are locked. If she takes the children for a walk or to the park, she should lock all doors and windows before she leaves. She should be sure to take the keys and some change with her. Inform the baby-sitter that she should never take the children to a deserted park or out alone after dark and that she must be wary of all strangers. Tell her that if she feels uncomfortable in a situation, she should leave with the children immediately. Finally, instruct her to look for anything unusual when she returns home—like a broken window, a ripped screen, or a door left ajar. If she does, tell her that she must not go in to investigate, but to take the children with her to a neighbor's home or public phone, and call the police at 911 or the operator.

CARPET CLEANERS

Obviously, you can hire a professional to clean your carpet or you can do it yourself. Ask friends, family, and neighbors about carpet-cleaning professionals they have used. When you get a few recommendations, start comparison shopping. Here are some of the facts you need to get to make a sound comparison of competing professional carpet cleaners.

PRICE

Naturally, you are concerned about the cost. Some professionals will quote a price by the square foot, some by the square yard and some by the room. Measure the area to be cleaned before you call anybody. By that, I mean every room, every closet, every hallway, and so on.

Use a yardstick or tape measure to check the length times the width of each area. That will give you the number of square feet. If you want to convert it to square yards remember to divide by *nine*. Yes, nine. There are nine square feet in a square yard.

When asking for a price, give your carpet measurements and find out how these areas are calculated by the cleaner. For example, he might quote the prices as "Four rooms for so much." What you want to know is, "What is a room?" If you have a dining area off the living room, is that one room or two rooms? What are closets—part of the main room or a separate room? What about hallways?

REFERENCES AND CONTRACT

I think it is important that you get references from the cleaner (you're going to live with his mistakes long after he's gone) and that you have a written contract that spells out the dimensions of each area to be cleaned.

Be sure the cleaner has insurance for damages to your carpets *and* other things in your house. You don't want to find out his insurance doesn't cover knocking over Aunt Tilly's Ming Dynasty vase. Hot water cleans carpets better than cold, so verify that the cleaner uses hot water.

PRECLEANING PREPARATIONS

Once you are set on the cleaner, it is your turn to do some work. Make your carpeted areas easily accessible to the cleaner. Normally, the cleaner will take care of temporarily moving all the heavy furniture, but you need to get all the small, personal stuff out of the way. Afterward, you should thoroughly ventilate the cleaned areas by opening windows and doors and running fans or air conditioners.

CONTRACTORS

For those times when you want to do a bigger job than you have the skill or time to do, you will hire an outside contractor to paint, rebuild, replace, or repair. Here are my tips on how to do this with the least exasperation and cost.

- Usually, a remodeling contractor is selected through a referral. When my wife and I last remodeled, we got our contractor's name from our friends Shelley and Mike Farrell. Other good sources include neighbors, business colleagues, architects/designers, real estate agents, and building materials suppliers.

- The key to a successful remodeling happens before a tool is lifted. It's a good set of plans and specifications. Insist on this.
- Hover. When the remodeling is started, visit the job frequently. Contractors and subcontractors don't think the way you do and mainly want to get the job done. If you watch as they go along, you can correct any errors early.
- As the remodeling progresses, make a written record and take video or still photos.
- You will get bids on much of the work and materials. Challenge every one and try for a better price. I do this all the time and usually get a lower price as a result.
- Do not hire a contractor who seems to have no roots. If you only get a post office box for an address and a cell phone to call, be suspicious. Do not hire anyone who has no references or who wants a big advance or who must always be paid in cash. Finally, don't hire a contractor who acts impatient or makes you feel uncomfortable.
- Be flexible. It is normal for contractors to work more than one job at a time and they cannot always show up when you expect them.
- Get color samples in advance for all painting, flooring, and stains to compare with the finished job. Ask for leftover paint and stains to be left with you so you can do touch-up work later if needed.
- Try to keep your sense of humor. This isn't the Taj Mahal you're building.

6

COOKING AND KITCHEN TIPS

The kitchen can be warm and friendly or a frustrating mess.
Here are hints on making it warm and friendly.

Many people say that the kitchen is their favorite room—perhaps because it is where many family traditions begin. Our associations with the kitchen may well relate to primitive tribal memories of gathering around the fire for warmth and nourishment. And while we have moved on from the open fire in the forest to the hibachi at the tailgate party, we still have all sorts of problems when it comes to food preparation. Here are tips and ideas on making your kitchen experience less work and more fun.

CLEAN KITCHEN IDEAS

I have lots of hints about keeping your kitchen tidy and germ-free. If you don't find what you're looking for here, check out Chapter 7.

COFFEEMAKERS

Clean lime deposits and calcium sludge from an automatic drip coffee maker by filling the reservoir with white vinegar and running the brew cycle. Rinse thoroughly with two cycles of cold water.

DISHCLOTHS

A quick way to clean bacteria out of your damp dishcloth is to zap it in the microwave for 30 seconds. Or tie it to one of the racks in your dishwasher and wash it along with the dishes.

SPILLS, PREVENTING

When mixing ingredients in a bowl, put a folded damp towel—cloth or paper—under the bowl to keep it from slip sliding around.

When frying greasy foods, put a metal colander or strainer upside down over the pan. Be careful when you remove it because will be hot.

STAINS, FOOD

Remove food stains from your hands by rubbing a cut raw potato on them.

COOKING TIPS

We're all so busy these days, we don't have a lot of time to spend over the stove. If you don't want to waste time in the kitchen, but want to make nutritious and delicious food, try my cooking tips.

CITRUS FRUIT

Dip citrus fruit in hot water for a few moments before using. If it's a tangerine or orange, it will peel much easier and if you are squeezing it for juice such as with a lime or lemon, more juice will come out.

CORN

To sweeten corn, drop a little sugar in the water in which the corn is boiled. An easy way to boil corn on the cob is to use a fryer basket to get the corn in and out of the pot of boiling water.

Corn on the cob can also be cooked with dry heat. Butter the shucked ears of corn and sprinkle a little sugar on to sweeten them if you like. Wrap in them foil and cook in the oven or a covered barbecue until tender. Be sure to poke several holes in the foil wrapping, because the moisture in the corn ear will turn to steam during this process, and if it can't escape, it will explode and go boom!

EGGS

- Prevent cracked hard-boiled eggs by adding two tablespoons of white vinegar per quart of water before boiling.
- The eggshells of boiled eggs will peel off more quickly and easily if cooked in water with salt added or with two tablespoons of vinegar added.
- Poaching eggs over salted water helps set the egg whites.
- To whip egg whites, check to make sure that there is not even a dot of egg yolk in among the whites. Even a tiny bit of yolk can make the difference. To remove the yolk, dip it out with a piece of broken eggshell (the yolk will often stick to it).

HAM

For a delicious, moist ham, some cola fans recommend wrapping the ham in foil and putting it in a pan into which you've emptied a can of cola. Remove the foil thirty minutes before the ham is done.

ONIONS

When peeling and slicing onions, the fumes from the cut onion float up and get into your eyes and nose. This is what causes you to cry. To prevent tearing up, put a slice of bread in your mouth to absorb the fumes or try peeling the onions under running water. An effective but admittedly goofy alternative is to wear goggles. But hey, everybody is entitled to a good laugh.

POTATOES

Stand potatoes on end in the oven to hasten their baking time.

SOUP

If soup has been oversalted, cut up a raw potato or two and drop the pieces into the soup. The potato will absorb the salt. (Thanks to the Morton Salt company for all the tips on ways to use salt. There are more than 10,000 uses for salt, and in the olden days, many of these were common knowledge. I'm sure my pioneer grandmothers knew of countless things to do with salt. Today chemicals have replaced many of its uses, but they're not always better. Salt is unique and much less costly than more "sophisticated" products.)

VEGETABLES

One way to prevent potatoes and some other vegetables from boiling over and burning is to add some butter or margarine.

If you have oversalted a vegetable you are cooking, cut up raw potatoes and drop them into the water (see **soup**).

SAVING TIME

When cooking one meal, pop in other items that you want to have cooked and on hand for future use. For example, when boiling pasta or vegetables, boil some eggs for breakfast as well. If you want to cook vegetables separately but still save time, put one vegetable in the bottom of the pot, add a metal colander, and put a second vegetable in that. Cook all together in one pot—you save clean-up time too.

SINGLES

If you've ever tried to buy groceries for one, you may find yourself wasting a lot of food. To minimize waste, cook up a complete package of pasta or rice or soup. Keep enough for your meal that day, divide the rest into resealable plastic containers, and pop them in the freezer. Now you have some extra TV dinners in your own style.

WHIPPED CREAM

Sprinkle a few drops of lemon juice into the whipping cream before you start whipping. Also, have the cream as cold as possible (but, obviously, not frozen). Both these tricks make it fluff up faster and easier.

KEEPING FOOD FRESH

Rule number one: do not refrigerate bananas. Rule number two: read the date on the package. You can't keep food fresh if it doesn't come that way.

BROWN SUGAR

I love brown sugar, but not when it gets hard as a rock. One solution is to put a slice of raw apple in the container. Pretty soon, the sugar should be manageable again.

CANNED GOODS

If you buy canned goods in large quantities—say a carton at a time—two good ideas are to 1) mark the tops with the date of purchase and 2) periodically turn them over while they are in your closet or on your shelf.

CELERY

Celery wrapped in foil will keep fresh in the refrigerator for several weeks.

EGGS

Place the egg in a cup of water to which two teaspoonfuls of salt has been added. A fresh egg sinks; a doubter will float.

To find out whether an egg has more than one yolk, or has blood in it, hold it next to a bright light in a darkened room (this is called "candling eggs" by the experts). You probably should discard an egg with blood in it because it is unacceptable to most egg consumers; on the other hand, a double-yolk egg is considered good luck.

If you're only using the white or yolks of eggs, freeze the part you are not using in an ice cube tray for later use.

FRUIT

Don't wash fruit until you are actually ready to use it. This may sound odd, but it will remain fresh longer that way.

GRAINS

Grandma Karn always said it was a good idea to check grains, flour, and spices from time to time after you store them. Sometimes little bugs sneak in there. Once they're in, you have to throw it all out. Be sure to open up the bags and look over the contents as soon as you get them home. Sometimes they have bugs in them at the store! To keep bugs away at home, try washing your closet shelves regularly with a vinegar solution. Also, take the food product out of the bag or carton it came in and store it in a plastic or metal container with a tight lid. Finally, some experts say it's a good idea to keep bay leaves in with these products because bugs hate their smell.

GREENS

This sounds silly, but here's how to keep lettuce and some salad greens fresher for a longer time. Keep them in a covered container—and here's the trick—along with a piece of stainless steel cutlery. Yes, it works.

LEFTOVERS

Mark the date and contents on boxes of restaurant leftovers. Write on the side of the box rather than (or in addition to) the top. That way you don't have to pull out the box to see what it is. Or, transfer it to a clear plastic container, but still mark the date and contents on the side.

MEAT

Kill bacteria in meat by marinating it in vinegar. The vinegar will also act as a tenderizer. Use one-quarter cup vinegar for a two- to three-pound roast, marinate overnight, and then cook without draining or rinsing the meat. Add herbs to the vinegar when marinating as desired.

POTATOES

Don't you hate it when the raw potatoes you've got in your storage bin start to sprout? This is, of course, natural from the potatoes' viewpoint, but not from yours. Drop some slices of raw apple in with the potatoes and they will stop budding.

REFRIGERATE RIGHT

Use shallow, loosely covered containers for food you put in the refrigerator. By doing so, the contents will cool quickly, after which you can tighten the covers. Layer food no more than two inches deep in each storage dish, or it will take too long to cool.

SPINACH

If spinach is washed in salted water, repeated cleanings will not be necessary.

STORING

It's very handy to have a handful of rubber bands, clothespins, extra wire twists, or alligator clips in a kitchen drawer so you can quickly and securely seal partially used bags and boxes of food like dry cereal, chips, and pasta. Some people keep empty used mason jars they have washed and stored in a kitchen cabinet for the same thing.

VEGETABLES

Line the bottom of your vegetable bin in the refrigerator with paper towels. They will soak up the moisture in the bin and the vegetables will stay fresh longer.

WAX PAPER

The wax liners in cereal, rice, and other boxes are good to save for wrapping and keeping lunches fresh.

WINE

Here's an interesting trick: save leftover wine by freezing it in an ice-cube tray. Next time you are cooking and want to add a savory wine flavor, drop the cubes into whatever you are cooking.

KITCHEN FRESHNESS

Probably the easiest way to prevent food odors from occurring in your kitchen is to eat out. But if you do cook on occasion, you may want a little help keeping your kitchen fresh.

DEODORIZING THE KITCHEN

Here are a few ways to eliminate cooking odors: try boiling one table-spoon of white vinegar with one cup of water or try cooking with a bowl of vinegar next to the stove. Another method is to cook brown sugar, cinnamon, and a little water in an open pot over a low flame. Another trick is to dip cotton balls in wintergreen oil or other scented oils and put them around the house.

DEODORIZING THE REFRIGERATOR

Absorb refrigerator odors by keeping an open box of baking soda, a few charcoal briquettes, coffee grounds, or some scented kitty litter—yes, scented kitty litter—in the fridge. These will also work well in closets, drawers, and other confined places.

TOOLS AND SUPPLIES

If you're like most people, you've extricated half a cork from a wine bottle and peeled off so much of the skin all you've got is the apple's core. We could all use a little help with our kitchen gadgets.

CAN OPENERS

Always keep a manually operated can opener in the kitchen for those times when the power goes off.

To sharpen up either a manual or an electric can opener, run some wax paper through it.

COFFEE FILTERS

If you run out of coffee filters, use a folded paper towel or paper napkin.

MICROWAVE MAXIMIZER

The shape of your container in the microwave matters. Round bowls are the best insurance for uniform cooking, because of the way the waves bombard the dish.

SHAKERS, PERSONALIZED

Fill an ordinary salt or pepper shaker or other such container with a personally selected blend of seasonings and use this combination shaker to season your food all at one time. (Don't overfill shakers with salt, pepper, or spices. Leave a little room at the top so the contents will mix when you shake, and come out of those little holes.)

WINE BOTTLES

When a cork is really stubborn, try putting a room temperature wine bottleneck under hot running water for a short time. This expands the glass and makes the cork easier to remove the cork. This also works for ordinary glass jars and bottles. Another, less advisable idea is to wrap the outside of the bottle in a towel and, while holding it firmly over the sink, smack it sharply on the bottom with your other open hand. This often loosens the seal and makes it easier to remove the cork or the screw cap. The reason for using the towel and sink is that you can actually break the bottle or jar when you hit it. So be firm, but careful. I wouldn't recommend this method unless you're really desperate.

7

CLEANING

Helpful hints to make cleaning as quick and easy as possible

Everybody likes a nice clean house, but who wants to spend every weekend with the vacuum? If you don't want to spend your leisure hours scrubbing the bathtub, and can't afford to pay someone else to do it, this chapter is for you. It's full of ideas to make cleaning less work.

DEVELOPING YOUR MODUS OPERANDI

My parents and grandparents taught me a lot of great cleaning and stain-removal tips. In fact, some of my relatives have devised their own house-cleaning systems. Maybe one of them will work for you.

TUESDAY BATHROOM APPOINTMENT

With the appointment system, you make regular appointments for different days with various parts of the house. For example, on Monday you might make an appointment with the vacuum cleaner to deal with what needs vacuuming. Tuesday might be an appointment with the toilet, bathtub, and bathroom sink. Wednesday might be the appointment with the deck or patio, and so on, until all the places needing attention are covered.

Something about the appointment system is quaint to me. It harkens back to a time when certain chores were assigned to certain days such as doing laundry on Monday and ironing on Tuesday. But then, everything old is new again.

THE BUCK STOPS THERE

Another approach is to assign cleaning chores to different members of the household. (I've found that they are more willing to accept the assignment if you keep a few chores for yourself—just a thought.)

If you delegate the work to children, be prepared to recognize their limitations. I learned a long time ago that the enthusiasm with which some children attack a project is often inversely proportional to their ability to do it. One important thing about passing the buck is that not everything will get done the way *you* would do it, but it will get done. You have to get over insisting the towels be folded your way. It's enough that the towels are folded and you didn't have to do it.

TIMER TEST

Another approach is based on the idea that efficient housekeeping is a matter of time management. With this method, you set a timer as you enter the room to be cleaned and see how much you can get done during that time frame. When it goes off, move on to the next room.

ANTI—MARTHA STEWART APPROACH

Happily, the value of housekeepers as human beings is no longer judged on the shine of the kitchen floor. This means not having the perfect house, but having a happy life. (Did you know Martha Stewart was a New York stockbroker before she became a lifestyle maven?) I have one friend, for example, who laughingly says his upholstered furniture is covered in a cat-hair pattern. Another friend says she's not a great cleaner but she is a wonderful cook and adorable person. She adds, no man ever kissed her because her windows sparkled.

My mother used to say that a washed window gets dirty twice as fast as an unwashed window, and I can attest from moving many times that the same amount of "stuff" that fills up a one-car garage also fills up a two-car garage. And so, perhaps the best method is the one that makes you (and not some phantom "Joneses") happy.

CLEANERS AND TOOLS

We expect our mops and brooms to take care of cleaning our homes, but what do we do to take care of them? As my father says, good tools are a job half done. Since your house cleaning tools are what you need to do the job inside the house, it is important to keep them in good shape. There are also many great cleaning alternatives out there you should know about.

BAKING SODA

With so many other uses around the house for baking soda, I wonder whether anybody ever uses it for baking anymore. Anyhow, baking soda—usually in conjunction with water or vinegar—has many household uses for cleaning and deodorizing.

For example, run a solution of warm water and baking soda down your garbage disposal to keep it fresh smelling. You can soak clothes in a baking-soda solution for thirty minutes before running them through the washing machine for a cleaner, softer result. You can clean and polish counter tops, silverware, dirty smudges, and crayon marks off the wall and counters with a paste of water and baking soda. Keep an open box of baking soda in your refrigerator to absorb odors and sprinkle in cat-litter boxes for same result.

BROOMS

The first rule of broom care is to store it upside down. You can do this by drilling a hole in the handle or tying a looped string in a ridge you make around the top of the handle. If you must keep it with the bristles pointing down, make sure that they don't touch the floor.

Brooms are not only important for cleaning, it's important that they are clean, too. Dip your new broom in a solution of hot salt water when you first get it, and then every few weeks dip it in hot water again. Shake it dry outside where the droplets won't make a mess. This will keep the bristles from getting brittle.

BRUSHES

Several kinds of brushes are handy for cleaning. You're used to using a large hand brush to scrub stone and tile floors when they get really dirty. Another great brush for cleaning is the toothbrush. A used toothbrush is perfect for scrubbing grout and small nooks and crannies. Buy a toothbrush for the kitchen as well as the bathroom. In the kitchen it's perfect for cleaning stuff from hard-to-reach places in your appliances and also from kitchen tools such as graters, blenders, and juicers, to name just a few. Finally, scrub brushes are popular for getting icky stuck-on stuff off pans and baking dishes. Scrub brushes can be sanitized and refreshed along with your dishes in the dishwasher, or try a 30-second zap in the microwave, as long as they have no metal parts.

CHEMICAL SAFETY

Using chemicals—commercial and natural—to fight the battle against dirt is unavoidable, but what must be avoided is mixing chemicals in dangerous combinations or using them in dangerous situations. Heed these two basic safety rules: 1) read the labels of all chemical products carefully and 2) never store household chemicals in anything but their original containers. Putting cleaners in unmarked containers is just asking for a disaster. If you transfer some chemical into a different container such as a spray bottle, mark the new bottle clearly with a label or marker so you, and anyone who touches it, will know what product is in it.

CLUB SODA

Club soda is the emergency spot remover you need handy to pour on spills and spots on carpets the minute they happen. Whether it's coffee, wine, juice, or whatever and whether it's on your carpeting, bedspread, or suit, it is club soda to the rescue and the drill is soak and sop. Soak the material heavily and repeatedly with the club soda, and keep sopping it up by blotting over and over again with a cloth or paper towels or tissues.

DISHCLOTHS

Wash dishcloths in the dishwasher with your regular loads or zap them in the microwave for 30 seconds or so.

DISH TOWELS

If the point is to dry off your clean dishes, you'll obviously want to use a clean towel or cloth, fresh from the washing machine.

DUST CLOTHS

Clearly, dust cloths must be clean to be of any use, so wash them in the washing machine when they start getting dirty. Almost any old fabric can be used for dusting. I like used athletic socks you slip over you hand. Another trick is to wrap an old sock around a tennis ball for tossing at out-of-reach spots—a good way to remove cobwebs and dustbunnies. You can also tie old cloths around the end of a broom and use it to reach high places. Some homemakers will give the dust cloth a light spray of furniture polish to enhance its effectiveness.

LEMONS

Lemon juice is a handy deodorizer and natural bleach. Your kitchen will smell wonderful if you heat some lemon slices in a pan on the stove. You can also use it, in combination with salt, to clean solid brass (not brass plate), chrome, and copper. Clean your hands with it.

PANTYHOSE

Save worn-out pantyhose and stockings for a variety of uses around the house. Many people stuff them with aromatics such as lemon, lime, or orange peels and hang them out of sight to rid a room of odors.

SPONGES

We use sponges to pick up dirt and bacteria, so it makes sense to sanitize them between uses. One way is to soak them in a combination of vinegar and water. My preferred method is to put them into the dishwasher and wash them every time you do the dishes.

SPONGE MOPS

Sponge mops should be washed and rinsed from time to time. They retain their texture and prevent the backing of the sponge from warping, and don't let the sponge completely dry out. One way to retain a little moisture and texture is to wrap your sponge mop in one of the many plastic bags you collect from the grocery store.

STEEL WOOL

Some homemakers swear by steel wool pads and others swear at them. One common objection is that they get rusty—sometimes to the point of leaving rust stains on your sink and countertops. If you like the cleaning power steel wool gives you, you might try keeping your steel wool pads—after you start using them—submerged in soapy water in a covered mason jar or air-tight plastic container. Some experts suggest using baking-soda solution in the container.

VACUUM CLEANER

A lot of people just whip out the vacuum and buzz around the room as if it were a tank. Actually, vacuums have to be cared for and handled correctly like any piece of machinery. The most obvious aspect of vacuum care is to change the bag before it gets too full. It's also a good idea to check the bristles every so often to make sure they are clean and functioning.

Your vacuum is designed to pick up dirt, not objects, so avoid running over crayons, hairpins, buttons, and similar stray objects that can flip into the rotor and damage the machine. Look over the carpet before vacuuming to see if there is anything you need to pick up first.

THE VACUUM VIP

You may appreciate your vacuum cleaner more when you learn that an inventor nearly died while demonstrating his early model. English engineer Hubert Cecil Booth observed big pumps and hoses being used to clean the inside of railroad cars in 1901. A similar technique was also used for homes—a large pump blew air through the carpets in the hope that some of it would fly out through exit tubes strung around the house. Booth decided that a machine that sucked up dirt, rather than blowing it out, might work better. Showing how a machine could suck the dirt off of floors in a London restaurant, he accidentally inhaled a mouthful of dust and just about choked to death. Fortunately, he recovered, and the vacuum cleaner is now an indispensable cleaning tool.

VINEGAR

Vinegar is one of the most versatile cleaners, deodorizers, and home companions you can have. You'll find me recommending it in various ways throughout this book. For example, use vinegar solutions to clean most surfaces in your bathroom and kitchen, including shower curtains and countertops. Add a few tablespoons to your dishwasher detergent to help do away with grease on dishes or half a cup in your laundry rinse cycle to make your clothes fresher and softer. Mix vinegar with baking soda to create a foaming cleanser for stainless steel. Add it to water for washing windows, mirrors, and glass tabletops. Vinegar is a natural air freshener when sprayed in a room.

WASTEBASKET LINERS

Instead of putting one plastic trash liner in your wastebasket, put in several at once. As one fills up, remove it as you normally would, and voilà! a fresh one is already in place!

CLEANING DANGERS

You can get sick or injured by not taking care of yourself while you're taking care of your house. Many cleaners can be dangerous. Read the label and pay attention. The following tips are not optional.

CAUSTIC PRODUCTS

Any product with the word *caustic* on the label should be treated carefully and, literally, with rubber gloves on your hands. Any substance that is caustic is corrosive—it can cause chemical burns.

CHILD PROTECTION

Keep all your cleaning chemicals out of sight and out of reach of children. Toddlers are notorious for getting into bottles, jars, cans, and sprays filled with dangerous material.

CHEMICAL COMBINATIONS

Do not *ever* combine chlorine bleach with a chemical for cleaning that nasty toilet bowl. For example, do not mix Clorox bleach with ammonia, vinegar, and other chemicals. The combination can produce *deadly* chlorine gas, which can kill you! The best advice is to *never* mix a cleaning product with anything that is not explicitly recommended on the label.

POOR VENTILATION

Whenever you're cleaning indoors, open up the windows, prop open the door (if it's safe to where you live). Chemical cleaning products often give off fumes that could make you and your family very sick when inhaled. If it's too hot or too cold to allow fresh air to circulate, you can either 1) open the windows anyhow or 2) do something more fun.

RAGS

When you use a rag with solvents, oils, or paint, be sure to dry it thoroughly outside the house before throwing it in the trash or storing for later reuse. Rags soaked in volatile or flammable fluids are self-combustible and accordingly are extremely dangerous.

SOLVENTS AND PAINTING PRODUCTS

When you're working with liquids that evaporate and give off explosive or dangerous fumes such as paint thinner, kerosene, alcohol, and turpentine, keep windows and doors open so there is good ventilation. You don't want to inhale the vapors. Store these volatile fluids in a cool place and keep them away from hot water heaters, furnaces, stoves, or any other open flame. The fumes could easily explode, causing fire, serious injury, or both.

VINEGAR

Vinegar, as I've said, is one of the handiest liquids around the house. But remarkably, even vinegar can pose a safety threat. *Never* combine it with another cleaning product such as chlorine bleach and *never* store it in a lead or copper container. When vinegar mixes with lead or copper, it can become poisonous. Keep it *only* in glass bottles.

BATHROOM BITS

The bathroom has lots of different kinds of surfaces that need to be cleaned, including the fixtures, the floor, and the various kinds of trim and accessories. For example, your bathroom may have chrome, aluminum, or brass towel racks and faucets; glass or stainless steel mirrors; glass or plastic shower doors; and, porcelain, marble, or tile tubs and basins. And all of these items collect some kind of dirt or scum on them such as soap film, rust, mildew, and even worse, germs.

Faced with this complex situation in the bathroom, here are some ideas for making cleaning a little easier.

SHOWER AND TUB

If you can, get everybody in the household to cooperate by cleaning and rinsing the tub or shower each time they use it so soap film doesn't form.

You might want to keep a spray bottle of cleaner and a sponge in the bath or shower to encourage bathers to wipe down the walls, faucets, and shower floor or tub. When not in use, leave shower doors or curtains open so air can circulate. This discourages mildew. If you spot any mildew forming, go after it immediately with vinegar or bleach.

Shower Walls

The car isn't the only place to use car wax. You can also use it to wax shower walls and doors. Don't wax the shower floor or you'll slip and hurt yourself.

To clean soap scum and dirt off the shower walls, simply wipe the surface with vinegar and rinse with water.

One easy way of handling chips and scratches to your bathtub or shower is to touch them up with what is called, cleverly, touch-up paint. These paints were created to cover chips and scratches on cars, and you should find them in most hardware or auto parts stores. They also works well on scratches to the sink or toilet.

Removing Decals and Stickers

If you want to resurface your bathtub, the little plastic flower stickers on the bottom are going to have to go. But they're tough to get off. One way to remove decals and stickers from your fixtures is to heat them with a blow dryer and peel them off. Peel them carefully with a plastic card, like an expired library or credit card. A razor blade will work, but *don't use it on fiberglass or plastic* tubs and showers. It will cut into them. Using a block of wood sometimes works and it won't hurt the tub or shower.

Shower Doors

Keep them sliding smoothly by putting a light coat of Vaseline on the shower door track. Keep the doors clean by occasionally wiping them down with white vinegar. Then rinse and dry.

Showerhead

In time, the water coming through your showerhead will deposit minerals and gradually clog the holes. Clean the showerhead periodically by taking it off—it should unscrew counterclockwise—and boil or wash in a one-to-one solution of vinegar and water. Or put it in the dishwasher.

Drain

The bathtub drain frequently clogs due to a build up of hair in the pipes. So, in the shower and sink, it's a good idea to put some kind of mesh or netting—even a hair net—over the drain when you shampoo your hair. Another way of preventing trouble is to clear out the drain from time to time *before* it gets clogged. Here is another opportunity to use that bubbly one-to-one mixture of vinegar and baking soda.

TOILETS

Toilets, of course, should be cleaned regularly but, as I mention elsewhere in this book, be careful not to mix poisonous cleaners together such as chlorine and ammonia. One of these products is enough to clean the toilet and two is enough to kill you when you inhale the poisonous gas created by the mixture.

There are alternatives to the traditional cleaners. Try pouring vinegar into the toilet bowl. Let it sit for an hour or more before brushing and flushing. Or, do the same thing using a cola drink. You can also use a tablet of Alka-Seltzer. Drop it in the toilet and let it sit for 30 minutes, scrub, and rinse.

To do a really thorough job, it's best to drain the water from the bowl. So, reach down under the water tank at the back, find the faucet handle, and turn off the water supply to the tank (the faucet handle is usually on the left side as you're facing it). Then flush. This will drain most of the water out of the bowl so you can get to it and clean it. You can use your favorite cleanser or even our buddy, white vinegar, and a long-handled brush.

Every six months clean the inside of your toilet tank. Never thought of *that*, did you? The tank will collect hard water deposits from your water supply and it will function better if you clean it. Turn off the water supply (see above). Then flush, so most of the water in the tank drains out. Splash some detergent in the water that remains so you can clean with a sponge or brush. When done, reverse the process. Turn the water back on, let the tank fill and, then, flush once or twice.

You may want to clean the holes under the toilet seat that hold the screws to the bowl rim. Unscrew the bolts, clean the holes and twist the screw shaft of the bolts in a paper towel with a little light oil. Reassemble.

I don't think it's a good idea to hang those deodorizer gimmicks inside your toilet tank or to put a brick in the tank to cut water usage. Either can harm the tank and result in the need for expensive repairs. If you want to reduce the amount of water you use with each flush, adjust the float arm inside the tank so it cuts off the incoming water supply sooner.

BATHROOM TILES

A good cleanser for ceramic tiles is two parts ammonia, two parts vinegar, and one part baking soda in warm water. Clean, rinse, and dry. Another nice cleanser is simply a splash of cider vinegar and a quart of water.

Tile Grout

Use a toothbrush to scrub the grout with a paste of my old dependable, baking soda, and water. If it's really dirty, make a paste of baking soda and chlorine bleach—*but be careful!* Have the windows and doors open and avoid breathing in the chlorine fumes. You can also try rubbing the grout with the folded edge of a piece of sandpaper. To get rid of mildew forming in the grout, pour hydrogen peroxide over the grout and wipe off it with paper towels. This is a quick and easy solution.

MIRRORS

Un-fog your mirror by wiping it off with shaving cream.

Because most food preparation takes place in the kitchen, it's the most likely room in the house to contain bacteria and so special care must be given to keeping it clean and sanitary. Happily, from pioneer days until now, most housekeepers have known this and there are many ways of doing it. Here are a bunch of basic tips for keeping your kitchen and the things you keep in it as clean as can be.

APPLIANCES

With the exception of your telephone, the first and most important rule about cleaning appliances is to *unplug them first!* If you starting cleaning your toaster, microwave, or coffeemaker while they are plugged in, it could turn out to be an electrifying experience!

That said, you can clean your kitchen appliances dry, or clean them wet, or both. By cleaning them dry, I mean you should dust them regularly. To clean them wet, usually the best method is to wipe them down with denatured alcohol which, you can buy at the drugstore or hardware store. Wipe and dry, using clean cloths. If you use a dirty cloth, the alcohol will transfer dirt to the appliance instead of removing it.

BLENDERS

Clean blenders with a touch of dishwashing detergent and a little hot water. Turn the blender on briefly and it should be clean. Of course, rinse with clean water.

BROILER PANS

Is there anything tougher than a dirty broiler pan or tray with grease baked onto it? One method is to spray it with cleaner or ammonia and seal it in a plastic bag (after the pan or tray has cooled, of course). Leave it in there for 10 or 12 hours, by which time the stuck on mess should have loosened. Remove it and wash. Another way to remove grease is to cover the pan with detergent powder and put a wet towel over it for a few hours. Then, give it a scrub. It will clean much more easily.

For burned-on food stuck to the scorched pan, cover the bottom with salty water and let it soak overnight. The next day, heat the water until it boils and the adhered food should wipe off with little effort.

CABINETS

You should clean out cabinets where you store your dishes, pots, and utensils two or three times a year. A small sponge or brush can be used to clean the spaces between cabinets. As you're cleaning and organizing, I recommend running the utility barometer on each thing in the cabinet. Suppose it's a cabinet where you store pots and pans. Are there certain items that you really never use? If so, why not dispose of them, and use the space for something else? After you wash and rinse the walls and shelves, line the shelves with shelf paper and reorganize everything in the cabinet.

As a conclusion to this shelf cleaning, you may want to introduce herbs or other substances to combat ants, roaches, and other unwanted critters. For example, you could put bits of tansy around the cabinets or sprinkle chili power or borax around. For roaches, use the lids of discarded small jars and fill with a mixture of sweets, such as sugar or cocoa, and poison, like boric acid. Obviously, don't use boric acid or other poisons anywhere that children or pets can get to. It can poison them, too.

COFFEE GRINDERS

If you grind your own coffee, one easy way to clean your coffee grinder is to occasionally run some uncooked rice—about half a cup—through the machine. It can be white or brown rice, instant or regular.

COFFEE POTS

Clean coffee pots by boiling baking soda and water in them for a minute and then rinsing the pot out.

COUNTERTOPS

Cleaning countertops is fairly easy with baking soda and water. For tough stains, let the mixture sit on the stain for 15 or 20 minutes and then rinse. Ceramic-tile countertops can be cleaned with abrasive cleansers, but they can scratch plastic countertops and should be avoided. Don't use abrasive cleaners on wood either. They can scratch the wood, if not rinsed thoroughly, some of the cleanser might remain in the crevices and get on the next food you place there.

Don't use cloth towels to clean countertops. After one or two uses, you may start simply spreading dirt and bacteria. Instead, wipe off counters with paper towels and discard them immediately.

CRYSTAL

Here are some tips to avoid cracking and breaking when you wash crystal. Slide the crystal pieces sideways into hot dishwashing water so they adjust to the temperature change gradually and won't crack. It's a good idea to line the bottom of the washbasin with a rubber mat or kitchen towel to cushion the crystal in the sink. One part white vinegar to three parts warm water is a good cleaning solution for crystal.

CUTTING BOARDS

After you use a cutting board for meats and poultry, wash the board in soapy water or cleanser immediately after you use it. If the cutting board is small enough (and *not* wood), wash it in the dishwasher too. Raw meats and poultry carry bacteria that easily spread from one surface to another and can make you and your family very ill.

Do not, however, use very strong or caustic cleaners on a cutting board. These types of cleaners can seep into the wood grain or other crevices and eventually wind up in your food. If you spill a strong cleaner on a cutting board or countertop, rinse it off immediately.

To refresh a wooden cutting board, rub it down with slices of lemon, lime, or both, then rinse.

DISHWASHERS

As you can tell, I'm big on cleaning the stuff you use to clean other stuff. To clean get great results from your dishwasher, place a cup of white vinegar on the bottom rack, run it for five minutes, then run though the full cycle. A cup of white vinegar run through the entire cycle once a month will also reduce soap scum on the inner workings and prevent soapy film from accumulating on your glassware.

ELECTRIC POTS

As with tea kettles, mineral deposits may form inside electric pots over time. To get rid of them, boil a half-water, half-vinegar mixture in the kettle for 8 to 10 minutes. Let it stand overnight and rinse thoroughly the next day.

FLATWARE

There are many tricks to cleaning your flatware. To get it shiny again, rub it with a cork or bathe it in water left over from boiling potatoes. Many stains can be removed by rubbing with a paste of water and salt.

Don't mix stainless steel and silverware in your dishwasher. Contrary to its name, stainless steel does stain the silverware.

GARBAGE DISPOSALS

To clean and freshen your garbage disposal from time to time, run some ice cubes and lemon peels through it. Or you might instead pour in one-half cup of baking soda and hot water and let it stand awhile. Another method is to mix one cup of vinegar in enough water to fill an ice cube tray, freeze the mixture, grind the cubes through the disposal, and flush with cold water. This both cleans the disposal and sharpens the blades.

MICROWAVE OVENS

There are many ways to sanitize your microwave. One is to put a microwave-safe cup or bowl in the microwave with a mild solution of one part baking soda and seven parts water. Then, zap it with the microwave on high for a few minutes. When you open the door, you'll see it has turned to steam and coated the inside of the microwave. Just wipe it down with a sponge and paper towels. Another method is to crumple up a handful of wet paper towels in the microwave and turn it on for 30 seconds or a minute. Here again, the resulting hot steam lines the walls of the oven so you can clean it easily by wiping with dry paper towels. Or, instead of paper towels, use a wet cloth. But be *careful!* The cloth will be hot. When it's cool enough to handle, use it to wipe down the inside. If you want to make the microwave smell nice, zap a bowl of water filled with lemon peels for half a minute or so.

If your microwave has a removable pan or disk in the bottom, wash it regularly in the dishwasher.

OVEN

Oven tops will clean up and shine with a bath of alcohol or ammonia thinned out one-to-one with water. When there are spills and drippings in the oven, sprinkle carefully with salt, which will absorb much of the drippings. When oven is cool, wipe it up. For a gentle, effective oven cleaner, make a paste of baking soda and water. (You'll probably have to do some scrubbing.) Coat the inside of oven windows with the baking soda paste and let the mixture sit for about ten minutes. Then rinse.

POTS AND PANS

To clean out food-stained pots and pans, fill them with white vinegar and let them stand for thirty minutes. Then rinse in hot, soapy water. If your pots and pans are covered with stubborn, baked-on stuff that doesn't want to scrub off, boil a solution of laundry soap and water in the pot for a few minutes. If the burned-on food doesn't boil right off, scrubbing it off will be much easier. Or, here again, baking soda can help. Boil a solution of baking soda and water and watch the baked-on guck break loose.

Another trick is to enclose the pot (don't do this with aluminum pots and pans) in a plastic bag with some ammonia. Seal the bag carefully and set it aside for several days. The ammonia fumes will "gas" the pot, which is why you should put this bag out of the way on the back porch or in the garage or wherever. After a few days, take the bag to a well-ventilated location—*outside is best*—and open it, being careful to avoid inhaling the ammonia fumes. Remove the pot and the baked-on mess should come off with a little scraping and scouring.

Cast-iron Pots and Pans

Here is an odd thing about cast iron pans: you shouldn't clean them with soap and water because they are porous and will absorb soap. The best way to clean is by boiling a 50–50 solution of water and vinegar in the pan and then let it cool for 2 or more hours. While the liquid is still in the pot, use a scrub pad to clean the inside of the pot before emptying and rinsing.

For greasy cast iron pans, put a little salt in it and wipe it with paper before cleaning. After, cover with a light coating of cooking oil. Note: You should break in cast iron pots before you cook in them. Coat the inside with cooking oil and set the pot on low heat for about an hour.

Copper-bottomed Pots and Pans

To clean the copper bases, try a paste of salt and lemon juice.

Non-stick Pots and Pans

Just because it's a nonstick surface doesn't mean it won't get stains on it. To clean it easily, boil a solution of 2 tablespoons baking soda, 1/2 cup bleach, and a cup of water in the vessel. After boiling for 10 minutes, drain and wash with soap and water as you would normally. After drying, coat the nonstick surface with cooking oil.

Stainless Steel

Coat the pan with vinegar, sprinkle salt on the inside, and scrub.

PLASTIC CONTAINERS

Plastic containers in which we store foods can get stained and become unsightly. To prevent stains, particularly those caused by tomatoes, soak the container—lid and all—in cold water for a few minutes before using. Dry the container, then take a paper towel soaked in cooking or vegetable oil and coat the inside of the container before putting the food stuff in. Or, after use, you can clean it with a paste made of baking soda and water. Scrub and rinse.

To rid plastic containers of unwanted smells, soak them for an hour or two in a mustard and water solution using enough mustard to give the solution a rich mustardy appearance. Then, wash as you normally would. Or ball up a piece of newspaper and seal inside. By the next day, the container should be odorless. No, it doesn't matter if you use the news, fashion, or sports sections of the newspaper.

REFRIGERATORS/FREEZERS

Take all the food out before you start cleaning the refrigerator or freezer. Also take out any removable shelves and the drawers. This will give you the maximum amount of elbow room to wipe down the walls and other inside parts. Generally, experts recommend cleaning using baking soda and lukewarm water instead of soap or detergent on these appliances. The manufacturer may state that the drawers and shelves should be washed in mild detergent and warm water. If so, that's fine. But I still prefer using baking soda and lukewarm water. The smell of many detergents can linger on and might be absorbed by some of the food in the refrigerator.

I always start by lining the bottom of the refrigerator with several layers of paper towels so the drips and slops that come from washing down the walls will be absorbed instead of spilling onto the floor to become an expanded cleaning problem.

Before replacing the food, you'll want to eliminate any odors in the fridge or freezer. As I mention elsewhere in the book, there are two ways of getting rid of unpleasant smells. One is to hide or overpower them with a stronger but nicer smell, and the other way—the one I recommend—is to have something else absorb the unwanted odors. For example, you could put a bowl of smell-absorbing charcoal briquettes in the refrigerator and freezer for an hour or two. In that case, of course, you may want to impose on a neighbor to let you keep some of your food in his units for a time.

SINKS

Traditionally, kitchen sinks are made of porcelain. To clean porcelain, use a spray-on foamy cleanser. Abrasive cleaners will ruin the finish in no time.

If your sink is stainless steel, you've undoubtedly discovered that it isn't really stainless. Two good stainless cleaners you can try are either baby oil or club soda. Once more use a paste made of my old friend baking soda and water. After rinsing, you may want to wipe it down with a dry cloth to eliminate water spots.

Drains

Here are two nontoxic drain cleaners for the kitchen sink. Pour a cup of any kind of salt and a cup of baking soda down the drain followed by hot, hot water. Don't use that drain for a few hours. About once a month. clean out your drains by combining my two favorites, baking soda and white vinegar. Pour in half a cup of each and stand back because there will be much bubbling and grubbling. In fact, you may want to cover the drain until the eruption ceases. Let things sit for half an hour, and then rinse with cold water.

TEA KETTLES

If you have minerals in your water, they will form deposits inside your tea kettle. To remove the deposits, boil a half-water, half-vinegar mixture in the kettle for 8 to 10 minutes. Let the mixture stand overnight and rinse the next day.

THERMOSES

Here are ways to clean your thermos. One, fill it with crumpled, dry egg shells and warm water. Shake vigorously, drain, and rinse. Two, fill with solution of two tablespoons of baking soda and warm water. Again, shake vigorously, drain, and rinse. Finally, a solution of water and a little splash of chlorine bleach will do the trick if you let it sit in there for about an hour. Rinse thoroughly because you don't want the taste of chlorine in your coffee.

WOODEN BOWLS

Don't wash wooden bowls in soap and water. Wood is porous and may absorb some of the soap, resulting in a salad à la soap bubble. Instead, wipe the inside with paper towels soaked in salad or cooking oil and then dry with more paper towels.

FLOORS AND WALLS

Yes, your house or apartment can look like you just moved in. Read these tips to discover how to make it happen.

ALUMINUM SIDING

The simplest way to clean aluminum siding on your house or garage is to hose it down. If this doesn't remove all the spots, try a solution of ordinary dishwasher detergent followed by a strong hose spray. Don't use scouring powder or abrasive cleaners because they can scratch the finish.

For particularly tough jobs, try this: use a solution of 1-tablespoon tri-sodium phosphate (TSP, available at most paint or hardware stores) with a dash of detergent soap. Scrub the aluminum siding with this solution using a good brush. Then rinse off with strong hose spray.

CARPETING

You never really appreciate carpeting until you live downstairs from someone who doesn't have it. I'm not going to make you a carpet expert (I'm not one either!) but here are a few basics that will help you take care of your carpeting.

Most home carpet is made of nylon, polyester, olefin, or wool fibers. The quality of a carpet is determined by the amount and spacing of the fibers, and the number of fiber twists per square inch. The number of fibers is called the carpet's "weight." The closeness of the fibers is called the carpet's "density." The number of twisted fibers per square inch is called, cleverly, "fiber twist." Carpets should be supported by padding, which, in a curious way, is the "carpeting" underneath the carpeting. The ideal carpet pad is neither too thick nor too thin. You want a medium thickness (a shade shy of $1/2$ inch, such as $7/16$ inch) for the best results.

Stains

When you spill something on the carpet, immediately blot the stain with vinegar and water, shaving cream, or club soda. Salt works on some fresh stains. Another good cleaner is a one-to-one paste mixture of salt and baking soda moistened with a little vinegar and water. Check the mixture on a remote corner to make sure it doesn't fade the carpet color. Then apply and let it dry. After it dries, brush or vacuum. In all cases, *blot, don't rub.* Rubbing spreads the stain.

Do *not* use dishwashing detergent to clean spots from your carpet because it is too sudsy. Also, it is hard to rinse out of the carpet and the residue of the detergent that remains will attract dirt, which is what you are trying to get rid of.

Chewing gum in carpet should be hardened before you try to remove it. Put some ice on the gum and when it gets very hard, squeeze it with pliers or crush it some other way and vacuum it up.

Nail polish remover will take off nail polish from the carpet, but it might also take off part of the carpet. Try it out on a remote, unseen part of the carpet to see how it tests out. If it works there, try small amounts on the nail polish and immediately blot—remember, *blot*—with a paper towel.

Wax on the carpet leaves me hot and cold. One approach is to do the same as you do with chewing gum, put ice on it to make it hard. Then, crush, scrape or break the wax off as best you can and immediately vacuum. To try the hot approach, put down some paper towels over the wax and *briefly* apply heat from an iron or hair dryer. You just want to melt the wax so you can scrape, scoop and, *blot* it up. Repeat if necessary but *don't use too much heat for too long.* Prolonged exposure could actually set fire to the carpet and burn down the house.

Vacuuming

As a general rule, you should vacuum your carpeted floors about once a week and "high traffic" areas such as hallways and entrances more frequently.

Most vacuums have an adjustment fixture that raises or lowers the suction lip. Adjust this for the kind of area you are cleaning. A vacuum does just what its name says; it creates a vacuum that sucks up loose things such as dirt at the mouth of the vacuum. On a bare floor, you want the vacuum mouth set low. You don't want it low when you are going over a carpet because the carpet fibers will bunch up and slow you down. It should ride just along the top of the carpet fibers.

Vacuuming is like mowing your lawn. You want to go back and forth making overlapping sweeps until you have covered the whole room. Repeat vacuuming over areas that are likely to be the dirtiest—high traffic spots and places where people rest their feet, such as in front of the living room couch.

One cleaning trick is to sprinkle baking soda lightly over your carpeting. Let it sit for 15 or 20 minutes and, then vacuum it up. This refreshes the carpeting (and will drive any bugs in the carpet to the surface so you can suck them up too).

FLOORS

The best method of cleaning a floor depends on the type of surface— I've covered the most common kinds in the next group of tips.

Ceramic tile and grout

To do a good job cleaning a tile floor, remember that the ceramic tile is not porous but the grout between is.

First, sweep or vacuum up loose dirt from the floor. Then, use a mixture of warm water with cleaners such as a tablespoon of borax and two tablespoons of ammonia as your cleaning fluid. This is one of those rare times when vinegar is not a good choice.

Next, mop with an ordinary rag mop that you rinse frequently to keep

it clean. You don't want to use a sponge mop because its material and design tends to squeeze dirty water down into the grout instead of swishing it out like the rag mop does.

Finally, finish the job by drying the floor using a dry mop or rag.

Linoleum

Use a regular sponge mop and warm soapy water. There is no need to clean with harsh chemicals and abrasives. Rinse and mop dry. Many scruff marks can be erased with one of those brown, cube-shaped art gum erasers or by rubbing with toothpaste on a clean, dry rag. Rinse and dry. A quick way to rinse is to sweep the floor with a broom dipped in clean water. A nice rinse for linoleum is a solution of the juice of one lemon in a quart of water.

VINYL

Use essentially the same method as for tile and grout floors. Sweep or vacuum dirt from the floor. Dilute your favorite floor cleaner, such as borax, with warm water and mop the floor with a rag mop. Rinse the mop often so that you aren't just spreading dirt around the floor. Finish the job by drying the floor with a dry mop or rag.

WOOD

The first step in cleaning a wood floor is to remove dust and loose dirt. *Don't* do it with a vacuum cleaner. The whirling brushes on the bottom of the vacuum cleaner can scratch the floor so use a dust mop instead.

If there are scratches, using a wax crayon the color of the floor is a good way to repair them. Rub it into the scratch, heat with a hair dyer and polish with a cloth rag.

When you're ready to wash your wood floor, try using a cup of brewed tea in a quart of warm water or a solution of vinegar and cool water. It's best not to clean wood floors with just plain water. Use a dampened cloth, but don't sop the floor with too much liquid. Dry with a clean cloth.

WALLS

There are several steps to washing down dirty walls just as there are to similar projects such as painting walls. Obviously, in the latter case, you are putting a coating *on* the wall while, in the former case, you are taking a coating *off* the wall.

Step one is to gather the right tools. They should include buckets for cleaning and rinsing solutions, baking soda, sponges (nylon sponges are popular, but natural ones are much better), fabric drop cloths (don't use plastic cloths that will get wet and slippery), cleaning solutions and materials (art gum eraser, alcohol, or hair spray), a ladder, and masking tape.

Next, prepare the wall and yourself. Drape the drop cloth over the floor and any furniture or items you can't conveniently move. Use masking tape to hold it in place against the wall and on the floor. You will be moving around on this drop cloth and, if you don't tape it into place it will slip and bunch up, leaving the floor and furniture unprotected.

Dress in appropriately old clothes and cover your hair. Wear old rubber-soled shoes. Don't wear flip-flops, step-in-sandals or shoes, or go barefoot. You are going to be stepping on wet surfaces on the floor and on the ladder, and you don't want to slip and fall. Remember you will be using a wet sponge with cleaning fluid in it and reaching over your head. This means liquid will be dripping on you from above. I recommend wearing safety goggles to keep liquid out of your eyes and tying strips of toweling or cloth around each bare wrist. Then, when the cleaning liquid drips down from your hand, it will not trickle all the way down your arm. Yuck.

Remove any marks you can with a brown, cube-shaped art gum eraser. Rub crayon marks gently with a paste of baking soda and water. Ink will usually give in to hair spray or alcohol.

Now mix your cleaning solution. An often-used mixture that I like consists of one gallon warm water, one cup ammonia, and one teaspoon dishwasher detergent. Next, go up the ladder and start washing. Work from the top of the wall to the bottom. If you wash bottom to top, the dirty liquid will drip from the top to the clean bottom. Not good.

Plow ahead and do one whole wall without stopping. If you stop to answer the phone or take a break, the cleaning will not be even.

Rinse the wall with clean water. If you really want a super job, dry the wall with soft, clean cloth.

WALLPAPER

Some marks can be cleaned off with a brown art gum eraser. Another trick involves rubbing the marks with rye bread. For tougher marks like crayons, try rubbing toothpaste (not the gel kind) with a soft cloth.

WOOD PANELING

Woodwork can be cleaned with cold tea (black, green, or oolong are all okay). Rinse with a solution of the juice of one lemon in a quart of water.

WINDOWS

To get windows clean, use undiluted vinegar in a spray bottle. Dry the windows with a soft cloth. If you have a canister vacuum cleaner that blows air out as well as in, use it to swoosh dirt out of the windowsills.

Most people understand that it's not a good idea to wash windows on a rainy day but many experts say it's not a good idea to wash windows on a sunny day either. The logic is that, on a warm, sunny day, the solution you put on the glass dries before you have time to wipe it all off and polish the glass. This makes sense. Besides, who wants to spend a nice sunny day washing windows?

A good window cleaner is 9 parts warm water and one part white vinegar. Dry the windows with crumbled up newspapers that you stroke vertically on one side of the window and horizontally on the other side. The alternating stroke pattern highlights any areas you miss. Another good window cleaner is kerosene. Again, dry with bunched up old newspapers. Or try 3 tablespoons ammonia in a gallon of water, or a solution of alcohol and water. Soapy solutions are not good for window washing because you will get streaks on the glass.

If you live where it gets freezing cold, try washing the windows of your house with the same solution that you use to wash the windows of your car, namely, windshield-washer fluid. Put some in a spray bottle and use like any other cleaning solution. But note: Windshield washer fluid is strong stuff, and it should be kept out of the reach of kids and pets.

WINDOW SCREENS

Notice how there is lots of advice on washing windows but not much on washing the screens that cover those windows? I suggest you remove the screens and lay them on a flat surface like the lawn or patio, so you have firm backing for the screen. Begin by brushing them with a stiff-bristle hand brush. Brush just hard enough to remove dirt and accumulated dust. End by rinsing with a hose or buckets of clean water. Then stand the screens on end so they can drain and dry before you put them back on the window. As an alternative clean window screens with ordinary kerosene brushed on from each side. Use a cloth to dry. Paper towels are all right too, but the screen will shred them if you rub too hard.

FURNITURE

Keeping your furniture looking brand-new is not as tough as you may think. Try the following advice on your prized possessions.

ANTIQUE FURNITURE

Try two-thirds turpentine and one-third boiled linseed oil (yes, you'll probably have to go to the hardware store for these products). Apply the mixture carefully with one soft cloth and polish it with a second soft cloth.

LEATHER FURNITURE

The standard cleaner for leather furniture, leather saddles, and leather anything is saddle soap. Follow the directions and use like most soap. Tradition has it one should polish leather monthly with some supple oil such as a touch of lanolin—a greasy extract from sheep's wool sold as an ointment, castor oil, or a two-to-one mixture of linseed oil (two parts) and vinegar (one part). To improve the appearance of their leather items after they have been cleaned, some country folk like to rub leather with a little milk applied to a soft cloth. Another barnyard leather tip is to rub grease spots away with a soft cloth and egg white.

MATTRESSES

You can't really wash your mattress, but a good airing and sun bath every few months is a good idea, as well. However, before you bring it in from outside, carefully inspect it on all sides to make sure you are also bringing in no unwanted critters such as ants, bullfrogs, spiders, or alligators. I also recommend vacuuming your mattress weekly. What? Vacuum the mattress? People aren't walking on it with their shoes on are they? Unpleasant as it may sound, experts tell us that it is not uncommon for tiny bed mites to snuggle down inside your mattress where it is warm and comfortable. If you run the vacuum over the stripped-down mattress (that is, with sheets, blankets, and pads removed), you can suck these critters out from where they might sometime bite you in the night.

By the way, I suggest that you turn your mattress over once every week or three. One time, turn it over in one direction (say from side to side) and the next time in another direction (end to end). By doing so, you avoid sleeping in the same spot night after night and help prevent the mattress from sagging.

PLASTIC FURNITURE

When it comes to holding up against harsh weather plastic is durable, but scratchy, harsh cleansers, stiff brushes, and abrasive chemicals can damage it. Actually, many experts suggest cleaning plastic with a little toothpaste and a soft cloth.

PATIO FURNITURE

Plastic upholstered patio furniture should be hosed off or vacuumed regularly to keep it clean. For a more thorough job, which you should also do regularly, make a spray-on solution from a quart of warm water with a teaspoon each of borax and liquid dishwashing detergent. Spray the plastic cushions thoroughly, let them sit for about 15 or 20 minutes, hose them down, and then dry!

UPHOLSTERY

Cleaning upholstered furniture is a job few people tackle, and I suspect it's because they either don't think about it or don't know how to do it. It really isn't any harder than most other cleaning jobs, provided you know a few basics. For example, manufacturers help by marking most upholstered furniture with a code that identifies the kind of material used and the basics of cleaning it. There are four different code letters printed on a label somewhere on most upholstered furniture—most likely these labels are under the cushions. Check it out. The labels should be marked with either a W for cleanable with water; S for cleanable with solvent (professional dry cleaning fluid only); S/W for either solvent or water (I'd recommend leaving this to a professional furniture cleaner); and, finally, X which means don't clean at all (you can dust but don't use any fluid cleaner).

With some pieces of upholstered furniture you will find the cushion and pillow coverings have zippers at the back, and this quite naturally seems to invite you to unzip the zippers, remove the fabric cushion cover, and toss it into the old washing machine. *Wrong.* The zippers are for the convenience of professional upholstery cleaners. Typically, we amateurs unzip, wash, and discover the fabric covers have shrunk, and we can't get the upholstery stuffed back into the cover. So don't be duped by zippers. Find and read the label on the furniture.

Upholstery Stains

Of course, you'll first *read the label* to discover if you can clean the upholstery at all. If so, to remove spilled grease, sprinkle heavily with salt right away and brush or vacuum off. For blood stains, apply cornstarch and water. When it dries, brush or vacuum the mixture off. This may have to be repeated. Some upholstery stains can be removed by applying white vinegar directly to the stain, and then wash as directed by the manufacturer's instructions.

WICKER FURNITURE

Clean wicker with a brush dipped in warm salt water. This will, among other things, keep it from turning yellow. Now you see why wicker is often popular at the seashore. To prevent it from drying out, apply lemon oil every so often. (To keep wicker in good shape, don't leave it outside in cold weather. It may split and come apart.)

WOOD FURNITURE

A good basic wooden furniture polish can be made with one-third lemon juice and two-thirds oil olive or cooking oil. Apply only when the furniture is dry. If you want to remove polish, try a solution of equal parts vinegar and water. Rinse and dry.

The downside of polishing wooden furniture with oil-based polishes is that you will ultimately get *too* much polish on it and it will attract dust.

Minimize attracting dust by buffing the furniture vigorously and not using too much polish. Later, if what they used to call in old-time TV commercials, "waxy yellow buildup" is a problem, rub the furniture down with turpentine and a clean rag.

PESTS

The only thing more unpleasant than ridding your home of pests is having to live with them. Before you call the exterminator, try my pest control tips.

ANTS

You can repel ants with several ordinary products. Try wiping your countertops, shelves, backboards, and baseboards with equal parts of water and vinegar or with a mixture of lemon juice and ground red pepper. To keep them from entering the house, spread crushed cloves, sage, or tansy at their entrances, or keep a potted tansy growing at these spots. Ants won't walk on some substances and you can keep them away with barriers made from chalk, sprinklings of baking soda, talcum powder, borax, dried mint, chili powder, cayenne pepper or scouring powder. Some experts say to leave around cut up pieces of apple around the ants' entrance points. Purportedly, the ants will take pieces of the apple back to the anthill, and the acid in the apple will kill them all.

Ants outside can be dealt with by soaking anthills in an equal mixture of hot water and coffee grounds.

To kill ants in the home, spray them with a light solution of detergent and water (one part detergent to sixteen parts water). Another, rather horrific method entails making a mixture of powdered sugar and boric acid—*this is poisonous so keep it away from children and pets!*. Put it in old jar lids or something that you can throw away. The ants will come and eat this mixture and die. Now for the horrible part. Apparently ants are cannibals and new ants arriving at the trap will eat the dead ants and die, too. This doomed march of ants will keep going until there aren't any more of them.

COCKROACHES

One good weapon against this disgusting insect is boric acid. Shake some underneath your cabinets, by the entrances to your home, or any other place you find them lurking. To make the poison even more enticing, try this: Mix boric acid one-to-one with flour or sugar and put it into little plastic containers or lids of used jars. Place them in areas where roaches like to congregate—often the refrigerator, the sink, or the dishwasher. The roaches will be attracted by and eat the sugar or flour, at the same time ingesting some of the deadly powdered boric acid. However, this is deadly not just to roaches, but also children and pets. *Do not leave boric acid anywhere kids or animals can get at it.*

FLIES

The conventional ways to get rid of flies include swatting, poison strips, sprays, traps, and so on. If you want to try an alternative, place a saucer containing a teaspoon each of milk and brown sugar mixed with one-half teaspoon black pepper on the floor, windowsills or wherever you see flies. This mixture should both attract and poison them. Another method is to attract birds (particularly swallows) to your yard with birdseeds or a bird feeder. Swallows and some other birds will also gobble up flies and other insects once you have their attention. Be aware that swallows do create noise and leave droppings, so they do have their downside.

Another weapon in the battle against flying insects is smoke. Most flying insects hate it, so try lighting incense or candles to drive them off. Perhaps you'll want to indulge in that fine cigar you've been saving.

FRUIT FLIES

If you're bothered by fruit flies in your kitchen, try keeping basil in a dish near your fruit bowl. It usually drives them away.

MICE, RATS, AND OTHER RODENTS

It seems everybody has a favorite way of getting rid of mice and rats. Traditional traps are still a favorite. Experts suggest that when you first start putting out mouse or rat traps, you should bait them but don't set them.

That is, put the cheese or whatever bait you are using into the trap and just let the varmints come and eat it. Do this for several days or weeks so the mice or rats become accustomed to the trap mechanism and are not frightened of it. After a time, the rodents will march boldly in to have a snack and *bam!* Some suggestions for bait include using peanut butter instead of cheese.

In cartoons, mice are invariably shown entering the walls through a little hole and, in fact, the cartoons are pretty accurate. Mice will crawl into any hole or crack available and set up housekeeping in walls, attics, floors, basements, boxes, and even pipes. So one important de-mousing step is to carefully inspect every wall, ceiling, and floor of your house and seal up any holes and cracks. Also check cabinets, stoves, and cars you don't use all the time. Often, they will take up residence wherever it's warm such as under the hood of your car or in an outside furnace or hot-water heater compartment.

There are a lot of alternatives to using commercial traps. Cotton or cloth soaked in peppermint extract is supposed to drive mice away. Another trick for spaces you don't often use is to lay down newspapers on the furniture and floors. Oddly enough, mice hate the sound of their own footsteps on newspapers. (Do you ever wonder who figures things like that out?)

Some suggest gluing small mirrors near the areas they inhabit because their own reflection frightens them away. An odd suggestion that I've been told absolutely works is another strange cola cure. The claim is that rats love cola drinks and will lap up large quantities of them, but are unable to belch and, therefore, they actually explode. Other animals and birds are apparently not attracted to the drink and so it is safe around domestic pets. I haven't tested the cola or mirror methods myself, but my sources claim they do work. Whether they work or not, they make good stories to tell your friends.

SILVERFISH

As with other pests, you can either try to keep silverfish away or kill them. To repel them, wipe down bookshelves, closets, bath areas, and any place they might congregate with turpentine. A trap that seems to work is a small glass on which you affix a strip of tape from bottom to top on the outside only. Put a little bit of flour on the inside bottom of the glass and place the glass wherever you see silverfish. Attracted by the flour, the little devils march to the glass, climb up the tape strip, and drop into the glass but can't get out.

SPIDERS

Spiders can often be driven away by certain odors, such as cedar, fragrant soap, and alcohol. Some people put alcohol in a spray bottle and squirt it around where spiders might be lurking such as in closets, windows, and the like. Scattering cedar chips and aromatic soap chips in those places often works, too.

SPIDER MITES

One of the few downsides to houseplants is that they may attract spider mites and other bugs. To rid your plants of spider mites, try spraying the plants with ice-cold water a few times a day. The mites hate it.

ODORS AND UNWANTED SMELLS

There are at least two ways of getting rid of unpleasant odors: one is to disguise the smell, the other is to absorb it. Use the following ideas to sweeten the air where you live.

DISGUISING ODORS

You can cover odors up by wiping down the place with a fresh-smelling solution. Try a mixture of equal parts vinegar and alcohol or equal parts lemon juice and alcohol. An open bar of scented soap or a perfume spray can help. Another way to mask odors is to put a few drops of perfume or cologne on the bulb of a lamp and turn it on. As the bulb heats up, the perfume will evaporate and permeate the room. Refresh drawers, furniture, and drapes by putting them out in the bright sunlight for a few hours. (Of course, you run the risk of bleaching fabrics by leaving them in the sun, so be mindful of this possibility.) Add some lemon juice to your humidifier's water and it will make things smell cleaner.

SOAKING UP SMELLS

The second way to get rid of odors is to absorb them. A sprinkling of scented kitty litter (odd as that may sound) can often do the trick. Leave it in the room for a few days and then vacuum it up. You may have to repeat this several times. Or, try using a tray of charcoal briquettes or old coffee grounds. You can leave the briquettes in a room or closet for months if you like—until it's summer and time to barbecue. Coffee grounds should be removed after a day or two and, if needed, replaced with others.

I recommend keeping an open box of baking soda in the refrigerator to absorb odors. Change this every few months. Charcoal briquettes work here, too, as do coffee grounds changed every day or so. Of course, wiping down the inside of the refrigerator with vinegar and water (equal parts) or baking soda and water is another solution.

Green plants in the home serve as natural air purifiers. Spider plants and English ivy, for example, soak up much of the carbon monoxide, formaldehyde, and other nasty vapors that can form indoors.

SKUNK ODOR

If you've been sprayed by a skunk, you'll be willing to bathe in tomato juice. A bath in equal parts of vinegar and water also works to get rid of the smell.

STAINS AND STUFF LIKE STAINS

I've found all sorts of answers to various stain problems, *but* I've also found that stains are like hiccups—everybody has a favorite solution but not all of them work all the time. Give them a try and find out what works best for you.

BLOOD

Wash the bloodstain immediately with detergent and cold water, or try applying cold water followed by meat tenderizer. Another method is to clean with a solution of salt water (one-half teaspoon of salt to a cup of water). For white clothing or fabric, get out the hydrogen peroxide. Soak and rinse. Getting blood out of velvet can be tough. If the stain is on velvet furniture, try to remove the fabric from the furniture, then aim some steam from the nozzle of a tea kettle through the *back* of the material and blot gently.

BURN MARKS

When you burn a wooden counter or piece of furniture with a hot pot or pan, you may be able to undo the damage. Try a paste of vegetable oil and powered pumice. Rub this gently into only the burned area. Rub back and forth with the grain of the wood so the mixture can get below the surface. When you're done, wipe it off with a cloth or paper towel, and polish. Some experts recommend using something as simple as toothpaste if the burn is only a minor one.

CHEWING GUM

The best first step in removing chewing gum is to make it hard and brittle. You do this by freezing it with ice cubes. If it will fit, just put the item in the freezer. You should be able to scrape the gum off when it becomes hard. Any residue will normally clean off with detergent and water.

CHOCOLATE AND COCOA

Here again, the key stain word is *immediately* as it is with many other types of stains. Wash the affected area with an ammonia solution right away.

COFFEE AND TEA

A simple, mechanical way of rinsing coffee and tea stains out of clothing or cloth is to do just that; namely, rinse it out. You want to get help because an extra set of hands makes this easier. Stretch the fabric with the stain taut over your sink and simply pour hot water through the stained area. That should do it.

GRASS

To get rid of grass stains from washable fabrics, simply wash with detergent. If the fabric is not washable, try using alcohol followed by a plain water rinse.

GREASE

A good grease cleaner is distilled water and soap. The distilled water penetrates the grease better than ordinary tap water and makes stain removal easier.

INK

For nonporous things, like countertops, walls, your body, and plastics, apply a little hair spray or alcohol and wipe clean with a paper towel. If the stain is on porous material such as cloth, put some paper towels or rags in back of the fabric and then apply the hair spray or alcohol.

JUICE STAINS

If you spill juice, immediately dab or blot—don't rub—the stain with a sponge dipped in cold water. Then do what I suggested for tea and coffee stains, pour hot water through the stain. All of this should be followed with a laundry detergent washing and rinsing.

LIPSTICK

Interestingly, this is one situation where one cosmetic can help with another. A simple solution to lipstick stains is to hit them with hair spray. After a few minutes, blot the stain away.

MILDEW

Here are two ideas for removing mildew from clothes and fabrics: lemon juice and salt or hydrogen peroxide. Sprinkle lemon juice and salt or hydrogen peroxide directly on the mildew and let it dry in the sunlight. Here again, it's always a good idea to test these methods on some out-of-sight portion of the material first.

NAIL POLISH

The answer here is obvious. To remove nail polish, use nail polish remover. Then, wash with soap and water. First, try the remover on an obscure spot to make sure it doesn't remove more than the polish. It is usually not a good idea to use it on cotton or polyester cloth.

PET HAIR

To get pet hair off of the furniture, moisten a chamois with plain water and rub it over the upholstery. That will take off most of Fido's hair.

SMUDGE MARKS

To get handprints, smudges, and smears off the wall, mist the mark with spray starch. When it dries, wipe the mark off with a towel or cloth.

MISCELLANEOUS ITEMS

Most of my favorite cleaning tips don't fit into a neat category—I guess that's why I like them. I hope you can use some of the ideas in the pages that follow.

ARTIFICIAL FLOWERS

Do you have some artificial flowers you'd like to bring back to life? Try this stunt: Put them inside a paper or plastic bag. Then pour in a little salt, close the mouth of the bag, and shake it vigorously for 15 to 30 seconds. When you're done, the flowers should be clean and bright once again.

BOOKS

You should occasionally take the books off your shelves, if not to read them, then to clean them. You can dust or wipe the covers down with a solution of one part vinegar and two parts water. Some people use waxed paper to rub their book covers, which gives them a nice coating and helps them stay cleaner longer. To protect against mildew and silverfish, take your books outside on a warm sunny day and let them relax in the sunshine for a little while. You might flip through the pages to air out the books as well. You can also sprinkle the pages with baking soda, talcum, or baby powder. After a few days, brush or riffle the pages to get the powder out and your books will love it for it. You can mend page tears by painting the tear with egg white and leaving the page open to dry.

BRASS

Mix equal parts of salt, flour, and vinegar to make a paste, rub the paste on the brass item, leave on for an hour or so, then clean with a soft cloth or brush and buff with a dry cloth. Worcestershire sauce, ketchup, and toothpaste, oddly enough, also work well as a brass polish.

CANDLESTICKS

The romance of candlelight fades fast when you're picking the dried wax out of your candlesticks. A couple of hints that will make it easier are the water and freezer techniques. The water technique involves putting a little bit of water in the bottom of the candlestick. When you are done with the candle, it should pull up from the holder easily. When you forget to put in the water, try putting the candlestick into the freezer for 15 minutes or so. This makes the wax contract and it should chip right out.

CEILING FANS

The easy way to clean ceiling fans is to buy a long-handled, twin-arm duster available at most hardware stores. You simply slip the twin arms over the fan blade and move them back and forth to clean them without climbing up on a ladder.

CHROME

One easy way to polish chrome is to rinse with cold water and use newspaper to buff it. You can also use alcohol, baby oil, a piece of lemon, white vinegar, or baking soda with water or club soda to clean it.

Polish vigorously with a cloth for that desirable shine.

COBWEBS

To get cobwebs down from unreachable places, wrap a tennis ball inside a dust cloth secured with a few rubber bands, and toss it at the distant cobweb. Or slip a plastic bag or cloth rag bag over the bristle end of your broom and scoop the cobwebs away without messing up your broom. Of course, there is always the vacuum with the extension tube.

COMPUTERS

With the computer off, use a handheld vacuum cleaner gently on the keyboard and mouse to keep them free of dirt and dust.

CONTACT LENSES

Is there anything more frustrating than losing a contact lens on the floor or, even worse, down the sink? To clean your contacts and actually keep them at the same time, take a small bottle and clean it thoroughly. Punch a couple of small drain holes in the lid and put your contacts in there to wash and rinse them.

COPPER

There is a great tip for cleaning tarnished copper that usually does the job as good or better than those fancy store-bought copper cleaners. Mix one part flour with one part salt and, using vinegar for moisture, kneed it together into a paste that you smear over the copper pots and pans. Rinse with water and the tarnish should be gone.

FIBERGLAS

Here is where my friend vinegar comes to work again. Spray hot vinegar all over the Fiberglas and follow that with a good scrubbing with more hot vinegar. Then finish up with a water rinse and dry everything off. The surface should be cleaner than ever.

GLASS TABLETOPS

To make glass-topped furniture shine, use lemon juice (not too much) and paper towels. After wiping, dry with more paper towels and polish with crumbled newspaper—I like using the sports section when I'm done with it, but any part of the paper will do.

HAIRBRUSHES

An easy way to clean your hairbrush is to use it on your hair while you are shampooing. Then "comb" it with your open fingers and rinse. Or comb hair out of the brush with a comb and soak in warm soapy water.

JEWELRY

Cleaning real jewelry is easy. Just soak it in a solution of dishwashing detergent, water, and a teaspoon of ammonia for a few minutes and clean with an old toothbrush. Then, rinse in clear water and dab dry—don't rub. Use the same solution to clean costume jewelry but don't soak it first, as doing so may loosen the stones. You should clean pearls by rubbing gently with an olive oil–dampened soft cloth.

LAMPSHADES

Surprisingly, many lampshades are fairly easy to wash. First, check whether the shade is glued or sewn to the lampshade frame. If it is glued, just clean it dry by wiping with a soft cloth. If it is sewn, you can do more. Remove it from the lamp—did we really have to tell you that?—and dip the shade in warm water that has a dash of detergent mixed in it. Then, rinse in clean water and dry as quickly as you can with a fan or by hand. If you just let it sit and dry, the chances are good—or, rather, bad—that the metal frame will rust.

PAINTINGS AND PICTURES

Don't spray cleaner on glass-covered pictures because the fluid can drip down behind the glass and attack the picture underneath. Use a cloth or paper towel lightly dampened with cleaner instead. Inexpensive oil paintings should be dusted and, if cleaned, use a soft cloth. Some experts even suggest using bread. (No report on which kind is the favorite: whole wheat, white, or sourdough.) If you have a valuable painting or one that means a lot to you, don't clean it yourself. Take it to a professional art restorer. No matter how careful you are with a painting, there's always the chance you will nick, mar, or chip the paint. Not worth the risk.

PEWTER

Old pewter was commonly used for pots in what my grandmother would call "the olden days," and it's a little tricky to clean because pewter is actually a combination of lead and tin. This means the combined metals are quite soft and easily scratched. One gentle method is to boil the pot in a dishwater mixture, remove, and wash and rinse.

New pewter is a different combination of metals—usually copper and antimony—that is not so tender. It should clean up nicely with regular silver polish or a mixture of baking soda and cooking oil. Rinse and store in a cabinet. Letting pewter sit out in the open tends to encourage tarnishing.

PIANO KEYS

Never tickle the ivories with soap. Instead run up and down the scale with half a lemon and dry the key with a soft cloth.

SHAVING CREAM CAN RINGS

I'm not sure why the bottoms of shaving cream cans tend to leave rust rings on shelves and counters in the bathroom. You can prevent the rings by taping the bottom with a short piece of duct tape or by painting it with nail polish.

SILVER

One thing that will help to prevent silver from tarnishing is to clean and dry it thoroughly, then wrap individual pieces in plastic or in a zip-locking bag. To fight tarnishing while silver is in the drawer or case waiting to be brought out for your next festive dinner, store it with some camphor, rice, or some other absorbent material to soak up the tarnishing moisture.

STICKERS

Have you ever removed a sticker from your bumper, or a decal from your window, only to be stuck with a patch of leftover glue? Get the glue off by sloshing some white vinegar on the spot and letting it soak for a while, say 20 to 30 minutes. Then it should come off easily when you scrape it with a knife or straight-edged surface.

STUFFED TOYS

Most stuffed toys are safe for washing in your washing machine; there may even be a washing-instruction tag sewn on to the toy (which, obviously, you should follow). Generally, stuffed toys should not be put in your dryer. Hang them up to dry the old-fashioned way. Some people prefer hanging them up by the ears and some prefer the feet. I don't think it makes a difference.

TABLECLOTHS

Here's a hint from my mother: For spots on tablecloths, apply lemon juice to the spot and then spread it out in the sun to dry.

TELEPHONES

Keep your phone germ-free by wiping it down with disinfectant mouthwash.

TELEVISIONS

It's nice when the screen is clean even if the program isn't. Wipe the screen down either with alcohol or a solution of one part vinegar and ten parts water. (If your TV has a wooden cabinet, don't use alcohol.)

VASES

Add a tablet of Alka-Seltzer to a water-filled vase, wait an hour, and rinse.

VENETIAN BLINDS

Clean venetian blinds with a long-handled, twin-arm duster. Insert the arms between the slats and move them back and forth. You can find the dusters at most hardware stores.

WAX DRIPPINGS

To get candle wax drippings off wooden furniture, use a hair dryer to warm the wax. When the drippings get soft, wipe with a cloth or paper towel. When you've gotten as much off as possible, go over the surface with vinegar and a towel or cloth. Then, polish the furniture as you usually would.

8

GARDENING

Guidance on how to make the outside of your home
as nice as the inside

Some people find gardening a great way to unwind. Others see yard work as just one more chore. Regardless of which side of the fence you fall on, here are some hints that will make gardening a happy experience with minimal effort. I outline some of the tricks experts use to make the work easier as well as the basic tools you'll need. Your reward will come when the flowers bloom and you are able to sit and enjoy what you and nature have done together (along with the help of a little fertilizer!).

PLANNING YOUR YARD

Some people hire landscape architects for a fee to plan out their yard, others have a natural knack and do it themselves, but the important thing is to have a plan.

THE NEEDS OF YOUR PLANTS

Obviously, your plants won't thrive if you put them into an unpleasing environment. Before you bring a bunch of plants home from the nursery, learn about the needs of those that you like. Plants that need a lot of sunlight can be grouped together in sunny areas of the yard; those that need shade should be grouped with other plants that need shade. Take into consideration the amount of water and fertilizer particular plants need and plant them together.

YOUR NEEDS

Group plants and trees by what you want from them. For example, in hot climates, you may want shade trees along the south and west sides of the house to help keep it cool. You may want trees that shed their leaves in the winter on the north side of the house so they can let warming sunlight in during cold days. Don't place fruit trees adjacent to walks or stairs where the ripe fruit may drop and become a safety hazard.

GROUND COVERS

Probably the first thing you need to decide when planning your yard is what kind of ground cover you would like. Not only does ground cover look good, it also keeps dust from blowing around and prevents soil slippage or runoff. Lawns are common as ground covers but there are places where low plants or vines are more convenient, particularly on slopes or rough ground and on places where maintaining a lawn would be bothersome.

Look at the homes in your area to see what types of ground cover are popular and ask at your local nursery for its recommendations. Crawling ivy and ice plant are popular ground covers in some places but, as with all plantings, you need to understand the advantages and the disadvantages of the plants fully. For example, with close-to-the-ground crawling plants such as ivy and ice plant, there is a tendency for rodents of various sorts to take up residence in the planting. So, you need to be prepared to respond should this occur.

After you have figured out how many plants you need for the area to be covered, prepare the soil by getting rid of weeds and other plants in the area. You'll probably need to use a mechanical tiller to turn and loosen the soil and you may also want to add a fertilizer and insecticide. Here again, consult your local nurseryman who understands soils and planting conditions in your area. Water the plants a few hours before you are going to plant them and dig planting holes. Gently remove the plants from their containers. Carefully untangle the roots and place the roots and plant in the hole, covering the roots with soil and pressing the dirt firmly in place around the plant. When you're done planting, water the plants thoroughly and lay down two or three inches of mulch mixture.

To prevent weeds from taking up residence in your fresh soil, you may need to cover the lawn for a while so the new plants can take hold. Lay down a plastic sheet and simply cut holes in the plastic to plant your ground cover plants.

LAWN MAINTENANCE

If you decide to plant a traditional lawn, start with good quality grass seed, then carefully follow professional advice on planting the grass. Once your grass has grown in, caring for it isn't too difficult.

Of course, you need to keep the grass watered. There are two easy ways to check if your lawn needs watering. One is to simply walk across it. If you leave footprints as if you were walking in snow, and they remain for a few minutes, your lawn needs water. Or you can get down on all fours and carefully inspect the blades of grass. If they are rolling or folding and changing color from dark green to a bluish green, your lawn needs watering.

A good deep soaking every week is much better that a half-hearted sprinkling a couple times a week. You need to get water not just to the grass on the surface but, more important, to the roots down an inch or two under the surface. A light watering may evaporate before the water can nourish the roots and it's the same as if you have not watered at all.

Although you should provide plenty of water, you don't want to do it too quickly. Water all over the lawn in a uniform way and watch to see that the water is being absorbed by the soil. If you flood the lawn with a rush job, the water may run off instead of penetrating down to the important roots.

MOWING

Mow your lawn regularly to keep the blades about 2¹/₂ inches high. It is best not to mow during very hot and dry weather.

If you're wondering, power mowers are just as dangerous as they sound. These mowers can rev up to 110 decibels—as loud as a rock concert and a lot less fun. The spinning blades of these tools can touch a rock or other hard item in the lawn, and propel it at enormous speed. If such an object gets thrown into your eye, it can cause serious damage. You may feel silly mowing the lawn in goggles, but it's a good idea. You should also wear sturdy shoes and earplugs when mowing the lawn.

FERTILIZING

Don't fertilize your lawn when it is wet from watering or the morning dew. The moisture tends to let the fertilizer burn your grass instead of encouraging it to grow.

BASIC YARD CARE

The purpose of the following hints is to help you keep your yard and garden looking great with little effort (and even less money). Why spend a fortune at the nursery when you don't have to?

FERTILIZERS

Some excellent fertilizers may already be around the house. For rose, for example, old bananas that have turned brown are excellent. Peel them and work them, peel and all, into the soil. Bananas are abundant in calcium, phosphates, sulfur, and magnesium, which are all very yummy to rose plants. The edible part works immediately while the peels will fertilize the plants more gradually.

Another secret fertilizer from the olden days is—ready?—urine. However distasteful this may sound initially, the fact is this is natural liquid waste very rich in nitrogen. Guess what that sack of fertilizer you bought at the nursery for $5 is rich in? Yup, nitrogen. Experts suggest diluting urine in half with water and sprinkling it on most of your flowers.

IVY-COVERED WALLS

Ivy-covered walls look so beautiful, but they can be difficult to maintain. The mortar used for building brick walls is less durable than that used for pouring concrete foundations and often is loosened by climbing vines poking into the cracks between the bricks. In time, this can make the bricks unstable and fall out. It is hard to patch such mortar holes and cracks without removing the vines. But if you must remove them, first cut off as much of the plant as you can. Then, let the rest of the vines dry out for several weeks followed by scrubbing the trimmed vines with a brush dipped in a solution of ¼ cup of trisodium phosphate (TSP) in half a gallon of water. You can get TSP at the hardware store.

If you want to avoid this insidious vine growth into the mortar, another approach is to put up trellises and train the vines and ivy to grow on them while keeping the area between the trellises and the brick wall trimmed and free of vines.

SEEDING

When you are spreading seeds by hand around your lawn or yard, mix in some clearly visible neutral material such as ashes or sawdust, so you can see what areas you've covered and which ones you have missed on the first try.

VEGETABLE GARDENS

If you want your vegetable garden to grow well, understand that vegetable seeds tend to like heat and sunshine in that order. When you first plant those vegetable seeds, keep them warm with a covering of a plastic sheet like a painting drop cloth, or even cover them with a layer of ordinary newspapers (weighed down, of course). Check daily and, when those little seeds have sprouted, they want light instead of heat, so remove the covers and let the seeds grow.

SCREEN DOORS

Many gardens are entered from the house through a screen door, which, over time, may begin to pull loose from the frame or get punctured. This becomes a passageway for insects and other unwanted critters. The easy solution—better than yelling at people not to push on the screen—is to nail a strip of wood or heavy gauge mesh wire across the inside of the door. Place the strip at about the height where most people push the screen.

WATERING

Often the water that comes out of the tap has chemicals in it that are detrimental to some plants. Water your garden with the freshest water possible. To capture fresh water, position buckets beneath your downspouts or shovel snow into barrels for use when it melts. Your plants will love you for it.

TOOLS AND GEAR

The most important part of any job is having the right tools. My list includes those that I think are mandatory.

- **Hand clippers:** Hand clippers are a basic tool for trimming shrubs and trees.
- **Heavy-duty clippers:** Heavy-duty clippers are for cutting branches

AZALEAS GALORE

To grow beautiful azaleas, occasionally water the plants with a mixture of two tablespoons white vinegar in one quart water. Azaleas love acidic soil.

up to an inch in thickness. You need them for pruning trees and large shrubs.

- **Hose:** Select a hose that's the right length for your purposes. Obviously, a hose that's too short isn't useful, but one that's too long will drive you nuts as it tangles up everywhere. If you want to get really organized, you'll include a hose reel mounted at the faucet so you can roll up the hose neatly when you're done with it. Check the safety labels on the hose guiding its use.

- **Protective clothing:** For working in the garden, you need at least one set of gardening gloves with leather lining. These are for handling thorny and rough plants. A pair of cotton gloves is also a good idea. I recommend wearing safety goggles when trimming larger shrubs and trees, and, of course, a hat.

- **Rake:** There are lots of different kinds of rakes including split bamboo, flexible metal, and rigid metal. I recommend the rigid metal kind. It's the most durable and can do the greatest variety of work.

- **Second-tier tools:** "Second-tier" tools are those that you'll probably want to add to your collection over time. They include a wheelbarrow (a must for shlepping fertilizer and the like), a hedge trimmer, and a saw. Obviously, if you have a lawn, you'll want a mower and, if you have a lot of potted plants, a sprinkling can for watering. A large broom is handy if your garden has a walkway or patio area to be kept clean.

- **Shovel:** There are two basic shapes of shovels, pointed spades for digging and straight-edged shovels. You'll probably want one of each. If you can only afford one, get the spade—you can use a dustpan or a plastic bottle with the bottom cut off for scooping.

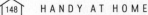

- **Sprayer:** A sprayer consisting of a reservoir or tank with a pump and nozzle hose is something you will use in most gardens for applying insecticides, fertilizer, and a variety of liquids.

GARDEN LIGHTS

Outdoor lights make the yard more enjoyable and safer. You may want to consider motion-sensitive lights that will come on automatically when they sense someone moving in the yard. They're a good safety measure.

Decorative lights are available as low-voltage strings of floodlights, tiny lights, or peanut bulbs. They can be used to outline a walkway or doorways, or to lighten up your street address at night. In addition to the strings of lights and electrical cable, the packaged units have a transformer with a built-in timer that allows you to set the lights to turn on and off at whatever time you wish.

After you visualize the lighting pattern you want, carefully measure the path where the connecting wires are to run and draw a simple map of your plan. Most lighting systems come with some kind of ground stake that lets you simply push the stake in and string the lighting wire through or around it. Normally, each light has two wires with a metal tipped tab. You simply put one of these tabs on each side of the wire and snap the tabs together.

Of course, you need to strip the insulation off the first half inch of the electrical wire and twist that around the appropriate screws on the transformer. Tighten down the screws and the wire. Plug the transformer into an outside GFCI (Ground Fault Circuit Interrupter) plug and set the timer. The transformer should have at least two on/off cycle settings so you can set the lights for both morning and evening. The three-pronged GFCI plug is to protect you from a sudden electrical shock. After you have checked that all the lights work, you may want to bury the wire in a shallow trench. It will look better and won't attract the attention of pets and kids.

CUT FLOWER CARE

To prolong the life of cut flowers, add two tablespoons of white vinegar plus three tablespoons of sugar per quart of warm water. The stems should rest in three to four inches of water.

POTTED PLANTS

Some people like to keep potted plants on their patio that they can move indoors when the weather gets cold. Here are some ideas for your indoor/outdoor plants.

POT SIZE

When it comes to containers for your potted plants, you want the plant to have lots of room. If not, the roots will get tangled up and the plant will become "root bound." You can check this periodically by grasping the stem of the plant and tapping the pot so it drops away from the plant. If it is root bound, you'll see it right away. There'll be a tangle of roots jammed all around the base of the plant, which are not able to nourish the plant properly. There are two easy solutions—you can move the plant to a bigger pot or cut back the roots and repot it.

MINI-GREENHOUSE

A funny bit of houseplant care advice from the experts concerns what to do when you're out of town and can't water. Try tying a plastic bag around the plant (loosely, of course). The bag will retain moisture in the air, providing a little eco-system until you return.

A SPECIAL LIGHT

One outside light that is very important to you and your family is the one by the front door. In time of an emergency you want the fire, police, or medics to use it to find you quickly. So, instead of an ordinary light bulb, put in a bright, colored bulb that is different from any other bulb on your street. That way you can call 9-1-1 for help, give your address, and add, "It's the house with the blue (green, yellow, or whatever) light." The colored light will serve as a beacon to those on the way.

9

MAKING STORAGE SPACE COUNT

Ideas for how to put things away, keep them in good shape,
and find them again when you need them

My mother used to say that she knew exactly when she would need some-thing—it was always a week after she had thrown it out. This is the type of experience that prompts us to keep things—sometimes more things than we'll ever need. The annoying aspect of this habit is that when we finally decide we need something we've put away, we can't find it (or we can find it and it's broken). Here are tips for efficient and safe storage ideas that will maximize your storage space and minimize your aggravation.

EXPANDING YOUR STORAGE SPACE

I've yet to hear someone complain—ever—that they have too much closet space. If you want (or need!) to create more room in your home, I've got great suggestions to help you do it.

CABINETS

With cabinets that come to a corner or are very deep, the storage space at the very back is inconvenient and hard to reach. At kitchen specialty shops you can get a lazy Susan unit that will make use of that space in the rear. There are lots of devices that swing, slide, or fold out to give you more room in cabinets and over counters. Check your community for storage stores that specialize in these items.

You can buy shallow fold-down racks to mount on the underside of your cabinets to increase storage space for spices and many small items. There are also large fold-up racks you can mount under counters in which you can store small appliances.

There may be a lot of "dead" space in cabinets that hold short items like coffee cups and juice glasses. If you have extra vertical space in a cabinet, buy an insert shelf with legs that will double the storage space. Or, you could screw in cup hooks on the bottom side of the upper shelf from which to hang more cups.

Sometimes kitchen cabinets don't go to the ceiling. This gives you a place for boxes, drawers, or other storage units you can reach with a small step-ladder.

Cabinet Clean-out

You'll have a lot more space if you clean out your cabinets. This advice is self-evident, so why can't you remember the last time you did it? If you're like most people, the tendency is to just come home from the store and shove your purchases into the refrigerator and cabinets as quickly as possible. Here are some suggestions.

For the cabinets where you normally store dry goods and canned foods, clean everything out at least three times a year. When the cabinet is empty, wash down the insides with soapy water, rinse, and dry. If you haven't lined the cabinets with shelf paper—preferably the self-sticking bug-repellent kind—this is a wonderful time to do that.

Then check over all the food you removed from the cabinet. Check the condition of each can and package. Are the containers still sealed? Are the cans still intact with no dents, seams sprung, or rusted? If dated, is the food still fresh? If the food is something your family will still use and the containers are in good condition, wipe the packages clean and replace them in your cabinets. Food storage experts recommend that you flip canned goods top to bottom, and then the reverse, each time you clean. This is also an excellent time to organize your foods into convenient groupings. You may want to do it by type of food (all vegetables together), how it's prepared (pasta and sauces together), or whatever way is convenient for you. A well-organized pantry cabinet is particularly handy when you're about to go shopping, as you won't have to search through everything to check whether you're out of an item.

SPACES IN THE KITCHEN

If you have room left over in the recessed space for your refrigerator, take advantage of it. Create or buy a tall, narrow roll-out storage unit on casters for this space.

Create shallow shelves in narrow places to store single rows of cans, condiments, and jars.

Mounting a peg board and hooks on the inside of kitchen cabinet doors and other closets can increase the space you have for hanging cleaning materials and other useful stuff.

You can get a wire dish rack to mount over your sink to use for storage, drying dishes, or both. Under the sink, keep your cleaning supplies—rags, sprays, cleansers, sponges, scrubbers, vinegar, baking soda, club soda—all together in one plastic tray or bucket with a handle so you can move them quickly and conveniently to where they are needed. This is especially handy in case of emergency spills and stains.

You can mount attractive suspended pots-and-pans racks from the ceiling over work areas and near the stove.

Make putting groceries away less cumbersome by adding a foldout counter in your kitchen. Everyone always needs more counter space, and it's particularly useful to have a counter that you can get out of the way.

SPACES IN THE BEDROOM

A lot of storage space in bedrooms can make your life more comfortable and make your home more desirable to future owners. And if you plan to *never* sell your house, you'll definitely want as much room as possible for all of your stuff. Which brings me back to storage space for the briefcases,

PLASTIC BAGS

Why devote valuable cabinet space to a mass of plastic bags? One way to store them neatly is to stuff them into paper-towel rolls, empty tissue boxes, or other empty containers such as coffee cans or cereal boxes.

athletic equipment, school books and back packs, CDs, and all the other things you keep in the bedroom.

You've probably noticed the increased interest in more and better storage space, which has given birth to a new facet of the home-improvement industry. It is an industry selling storage units, specialized gadgets, and inserts for inaccessible closet corners. You can now buy clothing trapezes to allow ceiling-high storage in bedroom closets and rolling "drawers" for under the bed. You can install lazy Susan shelves for hard to reach corners of closets and you can add shelves. Put in a hanging bar that you can raise and lower to reach clothes stored up high. Door hanging units are another source of extra space. Most closets have a single rod for hanging clothes, but the more organized have more than one rod. Add a second rod for at least part of the closet for hanging shirts, blouses, coats, and other short items.

Another popular item for more storage in the bedroom is the return of the individual man and woman walk-in closet. If you don't really need all the floor space in your master bedroom, why not consider building walk-ins? They're extremely practical yet they feel like a wonderful luxury. If a walk-in just takes up too much room, think about adding on an old-fashioned linen/accessories closet. Another trend in bedroom storage includes customizing closets—adding and removing racks and the like. Many people are installing pull-out jewelry drawers and/or hidden safes. Such safes are usually designed to hold both jewelry and important papers. This is an item you'll probably want to discuss with a locksmith.

A disadvantage to custom-designing storage space is that things in life change. Keep in mind that your clothing choices, leisure activities, and what have you will change over time. And in the case of storage in the children's room, remember that they are constantly growing and changing interests. You want storage space that's flexible, so think about adaptability when designing your closets.

Eliminating Closet Chaos

If there is one time and place where chaos, confusion, and clutter get us, it's in the bedroom in the morning when we're trying to wake up and pull ourselves together to go out and face the day. Pairs of shoes are separated, a sweater is here, and a jacket is somewhere over there. All this when you're just out of the shower and have 15 minutes to get coffee, kiss your spouse good-bye, and get on the road!

It's not the way you want to start your day and you vow that you'll organize it over the weekend. Some people pay professionals to redesign their closets and storage space. Here are some tips from the experts.

- **Applying the "toss it" principle:** I talked about the "toss it" principle in connection with cleaning out your kitchen cabinets. It's great for the bedroom. You need to set aside some time when you are not rushed or stressed—a rainy Saturday afternoon, perhaps, where you can pull everything out of the closet and sort it into three piles. One pile is for definite discards destined for the trash or charity. Another pile is for definite keepers. The third pile is the iffy stuff that you are not sure of. One test that many people use for the discard pile is the one-year rule. If you haven't worn it in the last year, toss it. As an alternative, one expert suggests an emotional gauge for putting items in the toss-it pile. If it doesn't make you feel good, if it makes you feel fat or unhappy, toss it. Before you proceed, remove pile number one. Stuff it in boxes or bags or whatever and remove it immediately! Just get it out of the room! With this one move, you have instantly made a major step toward more room and more order. Next, take the iffy pile and stuff it in a box or bag and set it aside—out of the way—in a corner. Leave it alone for at least a week, but no more than two weeks. After you've got your "new" closet space filled, sort out the clothes in the "maybe" pile. You may just find that you don't want to fill up your closet with questionable stuff.

- **Maintaining order:** Before you reassemble your hanging closet, you may want to wax the clothing rods with furniture wax or by rubbing lightly with bar soap. This will make the hangers slide more easily. You may also want to install one of those battery-powered stick-on lights unless the lighting in the bedroom illuminates the closet area. Having to pick clothes out of your closet when you can't see well might prove embarrassing once you get to the office. For a nice touch you may also want to hang a fragrant sachet or some spices and herbs in a perforated plastic bag to give the closet a nice smell.

Now, take the keep pile and sort it out according to type. Put each type of clothing, shoes, belts, and the like, in it's own part of the closet. That is, informal clothes in one group, work clothes in another, and dressy clothes in still another group. Within each group, it is a good idea to hang all the short items—shirts, blouses, jackets—together, so that you will have open space below them for storage of other appropriate things such as footwear, accessories, and so on. Then, color-coordinate the items within each category. Already things are better in that closet.

I've always found it convenient to have an empty hanging rod on the back of the closet door. That way, as you are deciding what to wear, you can hang possible alternatives on the rod, see how they work together, and make substitutions right there.

Hang your clothes with the hangers pointing the same way, that is, with the open end of the hanger hook toward the back of the closet. (You may have noticed that in some clothing stores, the hangers face in alternating directions. This is to prevent "grab-and-run" thieves from making off with a handful of expensive clothes.) You want maximum access and convenience so have all your hangers facing the back of the closet.

Organization is the key here, not more space. More space without organization does not address the problem you face on Monday morning. One expert recommends storing all clothes, including shoes and sweaters, openly rather than in boxes and bags. Easy access to your clothes helps you get dressed more quickly and makes it more likely you will wear them, or decide they don't fit your wardrobe and toss them.

Once you have organized the clothes in your closet, keep things where they are. If you remove a garment, leave the empty hanger in the same place so you will return that item of clothing to that same place.

MAKING NEW STORAGE SPACE

A common complaint about kitchens is there isn't enough space for storage and work. Here are some ways to create more space for relatively little money and effort.

CREATE A CUBBYHOLE

There might be lots of usable space literally hiding behind your kitchen wall. To create a cubbyhole for storage, first check for "blank" walls. These are usually walls made of drywall board nailed to a framework of 2 × 4 studs behind them. Find these vertical studs (the easiest way is to use a stud finder); check carefully for plumbing pipes or electrical switches, plugs, or wires in that section of the wall. When you find an area that's blank with nothing behind it, saw out and remove the drywall between the studs. You now have a shallow recess into which you can build shelves to hold canned goods, bottles, and other stuff. You could even add a door, but in any case, you've opened up more storage space.

TRANSFORM YOUR SINK INTO A COUNTER

You can expand your counter space by setting a cutting board into the top rim of the sink. It's a good idea to have a hole or slot in the cutting board so you can drain off liquids into the sink and to give yourself a grip for removing the board.

CREATE A PANTRY

More and more of us are buying items by the case. So, where to store it all? In the olden days many homes had a separate room off the kitchen for just that—the pantry. In most modern homes and apartments, you'll have to create your own.

Basically, there are two ways to create a pantry. You can buy one and install it in a hallway or closet or whatever spare room you can find. Often, shelving and storage stores will sell modular pantry units you can install at home. For example, the Scandinavian motif store, Ikea, sells pantry units for under $150.

Or, you can build a pantry or pantry units yourself. You can create shelves and bins in unused nooks and crannies in or near your kitchen—the back porch, the hallway, a nearby closet, or perhaps under the stairs.

Either way, you'll want to abide by the following rules my grandmother taught me. Before you do anything measure your space. After you have measured once, measure a second time; have someone else check your measurements, too. Silly? Not nearly as silly as spending a lot of money for cabinets or shelves that don't fit when you get them home. Also check the exact size of the major categories of things you are going to store in the pantry such as pots and pans or rarely used appliances. Generally, you can get by with 3-inch shelves for most canned and packaged goods but you may want spaces up to 18 inches deep for big pots and pans or large sacks of flour.

To maximize the room in your pantry, make it a habit to keep cans in one section, grains and flour in another section, utensils in another section, and so on. Neatness counts when it comes to saving space. Just as you should in your kitchen, make use of rollout shelves and rotating shelves to make maximum use of all the available space.

STORAGE RENTALS

One of the more interesting developments in America in the last few decades has been the blossoming of self-storage facilities, the endless barns that rent little units into which we stash all the stuff we don't have room to stuff around the house. Here are some helpful hints about using them.

AGREEMENT

When you rent storage space, you will probably have to sign a rental agreement just as if you were renting an office or apartment. Read it carefully and ask for an explanation of any part you don't understand. The landlord will probably ask for one or two months' payment in advance plus a cleaning or a security deposit. Check the details of the cleaning or security deposit provision. What are the terms for repayment?

It's best if the agreement has an arbitration clause that spells out how disputes will be resolved. It is much quicker and less costly to have a disagreement resolved through arbitration than by going to court. Make sure that any such clause entitles you to have a voice in the selection of one or more arbitrators. There should also be a clause requiring the owner to notify you in writing of changes in the management, intentions to evict, or clean out your space for nonpayment of rent. You must, of course, keep the owner notified of your current address.

ROUTINE CHECK-UPS

Make it a habit to visit your space every so often. It is relatively easy for people to steal from you even when you have your own lock on the place. You may want to install a motion alarm should a thief cut your lock off and get inside. These battery-powered alarms are reasonably inexpensive at most home-improvement stores. Many thieves operate by renting a space in a remote part of the complex and breaking into other people's storage at odd hours. They keep their pickings hidden in their own space for removal at a later time.

INSURANCE

The owner of the facility should have fire and casualty insurance on the building and should inform you of the policy number and insurer. However, this rarely covers the goods you have stored so you need to get fire, theft, and casualty insurance on your own property.

Storing dangerous items is probably illegal in your state and the storage contract will usually preclude you from storing certain things. To protect yourself from a lawsuit, and everyone who uses the space from an accident, you should not store live animals, perishables, liquids, explosives, flammable liquids and fuels, toxic materials, or other items that need a controlled environment. Remember to drain the fuel from gasoline engines before storage. (It might be silly to have to say this, but it needs to be said nonetheless.)

PACKING TIPS

Make the most of your storage space by using the following packing ideas.

Appliances

Things like refrigerators or freezers should be dried out before you store them. Keep the doors propped open a little bit. Fill the interior spaces with small, delicate items padded with towels. Clean all appliances before you store them. If you are storing machinery, drain all the gasoline or flammable liquids out of it.

Furniture

First, line the floor with corrugated cardboard, moving pallets, or plastic sheets. Sofas and mattresses are best stored on end. If you can take the furniture apart (unscrewing legs and tops, for example), do it. If you can't disassemble a table, store it top down. Use interior spaces. If you are storing a dresser or trunk fill up the insides. Put breakables in padded boxes and store on top of the heavy furniture.

Mirrors and Breakables

Glass tabletops, glass doors, and mirrors should all be stored on end. A good idea is to run strips of masking or duct tape over and around these items in several patterns to help keep them from breaking should they fall. It is best to do the same with other breakable items such as china and ceramic pieces. Then pack them securely. There's no point in having a storage locker full of useless broken glass.

PACKING WISELY

Pack boxes and barrels full, but not so full that they'll pop open. Divide heavy items into several small containers so none is too heavy to move conveniently. Seal and tape everything shut to keep from damage by vermin or water leaks. Label all boxes, barrels, and enclosed furniture with a list of their contents. Make an inventory list to keep at home, as well as a copy for another person you trust.

10

DECORATING

Some inexpensive decorating tips to make your
home even more beautiful

You've undoubtedly admired a clever element in the decor of a friend's home and wondered, why didn't *I* think of that? If you're looking for some simple ways to enhance the appearance of your home, read on.

A GOOD FIRST IMPRESSION—YOUR ENTRYWAY

As actors, my wife, Tudi, and I know that a good first impression (a good first act) makes a big difference to your guests. In our most recent home, we remodeled the entry hall. By raising the ceiling several feet, our foyer has an air of spaciousness. At the same time, we decorated with the very in vogue faux wall painting and created back-lit niches in which we have tasteful small statuary. The entrance is sophisticated and appealing.

One of my favorite ways of decorating the area outside the entryway is with plants. Try placing flowering potted plants by the door, or a tall, slender potted tree such as a cherry or dogwood or other tree appropriate to your area with small flowering plants around the tree's base. Note that for potted trees or plants (whether they're outdoors or inside), you need a pot that is about half the size across as the potted plant's height. For example, a four- to five-foot tall tree should be planted in a pot that is two feet in diameter. When it comes to the planter itself, each kind has its pros and cons. Most people like the appearance of a wood planter, but unless the planter is made of very expensive teak, it will likely deteriorate over time. It will definitely need occasional painting. Ceramics, concrete, and terra-cotta can chip and crack. These kinds of pots probably shouldn't be left outside in severe winter climates. Synthetic planters tend to be the most durable and you can find some that are quite attractive. For shady covered entries, try ferns in hanging pots.

A basic rule about planting outside your door is to not overcrowd the entry. You want plenty of room for access and you want to avoid brushing up against the various plants. The idea is to give visual appeal—not create a feeling of claustrophobia. A word of caution: Avoid plants and trees that will drop leaves alongside your walk or doorway. When leaves get wet, they tend to be very slippery.

If you don't want to bother with taking care of plants, try decorating with something else in pots or planters, like an array of colored balls or other decorative items. Another simple way of enhancing your home's entrance is to repaint the front door. Even if you repaint it the same color, it will look better with a fresh coat of paint. Or, you can add a surprising touch with an unusual paint design or color that distinguishes your home from others on the street and play up your creativity with plantings that compliment the new color. How about a bright yellow or powder blue or stunning white—whatever suits your temperament?

Play with your numbers. Instead of just those standard spray-on or hardware store numbers at the curb, put up fun, unusual, or intriguing numbers on the door, over the door, or alongside the door so people can find your place easily. Clean up, polish, and make your entranceway appealing to visitors with outdoor lights strung around the door frame, or an interesting doormat that goes beyond "Welcome" or "Wipe Your Feet."

If you have a front lawn or entry area, consider adding a gazebo, a fountain, an old wheelbarrow planted with flowers, a small windmill, waterfall, benches, or chairs.

THE ONE-DOLLAR DOORSTOP

To make an attractive doorstop out of an old ugly brick, cover it with a piece of leftover carpeting. A less decorative but effective doorstop is a sponge pushed under the door.

Porches and walkways can also contribute. A variety of materials and approaches—wood, concrete, brick, imprinted concrete blocks, various kinds of stone, or even a poem or welcoming thought drawn in the concrete while it's wet, or different colors and patterns in paving materials—can all be used to create a special look.

The point of it all is to distinguish you and where you live by setting a mood. It's just like setting the mood in the opening scene of a play.

FENG SHUI

At one time, feng shui was a trend. Now it's a fact of life for many of us. But if you're not familiar with the concept, you can get a clue from the way doorways are constructed in many Chinese buildings. You may have noticed that there is often a wall standing in front of the entrance and you have to go around it or zigzag to enter the building. This, I'm told, is because evil can only travel in a straight line, according to old Chinese beliefs.

In general terms, feng shui's purpose is to bring your home into maximum harmony with nature. Many of traditional feng shui masters think in terms of the "butterfly effect"—the notion that even small acts and events can have far-reaching consequences. Recall the old saying: "For want of a nail, the horse was lost and from want of the horse the rider was lost and for want of the rider the battle was lost and from want of the battle the kingdom was lost." Little things, such as the arrangement of our furniture and knickknacks can, say feng shui practitioners, affect our entire lives.

I'm told that authentic feng shui masters want to imbue each building with "chi" or good fortune. They use a compass to decide which direction the house should face and chart the chi or good fortune scheme of the house by doing what is called "star allocation." Also considered in the feng shui master's calculations is the birthday of the house, that is, when it was built and what cycle it is part of. The life pattern for everyone living in the house and the space occupied by each individual is also figured in.

Feng shui seeks to put your home into harmony to create the best environment for you. This begins with a preference for gentle objects. For example, tables with rounded corners are preferred over those with angular corners. Rooms filled with mementos of loved family members and friends bring loving, positive energy. You shouldn't keep your fireplace empty because a fireplace is associated with warmth and friendship. When you don't have a fire going, put some wood—preferably white birch—or a plant in the fireplace so it is a presence in the room. Conversely, the bedroom is a space for sleeping and should not be too busy or too cluttered with things. Keep it simple and clean.

I must hasten to warn you that, as with many popular but ill-defined practices, feng shui has attracted a lot of fakers, so don't hire just anyone to advise you. I do know many people, however, who have had a feng shui expert apply its theories to their homes and claim to be happier for it. As with so many esoteric disciplines, you will have to decide for yourself.

JAZZING UP THE WALLS

Decorating the walls is a lot of fun because it has no purpose other than to be pleasing. Here are some ideas on how to do it successfully.

HANGING PICTURES AND OTHER THINGS

Whether you're decorating with paintings, photos, or mirrors, or just putting up a towel rack, the basic techniques and principles are the same.

Remember that many of the things you hang on the wall are heavy, and you want to be sure you hang them in the right place so they won't fall down and leave a big hole. Ideally, you need to be driving the nail or screw

REFINISHING WOODEN FURNITURE

Sometimes the shade of a piece of furniture just isn't what you want. If you want to lighten a piece of wooden furniture, try carefully applying some ordinary bleach from the laundry. Put it on a little at a time so it doesn't work too well. A good rule is to always have a sponge and vinegar at your side, because the vinegar stops the bleach from bleaching and gives you better control. To make wood darker, try applying strongly brewed tea.

through the shell of the wall and anchoring it securely in one of the 2 × 4 stud beams that make up the wall's skeleton. On the inside of the wall where you are, you want to use the right kind of nail or screw. The easiest way to pick the right one is to talk to the expert at the hardware store. Tell him or her what kind of wall is involved. Is it drywall, plaster, or some kind of brick or masonry? If it is drywall, find out how thick it is, because that's a mark of its holding strength. Drywalls are usually ¹/₂ inch thick or ⁵/₈ inch thick. How can you tell? Well, you can drill a tiny hole in the wall at some inconspicuous place and carefully insert a tiny nail head into the hole. By wiggling the nail around a bit, you should be able to tell when the head catches in the inside of the hole at the back of the drywall. Mark the outside of the nail shank where it meets the outer surface of the wall. Withdraw the nail and measure the thickness of the wall that it indicates. If you just want to guess, tell the salesperson that the wall is ¹/₂ inch thick. This is the least strong of the two possibilities and you should be safe. If you want to cover up that little test hole, you can use a dab of toothpaste (not mint flavored).

As a rule, the best place to insert a nail or screw is into a stud. So, how do you find a stud hidden behind that wall? There are several ways. The thing to remember is that the stud is a solid 2 × 4 behind the wall and that it has nails in it. One approach is to buy a "stud finder" (which is not what you naughty ladies may think it is) and sweep across the wall until the magnet in the stud finder registers it has found something metallic like a

A ROOM WITHIN A ROOM

Add warmth and charm to a family room with a mini-library. This can usually be managed in one corner of the room with floor-to-ceiling bookcases readily available at lumberyards or home improvement stores. Mount some shelves in a corner at right angles, add one or two reading chairs, a small table, and a lamp, and you have a mini-library that will enhance the feel of the room. You may want to add an artistic touch with some small pieces of artwork scattered on the shelves among the books.

nail. Or, you could do same thing with your son's Boy Scout compass and watch for the needle to move. One builder friend of mine uses an electric razor. He turns it on and slowly passes it over the surface of the wall. When the tone of the buzzing razor changes, he has found the stud. Another approach, less accurate at times, is to tap gently across the wall until the hollow sound is replaced by a solid sound. Or do the "professional thing" and measure. In theory, most studs are built 16 inches apart. Thus, if you measure 17 inches from the edge of the wall, you should be right in the middle of a stud. If you want to find the next stud, measure 16 inches. You understand why don't you? It's because you're now going from mid-stud to mid-stud.

You can use other methods of finding studs. Most of them are basically common sense. For example, studs usually frame each side of a door or a window. Inspect the wall, if it is made of drywall sheets and you will find that the edge of each sheet of drywall should be nailed to a stud. The same is true of most electrical outlets. Plugs and switches are usually affixed to a stud. If you can't readily find where nails were driven to hold the wallboard to a stud because the wall was painted or papered over, check the baseboard. Sometimes you can see where nails were driven vertically up the wall and that will be where a stud is. But don't be fooled! Nails driven horizontally along the bottom of the wall and parallel to the floor are no help.

If you are going to hang a picture on the wall and there is no a stud where you want to hang it, you need to be sure it isn't too heavy for the wall material to hold. You should also use a bolt that will spread the pressure on the inside of the drywall or plaster as widely as possible. Too much pressure on a small area of the wall can result in a big chunk of the wall popping out.

There are several types of bolts or screw anchors that are commonly used for hanging pictures or mirrors or racks. Two of these are bolts designed for light loads on drywalls—the "winged toggle bolt" and the "molly bolt." To use them, drill a small hole in the wall and then insert the bolts. The winged toggle bolt has a pair of winglike arms that fold down and lie along the shaft of the bolt as you insert it in the hole. After you push or screw it in, the hole clears the wings and they spring open to press against the *inside* of the wall. So, as you tighten the bolt down, it penetrates further and further into the wing nut which is now inside the wall. As it penetrates, it forces the wings to spread and fit snuggly against the inside of the wall. The molly bolt has a similar approach in that it has a pointed tip and a frame around the bolt inside that pointed frame. After you push it all the way into the hole, the frame snaps and spreads so it cannot be pulled out. As with the winged toggle bolt, the bolt unit is pressing on both sides of the wall making for a strong, secure hold on which to hang a picture or whatever. Or you can use a wallboard anchor. You drill a hole and insert the anchor, which has a large spiral thread. As you screw it in, it grips the hold and hangs on much stronger than an ordinary nail or screw.

Other devices for lightweight hangings are the plastic anchor and the lead anchor. To use either one, drill a hole in the wall that is just barely big enough for the anchor and hammer the anchor into the hole. Then, insert a wood screw into the hole in the center of the anchor and tighten it up. As the screw goes in, it pushes the plastic or lead anchor outward making it grip the wall firmly. This can be used in masonry walls, as well as plaster, and drywall.

To hang things on masonry walls, you can use masonry nails, which are designed to hold light loads. As an alternative, you can use a wood or plastic plug, which is just what the name implies. You drill a hole in the masonry and hammer this plastic plug into the hole and screw a screw into the plug.

Another device you can use on masonry walls is an expansion shield, which is designed for heavy loads.

Finally, if you are hanging something on a wall that has metal studs, you obviously want to use a screw that is strong enough to penetrate metal and that is called the sheet metal screw. If you have a wooden stud, try using a lag bolt, which is designed just for that purpose. Both sheet metal screws and lag bolts are sturdy and can handle fairly heavy hangings.

Caution: When using any device that requires you to drill a hole into masonry or metal, please wear safety goggles and gloves. Even better, wear a safety mask. As you drill into hard materials, the spinning drill tends to fling out tiny stone or metal particles at high speed that can do serious damage to your beautiful face and irreplaceable eyes.

CHILD'S BEDROOM

An imaginative idea, which costs very little and is easy to do if you have any artistic skills, is to create a mural. Go to a bookstore and buy a large-sized coloring book featuring characters your child loves—Snow White, Robin Hood, Pokemon, Harry Potter, among many others. Select several pages in the book that would make an exciting mural in your child's room.

Take these pages to an office services outfit and have transparencies made of each page. Then, borrow or rent a transparency projector and project these images on the walls of your child's room with the lights dim. Using markers or paint, trace the images you have projected on the wall. You many want to leave it at that or you may want to use different colored paints to fill in the tracings.

In the end, you have created a whole new world of adventure in your child's room at relatively little cost. And of course, you can paint over it all and do it again later when your child's tastes change. Creative ideas for decorating abound in books available at the library and on Web sites, too. Try a few different search engines and punch in "kids room."

11

MAINTAINING YOUR CAR

You depend on your car for transportation and here are some ideas
to make sure it is dependable transportation.

When my family first settled in Seattle, Washington, the most common way of getting around was by horse. And today we still use horsepower—under the hood of our cars. Considering how much we rely on our cars and how much they cost—people are paying more for cars these days then they used to pay my father and grandfather for the houses they built—we want to take good care of them. Here are hints on car repair and maintenance that will save you money and keep your transportation safe and dependable.

TIPS FOR TRAVELERS AND TINKERERS

I've got lots of little ways to make car care simple and inexpensive. Check out the following ideas.

BATTERY CARE

Cola drinks are good for cleaning the two clamps of your car battery. However, don't touch clamps or both battery terminals at the same time. If you do, you'll have an unpleasant shock and electrifying experience.

BUMPER STICKERS

Remove decals or bumper stickers by soaking a cloth in vinegar or nail polish remover and covering the sticker for several minutes until the vinegar soaks in. You can also try covering them with peanut butter or mayonnaise. The decals and bumper stickers should peel off easily. Another way to loosen a sticker is to heat it with a hair dryer.

CHROME CARE

Polish the chrome on your car with cola drinks. Prevent a chrome trailer hitch from getting scratched by putting a slit tennis ball over the trailer hitch as a protective cover.

COLD ENGINE

On cold mornings, it may be hard to get your car to start. One reason for this is that the gasoline being sprayed into the engine cylinders from the carburetor may be too cold for the spark to ignite it. (Your engine causes a series of small explosions of air and gasoline that move the pistons that are connected to the drive shaft that's connected to the drive wheels.) So, try warming your engine's carburetor by blowing hot air on it from a hair dryer. After a minute or three, jump in the car and try starting it. It should catch and start running.

FIELD TRIPS WITH FIDO

One man has a clever way of keeping his dog's hairs on the dog and not all over the inside of his car. He literally puts one of his old shirts on his dog, covering the canine as much as possible. The car remains almost hair-free.

KITTY ALERT

In cold weather, cats (and wild animals like mice) may climb up under your warm car hood and curl up for the night. Before you start car in the morning, it might be a good idea to honk the horn a few times to clear out the unexpected guests.

PARKING

Hang a tennis ball on a string from the garage ceiling so it will hit the windshield at the spot where you should stop your car.

TAR STAINS

It's annoying to get tar or other tough stains on your car. You might try applying mayonnaise or rubbing alcohol to the spot and letting it soak. After soaking, the offending matter should wipe off with a cloth.

WINDSHIELD ICE

Prevent ice from forming on a car windshield overnight by coating the window with a solution of three parts white or apple cider vinegar to one part water. If you forget, and your windshield ices up, pour some cola over it and either rub the ice off with a paper towel or turn on the windshield wipers. If you elect to turn on the wipers, make sure the windows are rolled up or you'll get sprayed and splashed with a messy brown slush.

THE FIVE FLUIDS OF BASIC CAR CARE

As basic maintenance of your car you need only to regularly check five different fluids. It shouldn't take more than a few minutes in total.

OIL

If you keep your engine's oil at the right level, it will probably give you tens of thousands of miles of easy motoring. Oil is what keeps things moving smoothly in your engine. Somebody once likened it to using soothing hand lotion to keep things comfortable.

Oil changes are essential to keeping your car in working order. They don't cost much—certainly less than being without the use of your vehicle. I recommend changing your oil and the oil filter every 3,000 miles or every three months—whichever comes first.

In between oil changes, you should check the level once a week. *Only check your oil when the engine is cold!* When the engine is hot, the oil in the crankcase may be churning and you will not get an accurate reading. Open the hood, locate the dipstick that goes into the engine, and pull it out. Wipe it off and put it back in all the way. Then pull it out and check the oil level shown on the end of the dipstick. There are markers to show full, partially full, and empty.

Keep the level of oil in your engine at full. If it drops below full, you could cause damage to the engine. Changing the oil keeps it relatively clean, but it does not guarantee you are running with a full oil level. Those are two different things and you must pay attention to both.

RADIATOR COOLANT

As I mentioned earlier, your car engine runs by making tiny explosions every minute to turn the crankshaft that turns the drive shaft that turns the wheels of your car. All these explosions in the engine make it hot, and if it gets too hot it won't run. Coolant, incidentally, is water to which something such as alcohol or glucose has been added so the water won't freeze solid when you leave the car out in cold weather. If it freezes, you will have another big problem because ice expands and can crack your engine. This problem will require you to put a new engine in your car and will take a lot of money out of your bank account. Neither of these, putting in or taking out, is fun. So, you want to check the level of the coolant weekly.

TRANSMISSION FLUID

The transmission in your car shifts gears from one level to another. If you have an automatic transmission as most vehicles do these days, you need to check the diagram in your owner's manual to see where the automatic-transmission-fluid dipstick is located. Yes, I know you have never looked at your owner's manual since you bought the car, but now is the time to do it. If you don't have an owner's manual for your car, ask your local mechanic, gas station attendant, or salesperson at the local car-parts store where the transmission-fluid dipstick is. If your car has a manual transmission, things are both easier and harder. They are easier because you don't have to check the transmission fluid under the hood. They are harder because you usually need to get beneath the car to check it. Of course, if the person who changes your engine oil will check the transmission fluid (and he or she should check it for you), then we're back to easy again.

BRAKE FLUID

This is the fluid that transfers the pressure of your foot on the peddle to your car's brakes and makes the car stop. Here again, check your owner's manual to see where the brake-fluid dipstick is. Be very careful when opening the brake-fluid container. You don't want anything to fall in because it could affect the working of the brakes. You can tell you are checking the brake fluid because it is a different color than the engine oil. By the way, brake fluid can eat the paint off you car if you spill it. Naturally, I recommend not spilling it.

POWER STEERING FLUID

Finally, if you have power steering, you need to keep the power steering fluid at the right level so you can guide the car easily. Again, check your owner's manual.

So be sure to check these five fluids weekly. And note: These fluids are dangerous and you should store their containers up and out of reach of children and pets because, they can make people or pets sick. They can even make them dead.

GAS—THE SIXTH FLUID

You obviously know that you have to keep gas in your tank. But, do you know how to select the right gas for your car? Just to prevent us from getting bored, the oil refiners and government have given us the mystery of gasoline "octane." Check your owner's manual to determine the right octane level for your car. Regular octane is recommended for most cars. However, some cars with high compression engines, like sports cars and certain luxury cars, need midgrade or premium gasoline to prevent knock. A short version of all of this is to listen to your car's engine. If it doesn't knock when you use the recommended octane, you're using the right grade of gasoline.

As a rule, the FTC says, high-octane gasoline does not outperform regular octane in preventing engine deposits from forming, in removing them, or in cleaning your car's engine. In fact, the U.S. Environmental Protection Agency requires that all octane grades of all brands of gasoline contain engine-cleaning detergent additives to protect against the build-up of harmful levels of engine deposits during the expected life of your car.

WHEN YOU'RE LOCKED OUT

One of the most frustrating things in life is locking your car keys in your car. Not only are you locked out, but you feel like a complete fool.

There are several solutions to this feeling of frustration. One is the habit I've gotten into, and that's having an extra set of keys in my pocket. Ideally, you don't want your house keys on the same ring as your ignition key anyhow. An unscrupulous parking lot attendant could make an impression of your house key, and from that get a copy of the key made. He can get your home address with your license-plate number and presto—a snap, easy-to-do burglary! So you want to have one key ring for your car keys and a separate ring for your spare car key and your home.

Another solution is the famous wire-coat-hanger trick. This can be difficult and frustrating, but it can also work even if it takes some manipulating and some time. The idea is to unbend and straighten a wire coat hanger leaving the hook intact at one end. Bend the other end into a crude handle. Now, standing by one of the car doors—usually the one by the driver's seat—slip the hook end of the coat hanger between the top edge of the door and the car frame. This edge is "sealed" with a rubber strip but you can normally slip by that easily. Once the hook end of the coat hanger is inside the car, you fiddle and maneuver it until you can hook the inside door handle, and then gently pull it until it unlatches so you can get in the car and get your keys. It's really much easier to have an extra key.

A third approach is to call the Auto Club or an attendant from a nearby gas station. Many of them have a flat, flexible piece of metal called a "slim Jim." They slide this between the car window and the lower portion of the door into the door-lock mechanism. By slipping the slim Jim in there and fiddling around a bit, an expert can open the door. I've seen mechanics accomplish this in about 5 seconds.

You can also try hiding a key on the outside of your car. You can buy a small magnetic box for a spare car key that adheres to your car. Many people place them on the under side of the body or chassis. The flaws with using a magnetic box are several. For one thing, the box can pop off the body or frame if you are driving along and hit a bad bump. Of course, you don't miss it until you need that extra key and it's not there. Another problem is that mechanics who service your car can find and steal the box (and later, your car).

There is another hidden key trick but it isn't perfect either. Screw a spare key on your car frame behind one of the license plates. That is, have one of your license-plate bolts pass through the license plate, the key, and into the car frame. Use a bolt or screw that has a slot big enough to accommodate a penny, quarter, or other common coin. Then when you need a spare key, you can use a coin to unscrew the key and there you are. It is unlikely that anyone will spot the key, and if they do, it takes a long time to access it and so increases the chance of getting caught. This also panders to the basic rule about keeping your car from being stolen. That rule is you actually want to encourage the thief to steal somebody else's car by making yours too much trouble to steal.

TIRE TALES

Reading tires may not be as much fun as reading tea leaves or a novel but it can be instructive. With all the recent furor over dangerous tires, there should be a lot more interest in the care and feeding of tires.

TIRE TYPES

A step in that direction is to learn all the information tires have to give you about themselves. A lot of data about each tire is embossed on its side, and it's easy to understand the code. For example, a typical tire might have a long number/letter code like this on its side.

P215/65R15 89H

Broken down, that translates into the following information.

- "P" stands for passenger.
- 215" represents the width of the tire in millimeters.
- "65" is the ratio of height to width.
- "R" means radial.
- "15" is the diameter of the wheel in inches.
- "H" is the speed rating.

A "B" in place of the "R" means the tire is a belted tire, and a "D" in place of the "R" means it is a diagonal. The side information also shows the maximum air pressure in pounds per square inch that the tire should have. This maximum is also given in kilograms for those who use the metric system. If the tire has the letters DOT on it, that means it is up to the safety standards set by the U.S. Department of Transportation.

Also on the sidewall is the tire serial number, running up to 11 digits, that are a combination of numbers and letters. The sidewall also tells about the construction of the tire in terms of the kind of cords and the number of plies in the sidewall and under the tread.

Finally, the correct tire-inflation pressures are usually found on a form inside the driver's door. This lists the highest pressure you should have in your original equipment tires.

TIRE PERFORMANCE

The Department of Transportation requires tire manufacturers to report how tires do in three performance factors: tread wear, traction, and temperature resistance.

Tread wear is a measure of how fast the tire wears out as shown by DOT tests. For example, a tire with a grade of 100 wears only half as well as a tire with a grade of 200 in the DOT tests. However, the conditions of the DOT test may not match your driving habits and a tire might perform better or worse on your car. Traction is a test of how well the tire stops on wet pavement in the DOT tests. The best traction grade is A, middle is B, and lowest is C. Temperature resistance measures how well the tire resists getting hot while driving. These grades range from highest at A to lowest—C.

TRAVEL TIPS

Nothing's more fun than driving off for a vacation. Use these tips to make your road trip hassle-free.

MAPLESS DIRECTIONS

It's hard to read a map or other directions and drive at the same time. If you're traveling alone, record the directions to your destination on a tape recorder. You can play them back as you drive without having to stop.

COPY YOUR PERSONAL DOCUMENTS

Photocopy and record numbers of driver's licenses, passports, credit cards, and other important documents you're carrying with you. Leave a copy at home with a friend or family member you can call in case you lose them on the trip.

EMERGENCY PHONE CARD

If someone in your group of travelers doesn't have his own cell phone, make sure that he does have a prepaid phone card. And make sure that he doesn't keep it in his wallet. If the wallet is stolen, the card can still be used to call for help.

EXTRA KEY

Have extra car keys made for the other members of your group. You'll be glad you did if you lose yours.

KEEPING SAFE ON CAR TRIPS

When you're on the road, a little vigilance can go far to insure that your trip is goes smoothly. Abiding by my safety hints can only benefit you and your companions.

TAKING FIVE

Always stop in well-lit places with lots people about. No matter what kind of rush you're in, always shut off your car and lock the door when you get out. Never stop to "just run in" some store for something without shutting off your car and locking the doors. In the seconds you are gone, a criminal can steal stuff from your car or, worse yet, hide in the back seat to attack you when you come back. Carry a Mace spray on your key ring, approach your car with the keys in your hand, and be ready to get in quickly. The less time you spend fumbling, the less time you have to be mugged. *Before you get in the car,* check the backseat and under the car for anyone who might be hiding there. Finally, never leave your keys in the car. Never. Period.

ON THE ROAD

When you enter your car, don't fiddle or faddle, start up the engine right away, and get going. A moving target is less likely to be an invitation to a car jacker or mugger. In the car, never leave anything tempting to a thief in plain sight. Put purses, packages, cameras, and any tempting objects under the seat, in the trunk, or under a blanket.

Always drive with all doors locked and all windows rolled up completely. If you have to stop and talk to anyone, roll your window down just an inch or so. Never roll your window down enough for anyone to stick his hand in and grab you. If this happens, roll the window up as tight as you can and start slowly driving off pulling the intruder with you. After a moment, unroll the window just enough to allow the person to get away. Then report the incident to the police immediately. (By the way, be aware that it is quite easy to pose as a police officer. If you're stopped by someone who claims to be a policeman, ask to see his photo identification or insist on stopping at a well-lit place with lots of people around. If you get a signal to stop when on a busy highway, *do not* pull off onto a quiet street.)

The worst thing is to run out of gas when you are alone at night on a dark road. It takes only a moment to get gassed up.

Familiarize yourself with the inside of the trunk of your car. Sounds nuts, doesn't it? Unfortunately, some people have been kidnapped and locked up in the trunk of their own car as the criminals drive off in it. Car manufacturers have refused to put inside latches on car trunk doors until recently, and the chances are your car doesn't have one. So it makes sense to hide an escape kit in your trunk. This might include a small flashlight, a Mace spray, a portable screech alarm, a screwdriver, and pliers. Check out your trunk's inside lock to see what tools you need to open it.

The best investment for your safety is a cell phone. They are so inexpensive these days that it's inexcusable to be without one. Most styles can summon the auto club with the touch of one button and the police with another. Within a second or two of danger, help is on the way. Another great investment is an antitheft device. You could get something as simple as the Club that locks on the steering wheel or a more elaborate device that disables the electrical system if there is an attempt to steal your car. It depends on what you can afford, but the most expensive thing is nothing. If you do nothing to thwart thieves, you are inviting them to steal your car.

EMERGENCY KIT

Create an emergency kit for you and your car so the next emergency isn't a disaster. Include in your kit:

- Car and driving documents such as your driver's license, auto club membership card, car registration, and proof of insurance plus the owner's manual and road maps of your area.
- A flashlight, fire extinguisher (the dry chemical type), and window cleaning tool. The window cleaning tool, depending on your part of the country, might be an ice scraper, snow brush, or wiper blade. Keep a tire gauge for regularly checking your tires.
- Tissues and paper towels.
- Several votive candles in case you break down. They usually burn for about ten hours and can give you some warmth in the car without running the heater and draining the battery. *Warning:* Burning candles too long can use up the oxygen in the compartment.
- Some bottled water and something to eat in sealed containers like energy candy bars or trail mix.
- Emergency road flares are a must and a lifesaver.
- A police whistle and a few bright red or orange rags to tie on to your radio antenna or door. The rags can serve as beacons to help people

find you if you are stuck in the fog, or snow or rain. If you leave the car on foot, take a whistle and a signal rag with you.

- Pen, paper, and some change for a telephone in case your cell phone doesn't work.
- Two cans of tire inflator are an absolute must, in addition to the usual jack and tire changing equipment.
- Finally, if you really want to be ready for trouble, include tools such as two kinds of screwdrivers, hammer, pliers, and a knife along with a roll of duct tape.

TWO LIFESAVING ITEMS

Although these last two items aren't usually mentioned in lists like this, I think that they are absolute must-haves. They are:

Reflective Safety Jacket

Keep a high-glow safety jacket in your car. They are available in a universal size so they fit almost everyone. These jackets are made of reflective material that will make you visible at night in almost any kind of weather to other drivers; they're also inexpensive and waterproof. If you have trouble on the road at night, put it on immediately—you'll be much more visible to other drivers and can flag down help more easily. These jackets fold up into a small plastic packet and fit neatly into your glove compartment.

Escape Tool

What could be more horrible than to be in an accident and trapped in your car? Or to plunge into a river and sink in the car, because you can't get your seat belt off and the window or the door open. There is an amazingly small slash/smash tool that will help you escape. It is available in most auto-supply stores and is only about six inches long. At one end, it has a shielded sharp blade you can use to immediately cut your seat belt off. At the other end, it has a double-headed pointed hammer that will let you smash through the safety glass in your car and escape from the vehicle.

The important thing about this slash/smash tool is that you will need it in a car crash, so it should be where you can reach it easily in such an emergency. Don't keep it pushed down in a door-side pocket, as a side collision could crush in the door. If you have air bags, they get in the way if you keep it in the glove compartment or mounted under the dashboard. Inspect the inside of your particular car and envision the air bags deployed and the side doors crushed in. Where is the best place for the escape tool? You'll have to decide based on the kind of car you drive.

As a final thought, this handy tool is also good for fending off an attacker should you need to do so.

12

CARING FOR PETS AND THE HOMES THEY LIVE IN

Hints on caring for pet members of the family
to make their lives and yours easier

Most of us feel that our pets are truly members of the family and have endless stories about our relationships with our pets. Cat owners will tell you they are merely their cats' domestic help. Dog owners will tell you that they love their dogs because they wag their tails instead of their tongues. You want to keep your pets healthy and happy, and keep your home intact at the same time. Here are some ideas to help you do just that.

VISIT THE VETERINARIAN

The frequency with which Americans take their pets to the veterinarian is an indication of how much we dote on them. The rule of thumb (or rule of paw) has been to take Fido or Fluffy in once a year, but now some pet lovers say it should be more often. They contend that because pets age quickly, it is important for them to be examined often. Using the old formula that a pet year is equal to seven human years, how would it be if we only went in for our "annual" checkup once every seven years? Moreover, animals tend to hide their disabilities or illnesses as an instinctual form of self-protection. And when our pets do try to tell us that they are sick or hurt, their communication skills are not that strong. While most of us chat up our pets with silly conversation, the talking is mostly one-sided. Finally, studies of pets suggest that if you take two newborn animals from the same litter and give them to different families, one of them will grow up healthier and live longer than the other. Pet experts say a good part of that is due to one getting better care, better nutrition, and attention by a veterinarian. Seems reasonable. All this is why more pet advocates are urging that we take our pets into the veterinarian for checkups several times a year. So ask your veterinarian about how often you should bring your pet in.

FIRST AID FOR ANIMALS

There is one beloved member of the family who is at greatest risk from inadequate medical treatment and that's the family pet in an emergency. While there are 24-hour emergency veterinary hospitals in some parts of the country, you may not have time to get your pet in the car. Learning a few urgent-care techniques can make a big difference to your dog's or cat's well-being.

The American Red Cross in some 500 locations around the country now offers a four-hour course on managing emergencies. It teaches how to approach and handle a sick or injured pet, and how to read a pet's body language. The course covers CPR for dogs and cats: how to take an animal's pulse and feel for the heartbeat. You also learn how to take your pet's temperature and about the signs of poisoning and other injuries. Your observations can be critical to the veterinarian in treating the patient.

MANAGING VACATIONS

If you are traveling with your dog or cat and you feel you can leave him alone in your hotel room, here are some suggestions. Leave the radio or TV on low to keep him company. Rub a towel on yourself and leave it in his crate or carrier. An item with your scent is very comforting to an animal. (In fact, there is no reason not to do these things when you leave your pet alone in your own house.)

Put the Do Not Disturb sign on the door so the pet is not agitated by outsiders. Always leave a bowl of fresh water for your dog or cat. You may want to leave some newspapers laid down in a corner of the bathroom as a temporary "litter spot." So about the only thing left undone would be to teach him how to use the TV remote control and he may not care if you ever come back.

Finally, if you are taking a road trip with your dog or cat, be mindful of your pet's comfort and safety. Pet-care experts advise that you confine your pet while traveling—keep your dog in a crate and your cat in a carrier. If you must brake suddenly, your pet won't get thrown about the car. Confining your pet will also prevent him from crawling on your feet while you drive, and from falling out the window. Most everyone knows not to keep a pet locked up in a car during hot weather, but the same rule applies to the cold. So, if traveling with your pet in the car, bring along one of his blankets to keep him warm while you are away.

When you go on vacation and leave your pet with a pet-sitter, be sure you leave your itinerary and the veterinarian's name and phone number. You may also want to tell the vet who your sitter will be.

ORAL FIXATION

Cats and dogs love to chew on things and investigate them with their mouths. These habits not only destroy your stuff, but they also are dangerous to your pets. Just to cite a few examples, there have been cases of cats chewing, swallowing, and choking on ribbons, string, yarn, and dental floss. Dogs have been known to swallow pretty much everything, from tennis balls to TV remotes. The easiest way to prevent this is to put your stuff away and out of reach. If you have a dog, buy him his own chew toys. Don't give him an old sock or other item to chew on. He won't distinguish one sock from the next and every sock in the house becomes fair game.

CANINE CARE

Caring for your dog is more than just providing food and shelter. I can't address all aspects of good dog care in this book, so I'll stick to my favorites—looking after your dog's coat and keeping him out of harm's way.

A HEALTHY COAT

A healthy coat is neither too dry nor too oily and should not have a strong odor. If your dog has a doggie smell, a simple solution is to rub baking soda into his coat, then brush it out vigorously. You'll want to do this outdoors, obviously.

Your dog probably spends a fair amount of time outside, where he is likely to pick up stickers and burrs, which can be annoying to both you and him. A relatively easy way to get them out is to put a few drops of vegetable oil on each one, then comb his coat thoroughly.

Whenever your dog has been outside, look him over thoroughly afterward for ticks. Ticks can carry diseases and are a really big hazard in a really small package. If you find a tick on Fido, put on some rubber gloves to protect your hands. Comb slowly through the fur and work your comb gently so you unloosen the entire tick. Place a little bit of vegetable oil or rubbing alcohol on the tick and carefully pull the tick out. You must remove the entire tick. Do not squish it. If the tick is carrying a disease you don't want the germs on yourself or the dog. Flush the tick down the toilet. Keep

CHOCOLATE ALERT

Do not feed your dog any type of chocolate—*ever*. Most chocolate contains theobromine, which excites the dog's heart muscle and his central nervous system to the point that it can be lethal. Experts say as little as two ounces of milk chocolate can be fatal to a puppy.

a sharp eye on your dog during the following days to make sure he doesn't get sick.

When it comes to fleas, it is far better to prevent your dog from getting them than to try to eliminate them later. Several commercial products are now available that are very effective, and you can get them from your veterinarian. Some products prevent the fleas from breeding and some will kill them if they bite your pet. Ask your veterinarian about the best way for you to keep fleas away from your dog. These products work for cats too!

If your dog does get fleas, they are several home remedies to combat them. One is to put out a saucer with either liquid dishwashing soap like Joy or wine vinegar in a room where you have these pesky insects. At night turn off all the lights in that room except for one light that shines on the saucer. You'll be amazed at how many of these tiny critters dive in and drown themselves. Change the saucer and liquid as needed.

Yet another use for vinegar is to add a teaspoon to your dog's drinking water. Apparently, vinegar in your pet's system drives away fleas. Or put a teaspoon of brewer's yeast or a crushed 25 mg vitamin B tablet in the dog's food. You can also keep fleas away from your pets by sprinkling salt into nooks and crannies where your pet sleeps.

SAFETY FOR SPOT

Keeping the dog in the yard has always been a problem for dog owners. The old method of having a fence works well enough, but there are dogs that know how to dig under them or jump over them. Aside from not wanting your dog to run away or to bite a neighbor's child, you also don't want him stolen or hit by a car. If your dog has mastered getting around your fence, or if the zoning laws in your area don't allow traditional fences, you may want to try an invisible electronic dog fence. I must let you know up front that some dog lovers object to electronic fences, but there are others who swear by them. All types of electronic dog fences operate in the same fashion. The "fence" is actually a wire buried in the ground that outlines the yard. The dog wears an electronically triggered dog collar that warns him if he is straying too close to the fence with a beeping noise. If he steps beyond the confines of the fence, he receives a spike or a shock. These invisible fences run on a battery with a warning light to alert you when the battery gets too low. But be aware that these systems do not prevent others from entering your yard. If you are concerned that your dog might be stolen or attacked by other animals, you'll need a different method of keeping intruders away.

Many dog owners are trying alternative methods of identifying their pets. A collar tag is a must, but tags can fall off or be easily removed. You don't want your dog at the local animal shelter without identification. So like other careful pet owners, you may want to have an identification microchip implanted under the pet's skin by a veterinarian. Many animal shelters now have microchip scanners that they use for pets they process. These scanners can "read" your pet's identification through its skin.

KEEPING UP WITH THE CAT HAIR

Pets can really make for a lot of housework. Here are some ways to keep your home in great shape and your animal companions too.

ANTS
Do you sometimes find you are not just feeding your pet cat or dog but a lot of unwanted insects such as ants? The solution is to put your pet's food dish in a shallow pie pan with water in it. Your dog and cat can reach the food and the pesky insects cannot.

FLEAS

I talked earlier about how to get rid of fleas on your dog. Some of the old-fashioned ways to get rid of fleas in the home include dropping mothballs into your vacuum cleaner bag and thoroughly vacuuming your floors. The smell of the mothballs drives the fleas away. Of course, if the smell is too strong, it may also drive you away. Another technique is to sprinkle salt where fleas are. Fleas love salt and will gorge themselves on it to the point that they literally kill themselves.

HAIR ON UPHOLSTERY

You can remove pet hair from the couch in a variety of ways: wear a rubber glove and stroke the upholstered furniture; or wipe with a damp sponge; rub with a hand or other object wrapped in duct tape or masking tape—sticky side out, of course.

HOUSETRAINING LAPSES

It's really annoying when your dog or cat fails to use the right spot. To discourage this behavior it is important to remove the urine or solid waste without a trace. Any lingering odor will attract your pet to misuse that spot again. Many experts say the best approach is to buy an enzyme cleaning and deodorizing product at the pet store. Then apply it to the spot you have cleaned with paper towels. Soak it well because it has to get through the carpet and into the padding, just as the original mess probably did. Next cover the spot with clear plastic, which you weigh down on all sides to keep the enzyme cleaner from evaporating, and leave it covered for a day or two. Yes, a day or two seems like a long time, but you want to remove all odors so Fido or Kitty Cat doesn't come back to this spot again.

Finally, uncover and let it dry out thoroughly. This may also take several days. Yes, you can use club soda or plain water if you can't get the enzyme cleaner out for some reason. Another alternative for cleaning urine on the carpet is to blot up the urine, flush the area several times with lukewarm water, then apply a mixture of equal parts white vinegar and cool water. Blot up, rinse, and let dry.

Some people advise sprinkling red pepper in the areas where dogs urinate. To deter cats from using a particular spot, try hanging a cotton ball or other small cloth soaked in lemon juice at the location. Change the lemon-soaked item weekly until your cat has learned to use the litter box.

LITTER BOX ODORS

Minimize litter box odors by sprinkling baking soda on the bottom of the box before you add fresh litter.

SCRATCHING FURNITURE

Discourage your cat from scratching the furniture by rubbing it with chili sauce. This tip probably isn't great for upholstered items (you'd just need another tip on getting chili sauce off upholstery). For fabrics, discourage cats from scratching by spraying the item with perfume. Make sure it is a fragrance that your cat doesn't care for.

STRAY CATS

If you want to keep stray cats (or even your neighbors') out of your yard, keep a water-filled spray gun handy and blast the intruders when they show up. They'll quickly list your place as one of their least favorite yards to visit. Some people say that short pieces—say around 2 feet long—of black garden hose lying in the yard will often scare cats away because they think it is a snake.

13

MAINTAINING YOUR WARDROBE

Hints for keeping your clothing neat and clean without a lot of work

"The clothes make the man" was a popular adage from our parents' time. But while the saying may be old-fashioned, the message is still true today. People do judge us (at least in part) by our appearance and, in particular, our clothes. Here are ideas for taking care of your clothing so that it makes you look as good as you can.

LAUNDRY TIPS

Even with modern washers and dryers it seems like our whites are not white enough, our brights are not bright enough. Try my cleaning ideas for more pleasing results.

BLEACH

If your washer has a special compartment for adding bleach, use it. If there is no bleach compartment, add the clothes *after* the machine has filled with water and the bleach is completely mixed into it.

BRAS

Wash bras and other clothing with hooks on them in a pillow case to keep the hooks from catching on other clothing.

BRIGHTS

Before putting bright articles in the washing machine, soak them in white vinegar for ten minutes to keep them from fading. If the clothes are brand-new, keep them bright by soaking them in cold water for fifteen to thirty minutes before you wash them for the first time.

ENERGY SAVER

We all love the freshness of clothesline-dried clothes and the convenience of machine-dried clothes. Try combining the two for both freshness and saving energy. Hang your clothes up to dry in the backyard until they are mostly dry. For the final drying, toss them in the dryer and flip it on. It will dry them quicker and use less energy in the process.

HAND WASHABLES

Delicate things such as silk or lace garments are best washed by hand. Use delicate soap that is thoroughly dissolved in the basin you are using and avoid rubbing the garments. It is better to squeeze the soapy water through the fabric. Do the same with the rinse water. Rinse thoroughly.

JEANS

When you buy new jeans, you want to wash them first before putting them on, but even so, they come out of the drier stiff. Soften them up by adding 1/2 cup salt to the detergent water.

To keep jeans from fading, soak them in a vinegar solution for about 30 minutes before you wash them. A mixture of about a gallon of water and 1/2 cup vinegar ought to do it.

PERSONALIZED JEANS

At the time of this writing, people are wearing their jeans on the baggy side. But styles change, and when snug jeans are back in, here's how to get them skintight. Put the jeans on and get them soaking wet in the shower. Then, let them dry on your body. You'll need a shoehorn to get in and out of them, but they will show you off.

LABEL LESSON

If you remove a label because it sticks out of your clothes or into you, remove it and tape it to a 3 × 5 card, then post it on a corkboard in your laundry room for later referencing of its washing instructions.

LINT PREVENTION

Keep lint from clinging to clothes by adding one cup of white vinegar to each wash load.

MAXIMIZE YOUR MACHINE

To get your clothes their cleanest, put your garments into the machine loosely. A jammed load of laundry doesn't wash as well.

SOCKS

Bring dingy white socks back to life by adding a little dishwasher detergent to your regular wash load. An environmentally friendly alternative is to boil them in a pot with some sliced lemons.

One of life's great mysteries is where *does* the other sock go? One solution—offered by Doris Kearns Goodwin's father in her book *Wait Till Next Year*—is to glue a St. Christopher's medal to the washing machine so the family socks can find their way back home. It can't hurt. Another solution is to pin the socks together or wash them inside a pillowcase that is the same color as they are.

SORTING SMART

Check the washing instructions for each item of clothing and sort each type into piles to wash separately. Generally, you can apply the following rules:

Silk	Hand wash in warm water and mild soap
Synthetics	Warm water
White natural fabric (cotton, linen)	Use hot water
Woolens	Warm water, mild soap, and rinse several times

WHITES

If your white items have a yellow cast when they come out of the wash, it means you washed them for too long and at a too high a temperature. Rewash for a shorter time and at a lower temperature.

WOOL SWEATERS

After washing, rinse wool sweaters in equal parts vinegar and water to remove odor.

WRINKLE PREVENTION

Mount a high clothing rod in your laundry near the dryer or ironing board for hanging permanent press or freshly ironed clothes.

STAINS

Unfortunately, stains often get stuck in the fabric for good (I mean bad) once the garment has been washed. So before throwing your clothes into

SHOE STORIES

Here are some shoe-care tricks that will give you happy feet. For example, did you know that you can quickly clean and shine your shoes using a banana peel? Sounds slippery, but it works. To keep uncooperative shoelaces tied, moisten them before you tie them. To scuff up the bottom of slippery shoes, scratch them a bit with a knife, screwdriver, or other tool. Or stand on a rough, hard surface (like cement) twist your feet back and forth. If you live in a humid climate and/or your feet tend to perspire, sprinkle a little bit of salt into your shoes to soak up the moisture. If your shoes are stiff and dry, rubbing them with a sliced potato will add a little moisture and make them more pliable. To keep new tennis shoes looking new, spray laundry starch on the canvas areas before first wearing them.

the washing machine, look them over carefully. If you find a stain, remove it before you wash the item.

Generally, use cold water to remove stains, work from the inside of the fabric out, and as you do with carpet stains, *blot the stain—don't rub!*

Stain solutions in a nutshell:

Blood	Blot frequently with soda water or ammonia
Chewing gum	Freeze in freezer and scrape off
Chocolate	Club soda or salt immediately, then cold water and detergent
Coffee	Hairspray
Grease	Club soda or gentle shampoo
Ink	Alcohol or hairspray

Lipstick	Hairspray
Red wine	Club soda or salt immediately, then cold water and detergent
Tea	Hairspray
Wax	Freeze in freezer and scrape off

COLLARS 'n' CUFFS

Squirt a little extra liquid soap on dirty collars, cuffs, underarms, pockets, and areas that tend to get extra dirty. Some people keep a squirt bottle full of soap by the washing machine just for this purpose.

PERSPIRATION

White vinegar (amazing stuff, isn't it?) can remove perspiration stains from clothes. Apply one part vinegar to four parts water, then rinse.

SCORCH MARKS

To remove light scorch marks from fabrics, rub the burned area lightly with white vinegar, then wipe with a clean cloth. Another method to try is to immediately soak the area that is scorched and cover it with cornstarch. Let it dry and then scrape the cornstarch off. If you moved quickly enough and you're lucky, the mark should be gone.

ZIPPING ZIPPER

If you want your zippers to zip, try rubbing them with a little bar soap. Other effective ways to lubricate a zipper are rubbing it with tip of a pencil (pencil lead is graphite, which is a good lubricant) or spraying with laundry starch.

SEWING AND STUFF

You can have your cleaner sew on buttons or press your clothes, but these services get pretty pricey. Use my tips to get the jobs done quickly and done well.

BUTTONS

Buttons on clothes made of heavy material often strain the thread holding them on. So, when sewing buttons on in this situation, put a large safety pin in the material where the button will be sewn and sew keeping the buttonholes on either side of the pin. Afterward, simply pull the pin out. (Make sure you do your sewing on the side the pin opens on or it will be sewn on with the button!) The result is a thread with some slack in it so that it can easily accommodate the heavy material.

When a button gets torn off a garment leaving a hole, take a piece of cloth from the garment's hem and cut out a patch bigger than the hole. Then sew the torn-off button onto this patch and push the button through the torn hole from the backside. Now, sew the patch in place and everything should be fine.

To prevent buttons from getting ripped off, iron some iron-on patch material on the backside of the fabric. This reinforces the material and makes it less likely the button will pull out and the material tear.

When sewing new buttons on any clothing, sew an extra button or two in some inconspicuous place. Manufacturers often place extra buttons on the front shirttails of dress shirts and on the hems of dresses and skirts.

IRONING

When you are ironing a garment with plastic buttons, protect the buttons by laying the bowl of a spoon upside down over them.

An interesting ironing board trick is to line the board with aluminum foil (shiny side up) and then replace the cloth cover. When you iron, the heat from your iron is bounced back by the foil onto the fabric, which will enhance your ironing jobs.

A rushing-out-the-door "ironing" trick is to put the garment into the dryer with something damp and turn it on for a few minutes. This isn't the best solution, but it will get some of the wrinkles out.

SEWING SUPPLIES

An egg carton is useful for storing buttons, pins, and small sewing items.

Keep a small magnet handy in your sewing basket or box. It will be very convenient for picking up dropped pins and needles.

Use sandpaper to sharpen needles and scissors. Snip the sandpaper several times and the scissors will have sharper edges. For needles just plunge them through sandpaper a few times and you'll have sharper needles and easier sewing.

APPLIANCE CARE

You can't get clean socks out of a dirty washer. Take care of your appliances so they take care of your clothes.

CLOTHES HAMPERS

Keep hampers fresh by sprinkling baking soda in with the dirty clothes. You don't need to shake the clothes out before washing.

DRYERS

Clean your dryer's lint screen frequently. It will dry your clothes faster (and save energy). Moreover, the accumulated lint can be a fire hazard. In fact, not long ago a luxury cruise ship was disabled in the Caribbean when a fire broke out because the crew didn't know enough to keep the lint filters of their clothes dryers clean! Anyhow, you can go a step further in fire safety by getting a wire coat hanger, straightening it and bending a hook at one end. Then, use this to poke around those big vents from the dryer and through the wall to the outside of your house. This helps to clean out any lint that might have accumulated there.

IRONS

To remove starch stuck to the bottom of your iron, rub the cold iron with toothpaste (don't use the gel kind) and rinse and dry. Or try steel wool dipped in vinegar. If the buildup on the iron is significant, wrap all of the iron except the bottom surface in a bag, go outside and spray the ironing surface with oven cleaner. *Avoid inhaling any of the toxic oven cleaner!* Then, sponge off with water and dry.

IRONING BOARD COVERS

The cover on your ironing board will last longer if you starch it.

STEAM IRONS

Clean mineral deposits from a steam iron by filling the water tank with white vinegar. Turn the iron to the steam setting and steam iron a soft utility rag to clean the steam ports. Repeat the process with water, then thoroughly rinse out the inside of your iron. Another method is to fill it with a mixture of $1/2$ cup vinegar and 1 tablespoon baking soda. Heat for a few minutes, drain, and then flush with warm water. Clean starch buildup from the bottom by cleaning with a paste of baking soda and water or by putting a thin layer of salt on a clean piece of paper and ironing that for a minute or two.

WASHING MACHINE

The detergents used in the washing machine tend to build up deposits in the machine itself. To get rid of them, pour a cup of white vinegar into the washer and run it set on hot. (Don't put any clothes in.) Probably doing this once a month will do the trick.

CLEAN WATER TIP

Your hot-water heater takes in water from outside water pipes and this water is not always completely clean. So open up that faucet at the bottom of your water heater (you didn't know you had a faucet down there, did you?) and drain off a bucket of water every six months or so. This will take out impurities that have settled at the bottom and extend the life of your hot-water heater. It will also send cleaner water to your shower and your washing machine.

When you are not actually doing laundry, turn off the water-line valves that go into your washing machine. It only takes a few seconds and it will relieve the constant water pressure on parts of the washer such as its solenoid (you don't have to know exactly what that is, just that it's good to relieve the pressure on it). This can also keep the water hoses from bursting.

WHEN YOUR HOUSE IS NOT JUST A HOME

Tips on "alternative" home uses—the party site and the home office

Our homes aren't just where we hang out at night. We use our homes to entertain and we use them as a place to earn a living. Although entertaining is supposed to be "play," it falls into the "work" category for many of us. This chapter will provide ideas on how to make both activities less stressful, less costly, and more fun.

THINK OF YOUR GUESTS

It doesn't have to be a formal affair to be fun. It can be an informal cocktail party, a backyard barbecue, or a picnic at the beach. The important thing is to think of your party from the guest's viewpoint. Check the calendar to make sure that your date doesn't conflict with others' religious observances. Is it a good time of the week or month for your guests? For example, avoid times and places where guests have to fight traffic jams, and so may arrive late and annoyed they had to come to your party at all. Does the place for the party have enough convenient parking? In other words, put yourself in the place of your guests coming to your party and make it easy and comfortable for them. A friend of mine lives at the end of a narrow street in the Hollywood Hills and has parties every month. Two secrets of his success are that he always invites the neighbors and he always has valet parking. His neighbors are never annoyed by the noise and his guests don't spend half the night looking for a parking place. Everyone arrives feeling good and ready for fun.

CREATING A MOOD

Once your guests arrive, set the mood immediately to make them feel comfortable and entertained. Create atmosphere with flowers, decorations, candles, appealing place settings, and table arrangements. To the visual mood, add a little olfactory sensation with a delicate scent or perfume—not overpowering and, probably, not too exotic. Auditory mood setters are, of course, music and—like the scents you use—should be tasteful for the occasion. I've found that live music sets a wonderful tone for a party and guests love it. A guitar player or pianist adds drama. And if you want them talking about your party weeks afterward, engage a lady harpist to play. Knocks them out!

FOOD AND DRINK

Food and drink, of course, are central to most parties. What's served will vary according to the taste of the crowd. Who will serve? Will the guests serve themselves or will you see to that? Again, put yourself in the shoes of your guests. If you are going to do it buffet style and let them serve themselves, provide them with the material they need to do it easily. Don't have your guests tottering around balancing several plates, glasses, silverware, and so on. Put silverware, glasses, condiments, and drinks in bottles or pitchers at each table so all the guest needs to do is handle one plate for his or her food. Have someone by the entrée table to help serve. Make mini-buffets at each table. To make the food interesting, try a theme buffet or an array of unusual foods.

If you are going to cook and serve, limit yourself to three dishes and bring in a friend or relative to help. Our rule is to always have one more helper than you think you're going to need to prepare and serve. You are, after all, not just the cook and server, but also the host. You will need the flexibility, because if you're not having a good time at your own party, chances are nobody else will either.

FOOD AND DRINK SAFETY

Nothing can spoil a wonderful dinner or party at home than having everybody getting sick from the food and drink. Here are guidelines to avoid that happening at your next party.

Keep It Small

Yes, we know it is easier on you if you can pile all the food on one or two big trays and set them out for the whole time of the party. Yet, this is a possible invitation to trouble. It is much safer to put modest-sized portions on small plates and dishes and replace them frequently from the refrigerator. As a rule, never put out more than what will be eaten in a half an hour. This system has the added advantage that guests arriving later will enjoy the same quality of appetizing foods as the early arrivals.

Keep Hot, Hot—and Cold, Cold

It is important to keep hot foods hot using warming trays, candles, or canned heat that keeps the food at 140 degrees F or more. Hot foods will taste and look better and should remain fresh if you don't leave them out for more than two hours. Then, it's best to discard them or refrigerate and reheat when ready to serve again. Put cold foods in a nest of ice or in a dish that you rest inside a larger dish with ice in it.

BARBECUE

We Americans have a love-hate relationship with our barbecues. We love barbecue cooking and we hate barbecue cleanup. Here are my tips for both.

COOKING

When you put meat on the grill without trimming unneeded fat, the fat will drip onto the coals causing flare-ups and uneven cooking. So, trim before you grill. If your fire does flare up from dripping meat, throw a handful of salt on the flames to temper them. Also, use tongs instead of forks because piercing the meat will let juices drip and make meat dry out.

When you see white ash forming on the coals, knock it off with tongs. You'll get more heat from the coals that way. When you decide the fire needs more coals, add them around the edges of your existing coals—not on top of them. If your coals die out on you, sprinkle a little cooking oil on them to get them going again.

STARTING THE FIRE

For some, the fun of barbecuing is to soak the briquettes with gasoline or lighter fluid, then stand back throwing lit matches. This often leads to singed eyebrows and a blackened face. There are other less spectacular and safer ways to light the charcoal. First, be sure the charcoal is dry; not surprisingly, damp coals won't light. One safe way to light the charcoal is to stuff newspapers into milk cartons, cover them with charcoal and light. The waxed milk cartons will burn easily and hot, igniting the charcoal. Or soak some briquettes in starter fluid in advance in a can with a lid. When ready, pour out the soaked briquettes, cover with dry briquettes and light. Soaking the starter briquettes ensures that there is enough lighter fluid to produce a lasting, hot flame to light the dry briquettes. Keeping them sealed in a can until you are ready to cook keeps the lighter fluid from evaporating.

SERVING TIPS

As I mentioned earlier, good hosts think of their guests' comfort when planning a party. So visualize your guests. They probably will have a plate in one hand and a drink in the other looking for a place to sit down. Don't make them try to juggle a lot of things such as three pieces of silverware, condiments, and so on. In fact, the best eating arrangement at a barbecue is with hands only or just a fork. If it's a fancy barbecue featuring steaks or chicken or roasts, have seats for the guests with napkin-rolled cutlery awaiting them.

PUTTING THE FIRE OUT

A basic rule for engines is not to start one unless you know how to turn it off. Apply the same rule for barbecues. Never start one unless you have a full box of baking soda at hand, which you can use to put out the fire if it gets out of control.

When you're done cooking, you can save the coals for use at the next barbecue by spraying carefully with water. They will dry out and be ready to burn again another day. Whether you plan to save them or not, put out the coals. They can be a hazard when not attended. The best way is to simply smother them by closing the barbecue's vents and putting on the lid. *Do not dump them on the ground or in the sand.* More about that in a moment.

CLEANUP

Start by spraying a nonstick cooking product on the grill. Immediately after cooking, while the grill is still warm, rub it *carefully* with a wad of crumpled aluminum foil. This will remove a lot of the immediate mess. Another aluminum foil trick is to remove the grill and wrap it in heavy aluminum foil with the shiny side inward. Fire up the barbecue and put the wrapped grill back in place for about ten minutes. Later, when you've turned the flame off and the wrapped grill has cooled down, unwrap the foil carefully. Much of the mess stuck on the grill should come off with the foil.

If you are barbecuing over a cement patio or wood deck or someplace nice like that, you want to guard against barbecue splatters. Keep a big box of salt handy and cover such accidents with salt immediately. The salt soaks up the mess and can be swept up.

INSECT REPELLENT AT BARBECUES

A simple and effective insect repellent is to rub your exposed skin with vinegar. Yes, it will smell vinegary, but that will go away as it dries.

If you have to cope with mosquitoes or flies, you may be able to drive them away with smoking candles or incense (many flying bugs hate smoke). Or spray bug repellent before the guests arrive (making sure that no food, plates, or other utensils get sprayed in the process).

BEACH BARBECUE SAFETY

If you are barbecuing at the beach, throw water on the coals after you are done. *Do not dump the coals in the sand!* Even though covered with sand, they are still hot for a long time and can cause a serious burn if stepped on.

Some candle drippings can be easily scraped off your tablecloth. Others may need you to rub them down with lots of vegetable oil followed by paper towels.

DEALING WITH THE DINING ROOM

I sometimes call the dining room the "split-personality room." As a separate room, the dining room has a somewhat formal, dignified atmosphere—shielding diners from the messy kitchen. But some people say formal dining rooms are rarely used except on special occasions and are an enormous waste of space. Moreover, they smack of a family with servants, which most American families don't have. On the other hand, the open dining area has a warm, all-American family feel to it as part of a big casual gathering place.

Some people try to compromise and make it both by having open "pass through" spaces with a partial divider. These allow people in the kitchen to converse with those in the dining area in a congenial atmosphere and it makes serving easy because guests can help themselves from dishes on the pass-through countertop.

Are there other middle-ground solutions? Sure. One of the easiest methods is to use lighting or lack of it. Make sure the dining room or dining area is on a different circuit from the kitchen. When you are done working in the kitchen, dim or turn out the lights. Or, have a shade or set of shutters with interesting colors and designs that you can draw to block out the views of the kitchen. Another choice is floor-to-ceiling folding doors done in the same material and design as the rest of the dining area. These can give the impression that there is no opening to the kitchen. In lieu of shades and shutters, you might have a stained-glass divider you can open up or a glass-beaded curtain you can use. Other approaches include having a deep sink so dirty pots and dishes can't be seen from the dining area or have the pass-through counter higher on the dining area side so people in the dining area can't see directly into the kitchen. Also, sliding pocket dividers in the pass-through divider counter are an idea. In planning the relationship of the dining area and the open kitchen, some designers recommend that the rooms be at right angles to each other. That is, the narrower wall of the dining area should abut the kitchen area. This will automatically obscure much of the kitchen from most of the diners.

FIREPLACE FIRES

It's always good to know how to put out a fire before you start one. Keep a supply of salt or baking soda near your fireplace to douse the flames if necessary.

HOW TO BUILD A GOOD FIRE

Start with a clean fireplace and make sure the damper is open. You need a fireplace grate. Ball up some newspaper under the grate and between the openings. Take two firestarter bricks and break them up on top of the paper. Then put four pieces of kindling that are maybe an inch in diameter on the grate. Crisscross this small kindling wood so air has room to circulate. Take three pieces of firewood and lay them in the opposite direction from the kindling, with spaces between the pieces. Put two more pieces over them, going the other way. Put a last one on top in the opposite direction. Never lay wood tightly together because it will not draw the air circulation it needs. It's best to hold back on the big heavy logs until you've got the fire going well.

You'll want to place some old newspapers rolled up into paper-towel tubes or milk cartons underneath the kindling to get the fire going. However, do *not* use paper of any kind that has colored ink printed on it. Colored ink contains lead, and when you burn it, the lead gets in the air of your home and is dangerous to everybody, particularly children.

FIREPLACE POTPOURRI

If you want to give a decorative note to a room without building a fire, you can line the inside front of your fireplace with lit candles. You get the same kind of magical effect without the trouble and heat.

Add an aroma for an extra flair with your fire. You can burn the peels of aromatic fruits (oranges, lemons, and limes); aromatic wood such as sandalwood or cedar; or aromatic spices such as basil, cinnamon, vanilla, and so on.

FIREPLACE SAFETY

As the soot builds up on the inside of your chimney, it becomes a fire hazard. Protect against this by having it cleaned, or as the professionals say, "swept," at least once a year. Besides, think of Santa Claus. You don't want him getting all sooty sliding down your chimney. Santa aside, many say that soot is a good fertilizer for your garden, so you may just want to clean it out of your chimney and spread it among your plants.

Clean the hearth and the fireplace regularly by brushing the sides of the fireplace clean and sweeping out the dust. Some recommend vacuuming the fireplace, but blowing air around a box of ashes isn't my idea of a good method of cleaning. Sweeping carefully makes more sense to me. In fact, some people will lightly spray the fireplace ashes with a fine mist of water to keep them from flying all over the room. While you're at it, you may want to wipe down the fireplace tools and gently brush the fireplace screen, too.

GOOD FIREWOOD

It's a mark of how much we love the cheer of a fireplace that half of all homes in the United States have at least one fireplace. Incidentally, you are allowed to collect up to six cords of downed or dead wood from a national forest if you have one handy. Call the U.S. Forest Service for a permit.

But you can't enjoy a fireplace unless you get good firewood, and most of us can't tell one fire log from another although I have an edge having been brought up in Seattle. Of course, that's not true of my lovely wife,

Tudi, who was raised in Texas where they think a fireplace is where the firemen live.

First, you should know that the basic measurement for firewood is a unit called a "cord," which is technically a pile of wood four feet high, four feet wide, and eight feet long or 128 cubic feet. The easiest way to stack wood up into a standard cord is by using logs two feet long (which are too big for most standard fireplaces). So a different measurement is often used called a "face cord," which uses pieces of wood 12 to 18 inches long. When you stack this shorter wood into a pile, it is four feet high and eight feet wide, making it more convenient for the homeowner to use, but also a lot less than a "standard cord." If you stack the pile with logs one foot long, you get 32 cubic feet or one-quarter of a standard cord and with 18-inch logs, you get 48 cubic feet or one-third of a standard cord. Be sure you know what you're buying before you open your wallet. In some states it is illegal to sell any measurement other than a standard cord or a fraction thereof.

Marshall McLuhan said that "art is anything you can get away with," and I would argue that the same goes for a cord of firewood.

It is not uncommon to buy firewood from traveling purveyors who sell the wood from their truck. There is a certain earthy charm to getting your wood this way, but be careful when you do so. If you're wise, you won't do business with strangers who take your money and disappear.

Of course, price is only one factor to consider when buying firewood. You want to be sure to get a good product that suits your needs. Unsplit logs may burn all day while split logs burn more easily. Some people like a mixture of both. Smart firewood buyers also look for seasoned wood or aged cut logs. They warn against wood that has been cut recently because it is "green" meaning it is loaded with water and very difficult to light. Seasoned wood has been drying out (under cover) for at least six months or longer. You can spot seasoned wood because it is lighter than green wood, and it has natural cracks at the ends of the logs.

Remember these tips when buying wood:
- Green wood is real clean, not dirty. If its bark doesn't come off, it's green.

- Hardwood, which is dense, is best, because it burns slowly, cleanly, and produces the most heat. Good hardwoods include red oak, black oak, white oak, locust, cherry, and apple. Don't buy pin oak. It will stink up your house.
- Softwood is cheaper than hard. Some consumers mix the two to save money.
- Softwoods sometimes produce a residue that coats the chimney with tar like creosote. This creosote builds up inside chimneys and can catch on fire and burn your house down. But, aside from that, no problem.
- A small amount of softwood makes excellent kindling. L. L. Bean has been selling millions of pounds of one kind called "Georgia fatwood."
- Cedar also makes good kindling and has a wonderful aroma.

Storage wood tends to attract insects so don't keep your wood in, or against, the house.

WORKING AT HOME

More and more of us are working at home and the need for an efficient and comfortable arrangement is increasingly important. Of course, much depends on what kind of space you have available in your home, but the old kitchen table probably won't do anymore. Here are some guides to keep in mind to make your at-home office work best for you.

LOVE THAT "L"

It's generally agreed that having your layout in an L-shape is usually the most efficient. That way you can sit in the middle and have your immediate work area right in front of you with an accessory work area just a simple little turn to one side or the other.

COMFORT IS THE KEY

Do not skimp on comfort. You want a chair that is comfortable, that gives you the right back support, and that is ergonomically correct. You'll want a chair with good upholstery and proper wheels so you can move around easily. Have one with adjustable height so your feet are on the floor. To relieve yourself of aches and pains, don't stay seated in the same chair and in the same position all day long. For your body and your mental outlook, get up every hour or so and take a short stroll outside or, at least, do a little stretching and bending.

AVOID CUBBYHOLE SYNDROME

Don't put your home office in the smallest, darkest room in the house. You're going to spend hours and hours there, so good lighting and ventilation are musts. A nice view is also good for the spirit rather than staring at the neighbor's fence or garbage cans for eight hours.

Good lighting is very important when you are working in the confined conditions of most home offices, so make sure you have a light fixture or system that is bright and focused on where you are working. Not only will it eliminate eyestrain, it will also make your at-home workplace cheerier.

KEEP IT MOBILE

Invest in a cordless phone. You can fold laundry, chop veggies, and do lots of other things when your hands are free. Rolling files are also a great convenience—if you decide to move your office space into another room, you'll be glad that you can just slide the furniture to its new location.

PLEASANT AND PERSONABLE

Experts recommend fixing up the home office with family pictures, artwork, photos, lively colors, or whatever you think makes it a cheerful place. I know of major corporations that allow only one or two modest family photos in their employees' offices. Everything else decorative must be strictly company issue or the janitors throw it out at night. Ugh! There's nothing wrong with being happy while you're working. I used to work at

Disney Studios and they had seven dwarfs who believed in that along with whistling.

PRIVATE AND OFF-LIMITS

It is important that your family respect the time you need in your office and give you the quiet and the privacy you must have. Everyone—children and adults alike—must be taught that the office is off limits even though it's in the house. You don't need your grade-schooler erasing your company's sales promotion plan for the next year when you step away. In other words, the home office is serious business and not a playroom.

HOME OFFICE TELEPHONE TIPS

Ideally, your home office should have its own private phone line if you are going to present a professional image. In fact, chances are good that you'll want two phone lines. For most professional home offices the basic items of equipment include a telephone, a computer, printer, answering machine, and fax machine. (Remember when we all got along with just a manual typewriter?) If you are on the Internet a lot, you'll want a separate line for that purpose so you don't miss a lot of calls. You also may need a phone line for the fax machine. We are all very busy these days, and you don't want a client to give up on you because you're hard to get in touch with.

PLUMBING

Is there anything worse than plumbing out of control?
Here are some ideas on easing the pain and the problem.

Of the various things that can go wrong around the house, there is probably nothing more annoying (or inconvenient) than a plumbing disaster. And without fail, major plumbing catastrophes must happen on three-day weekends when whatever plumber you can find will charge you an astronomical fee. There is the joke about the man who called in a plumber and was astonished at the bill. He complained, "I don't make this much an hour and I'm a heart surgeon." The plumber replied, "Neither did I when I was a heart surgeon." This chapter will help you handling plumbing problems without some of those stunning bills.

THE ALL-IMPORTANT BATHROOM AND KITCHEN PLUMBING

UNCLOGGING A SHOWERHEAD

Unscrew the showerhead, remove the rubber washer, place the head in a pot filled with equal parts vinegar and water, bring to a boil, then simmer for five minutes. Wait until cool and replace.

TOILET OVERFLOW

This next may be a touch indelicate, but it deals with something that can be very awkward and troublesome so we think we should talk about it. If you are ever sitting on the toilet and flush it, only to suddenly become aware the water and waste is swirling *upward* and filling the bowl, instead of swirling downward and emptying the bowl, here's what to do:

- Stand up immediately and take the lid off the tank
- Reach in the tank and find the flap ball closer at the bottom of the tank, and push it back into the tank hole to stop water coming out of the tank.
- Next, reach down under the tank to the turn-off value and turn it to the right (clockwise) until you have turned off the water.

Then, wait a few minutes. The water in the bowl may gradually seep out the exhaust pipe. Whether it does or not, you probably should use a bathroom plunger to clear whatever is jamming the drain.

PREVENTING TOILET CLOGS

The toilet and its proper use is a delicate subject.

Without my getting overly graphic, the toilet is not a universal waste disposal system and not every thing should be deposited into it. Basically, the only two things that should go down the toilet are the human waste it was intended to dispose of and toilet tissue because these tissues are made of paper that is designed to disintegrate quickly and flow readily. Everything else should *not* go in the toilet. Kleenex or facial tissues, sanitary napkins, Q-Tips, and everything else should be disposed of in the trashcan. Sound silly? It isn't. When I was managing a 30-unit apartment building, I had lots of unpleasant experiences with this. Once a tenant laughed when I said not to throw Q-Tips down the toilet and a while later that tenant was having a serious toilet backup problem. Had to call a plumber, who took the toilet apart and found—guess what?—crisscrossed Q-Tips that had created a trap that caught other waste and bottled up the flow of the drain.

The Q-Tips going into the toilet cost less than a penny, but jammed up in the toilet they cost many, many dollars to remove.

WATER MASTER VALVE

Your water system is a simple in-and-out arrangement. A small pipe brings fresh water into the house from a main outside line that serves many homes in your area. One of the most important things for you to know is that there is a valve outside of your home that controls the flow into the house. This is a valve you should know the location of and know how to turn on and off, which is easy since it's usually an ordinary faucet handle.

BASIC PLUMBING FACTS

Here are some of the basics about your plumbing system.

1. When you are working on fixing such things as leaks, turn off the water at the master valve before you begin.

2. Water expands when it freezes. In freezing weather drain pipes are subject to the cold, and you must warm them to keep the water from freezing. If the water inside your pipes freezes, it will expand and may split open your pipes and you will have expensive trouble. Ways of warming water pipes are to wrap them with cloth to insulate them from the cold, warm them with a hair dryer, or wrap them with warming tape. This last is a strip that has a heating element embedded in it and you spiral wrap it around pipes subject to freezing and turn on the heating element. This keeps the water in the pipe warm enough not to freeze.

3. There is a problem with pipes in older homes that many people are unaware of called electrolysis. Old pipes tend to be made of steel or iron but in more recent times people have been using copper tubing for water pipes. When you connect copper tubing to steel pipe, an electrochemical reaction sets in corroding the connection. So, you need to convert all your piping to either steel or copper, or you need to install a device that neutralizes the reaction.

The other end of the water cycle in your home is the bigger pipes that carry waste out of your house and into the sewer or septic tank. The important thing from the viewpoint of your comfort and convenience is to keep these drain pipes open and running freely. Basically, you want to avoid clogging these drains. That means not putting anything down them that will stop them up, such as the wrong kind of material in the toilet; hair and soap in the shower, bath, or sink; and materials the garbage disposal can't handle down the kitchen sink.

DRIPPING FAUCETS

A typical plumbing job that comes up periodically is fixing a dripping faucet. Ultimately, you will want to fix it, but if you need a quick fix to keep the dripping from driving you nuts at night, tie a string around the end of the faucet and drape it into the sink so the water runs down the string silently instead of dripping.

Ultimately, of course, you need to fix the drip. To understand what needs to be done, you have to understand the simple basics of a faucet. There are two general types of faucets. One type has two spigots and two handles that turn with one spigot being for hot water and the other being for cold. The other type has one spigot and one handle with which you can adjust the mixture of hot and cold water, as you like. This second type is referred to in the plumbing trade as a "washer less" faucet.

Let's start by looking at the first type, which is called the "compression" faucet, because it compresses a rubber washer in the water supply hole to seal it off. It has two spigots: one for hot water and one for cold. When you turn the handle one way (usually clockwise when viewed from directly above) it unscrews the washer, raising the washer assembly from its seat on the incoming water pipe and letting water flow through and out the faucet. When you turn the handle the other way, it seats the washer assembly tightly over the incoming water hole and stops water from flowing. It is really fairly simple.

When this kind of faucet begins leaking, its because the rubber washer assembly has worn out from use. To repair it, start under the sink where there should be two more faucet handles as a control for the incoming water.

Turn these off so you don't spray geysers of water all over when you undo the faucets at the top of the sink.

Then, back to the top faucets.

Open both of them to drain out what little water may be in the line. Put stoppers in place in the sink drain and maybe even spread a towel or paper towel on the bottom of the sink so, when you accidentally drop a washer or a screw (it seems like everybody does), it will not drop down the drain and make for a bigger job than you contemplated.

Next remove the faucet handle. This is normally held in place by a screw in center. If the center appears smooth, it's probably a decorative cup that is snapped in place to cover the screw head. Carefully pry off the decorative cap and unscrew the screw beneath it. A screw on the side holds some faucets in place. In either case, loosen the screw. Then, gently pull or pry the faucet handle up and it should reveal the washer assembly.

Now, here comes our smartest advice for this kind of job. We know this just as we also know you will ignore it. At least, at first. Ultimately, you go along with our suggestion. Here it is. Take the faucet assembly including the washer assembly to your friendly hardware or home-improvement store. Show it to the clerk and tell him or her you want two exact duplicates of the washer assembly if possible. Or at least two as close to exact duplicates as possible.

Then, return home and open one duplicate package in the way we instructed you elsewhere. Namely, slit open the plastic package very carefully so you can put it back together if the part turns out to be wrong.

Assuming the part is the correct replacement, reverse the order of what we did a minute ago in removing the faucet and washer assembly. When you are done, the next washer assembly should fit snuggly and the leak should be gone.

Oh, yes. What about the second duplicate washer assembly you bought? As soon as you are done with repairing the faucet that leaks, repeat the process with the other faucet that doesn't leak—yet. If the first washer assembly has worn enough for it to leak, you can know the second isn't far behind, so let's fix it before it needs fixing. It will save you time and annoyance to do it now.

This brings us to the "washer less" faucets of which there are four common types and all of which is an outgrowth of plumbing fixture manufacturers making fancier and more expensive faucets. The four types of washer less faucets are called ball, cartridge, ceramic disk, and tipping valve—each of which describes its mechanism in part. Our suggestion, because each manufacturer makes each of these single faucet mechanisms different than its competitors, is that you get the name of the faucet maker from the faucet, take a photo of it from several angles, and then go to the plumbing supply or home-improvement store. Talk to the department clerk and see if you can identify your faucet type and read the instructions on how to install it and to repair a leak.

Of course, when you are home, you should follow the same early steps as we did with the two-faucet "compression" system. Namely, shut off the water under the sink, close the drain, and line the sink with a towel or paper towels. Then, follow the instructions to repair and replace the leak.

JAMMED GARBAGE DISPOSAL

The garbage disposal is a wonderful gadget except when it isn't working. Sometimes it jams all by itself, but usually you help it jam by not using it correctly. Here are some of the things you shouldn't do because it can make the disposal stop working.

- No harsh chemicals or drain cleaners. Don't put corrosive stuff in the disposal because it can hurt the seals and make the disposal leak.
- No fibrous garbage such as cornhusks, banana peels, et cetera. These can get under the rotating blades and jam the disposal.
- Too much stuff at one time. That's self-explanatory. Feed it a little at a time.
- Water. Water. Water. The garbage disposal needs water to work right. Don't turn it on unless you are running water into it. If you are dumping greasy stuff in the disposal, run hot water—lots of hot, soapy water to keep it liquid until it is flushed out to the main sewer line. That will help. Generally, it's best not to pour grease down any plumbing because, when it cools, it hardens and clogs the plumbing

line. It also enriches plumbers. Instead, pour grease into a can to save for future cooking, or to let cool and harden so you can throw it out in the trash.

Fortunately, when you ignore most of the things we have just told you and the disposal jams, it will usually stop running automatically. A built-in circuit breaker shuts off the power to the disposal motor. Otherwise, the disposal motor might burn out, or, worse, catch on fire. So, now you have a disposal with TWO things wrong with it: It's jammed and there's no power.

1. You want to un-jam it but, before you do anything, turn off the disposal switch. Yes, yes, the electricity went off automatically, but turn off the switch in case it comes back on automatically while your hand is down in the disposal. Ouch! There go some fingers!

2. Next, open the sink closet door and get down to where you can see the bottom of the disposal. Sometimes a flashlight is handy at this point. In most disposals these days, you will find a hexagon-shaped slot in the middle or at the very bottom of the unit. So, the easy way to unjam the unit is to use a hexagon wrench and turn the disposal blades by hand. A hexagon wrench should have come with the disposal unit when it was installed but it may have been lost. In that case, it means a trip to the hardware store for a replacement.

Almost everything in the Northern Hemisphere (that's us) turns clockwise when it's working. However, you want the blades in the disposal to go backward so they can unjam. Thus, you will want to use the hexagon wrench to turn the disposal blades counter-clockwise. A little effort and the blades should be free.

3. We don't want the disposal to jam up again. That's why you should now remove some of what you jammed down there before. Sometimes you can do this with a pair of tongs and sometimes you just have to put your dainty little hand in there and pull out what jammed the disposal. BE SURE THE ELECTRICAL SWITCH IS OFF! Actually, we are so safety minded that we not only turn off the wall switch in the kitchen near the garbage disposal,

we also flip the fuse or circuit breaker for the disposal. Does that sound overly cautious? Perhaps, but we still have all of our fingers.

4. Now, with the disposal blades able to turn and the jammed material out, we're ready to try again. Make sure you're not putting any fibrous waste into the disposal and that you are only putting a small amount of waste in at a time.

5. With your hands out of the disposal, go back under the sink and check the bottom side of the disposal again. There should be a red reset button. Push this button. You should hear a click. Then, you should be able to start the disposal again by flipping the regular start switch. Remember to run the water first.

One last thing you might want to do: Use a piece of duct tape to attach the hexagon wench to the disposal so it's easy to find next time. Yes. There will be a next time. Trust me.

SLOW FAUCET FLOW

From time to time you will notice that the water flow out of your faucets seems to be diminishing. This is often the fault of aerator guck. The aerator is a set of several filters at the nozzle of your faucet designed to strain out solid particles and other irritants. The trouble is that it keeps catching this stuff and holding it there until you have a buildup of guck that restricts the flow of water. The solution is simple, you need to unscrew the filter, rinse it and screw it back on. This, of course, assumes you have an unscrewable aerator. Most homes do, but some don't. So, if it doesn't unscrew readily, don't force it.

Often, you can unscrew the aerator with your hand, but if it is very tight, you may have to use a pair of pliers. Before you unscrew it with either your hand or pliers, put a drain stopper over the drain in the bottom of the sink and/or layer a couple or three folded paper towels in the bottom of the sink. This tiny precaution will save you much time and aggravation because it will prevent you losing a part of the aerator down the drain and into the garbage disposal.

Also, if you are going to use pliers, wrap a folded paper towel or a cloth around the outside of the aerator so your pliers teeth don't mark up the chrome finish. Now, unscrew the aerator and take it apart, remembering the order in which each screen goes. Then rinse them all, reassemble and screw it back on to the end of the faucet.

TOILET REPAIR

The bathroom is one the most private rooms in the house and, for many, it contains the most mysterious of devices, the flush toilet which we have recently learned was originally invented by the Chinese some 4,500 years ago. Yet, old as it is, everybody wants it to work properly and panics when it doesn't. Actually, the toilet is a fairly simple device and its problems are generally one of two types: either it doesn't work or it won't stop working.

The toilet normally works with two reservoirs of water: one in the bowl and one in the tank. The water for the tank comes in from your regular water supply line and a long, thin metal handle controls it with a large floating ball attached to the end. As the water fills up, the large ball floats on the top of it and, when the tank is full, the floating ball has turned the metal handle up enough to stop the water coming in. Sometimes the metal handle does not turn off the incoming water completely. To fix that, remove the lid of the tank and use your hands to gently bend the metal handle a little bit so the large ball is a little lower. That should turn off the water running into the tank.

When it is time to flush the toilet, we all know how to push down on the control level outside the tank. This is connected inside to a small chain that, in turn, is connected to the stopper at the inside bottom of the tank. When you push down the handle, this raises the little chain and the rubber stopper that releases all that water in the tank into the bowl, where it washes the contents of the bowl into our waste or sewer line. It's that simple.

One other basic everybody should know is that there is a safety or back-up value handle to control the incoming water going into the tank. This is usually a regular faucet handle down near the floor against the wall under the tank. To stop all incoming water to the toilet, simple turn this handle to the right as far as you can.

When It Doesn't Work

When the toilet doesn't work, it's because (1) the simple system of flushing water from the tank to the bowl has not happened; (2) the plug at the bottom of the tank is not opening to let the water into the bowl; or (3) something is keeping the water in the bowl from going into the sewer pipe.

Lift the tank lid and see what is or isn't going on in there. If there is no water in the tank, check the floating ball handle to make sure the lower faucet on the incoming water pipe is open by turning it to the left as far as it will go. If the tank is filled with water but not draining into the bowl, it's because the stopper at the bottom of the tank is not opening. Check the flushing handle outside the tank. Check the little chain connecting the flushing handle to the stopper at the bottom of the tank. Sometimes this little chain gets disconnected. If so, reach into the water with your hand, pull up the stopper to drain the water and, then, reconnect the chain between the flushing handle and the stopper.

Probably, the most common and most distressing problem is the third one, namely, the water is filling up the bowl from the tank but not draining out the sewer pipe. Immediately, take the tank lid off, reach down into the water and push the stopper into place. This will stop more water from flowing into the bowl and, ugh, out on the floor. Then, reach down and turn off the incoming water at the faucet below the tank. Otherwise, everything will overflow and that's one royal mess. After you have stopped more water from coming in, you should try to get the water in the bowl out through the sewer pipe. It is probably not draining because it is clogged by some obstruction. The ordinary ways of clearing a sewer outlet obstruction is to use the so-called "plumber's helper" or plunger. By putting it against the sewer line exit hole in the toilet bowl and pumping, you may force the obstruction that is lower in the sewer line to clear. If you can't clear the line this way after 25 or so plunges, the next choice is what is called a hand "snake," which is a thin, flexible wire with which you can probe into the sewer line and try to clear the outlet. As an emergency measure, some people will try creating a makeshift snake by straightening a wire coat hanger but this usually doesn't work too well.

The final choice is to call a plumber.

One thing *not* to do to clear a clogged sewer exit line includes using an electric snake because these are often so powerful that they can crack the porcelain toilet bowl and *then* you have a major problem! Another thing NOT to do is to start pouring caustic chemical drain openers into the water in the bowl. If these don't work, and often they don't, you then are dealing with caustic tainted water that can burn your eyes and skin and those of anyone else working to clear the stoppage. NOT A GOOD IDEA!

When It Doesn't Stop Working

Another irritation with toilets is when they don't stop working. They either keep on running or they leak water onto the floor. Both are irritating but not as bad as when they stop working all together.

When the water continues to seep into the bowl even after the tank is filled, the large float bulb inside the tank needs adjusting as we described a few paragraphs ago. That is a simple leak.

Then there are the complicated leaks. One may be caused by a crack in the porcelain bowl or tank created by a hard knock or a mishandled tool or electric snake. This is a lot of work to fix because you have to replace the cracked bowl or tank or both.

Another source of toilet leaks onto the floor is when it's coming from around the base of the toilet bowl. The toilet unit is basically the toilet tank sitting on top of the toilet bowl. The toilet tank sits on top of and is bolted to the toilet bowl. The bowl sits on top of the sewer line hole in the floor and is usually bolted to the floor with two or four bolts. It has a gasket of some kind between the bottom of the bowl and the floor to seal it tight. When that gasket gets old and disintegrates or is disturbed some other way, it sometimes starts to leak. To repair this is a job, but it can be done fairly easily. You'll need to get a new bowl gasket from the hardware store. Try to measure the bowl carefully and note the brand name and model number so you know the right gasket to get. Then, you go to work with paper cup, wrench, and a paint or putty scraper.

1. First, turn off the incoming water faucet underneath the tank.
2. Then, flush the toilet and, using a paper cup or other small re-

ceptacle, bail out all of the water that you can. This is because you are going to unbolt the toilet bowl from the floor and any water in the bowl is going to run out on the floor.

3. Now, remove the lip of the toilet tank and set it aside in a safe place. Then, unbolt the toilet tank and lift it off the toilet bowl. Careful. You have to unbolt it from the toilet bowl AND disconnect it from the incoming water line. Set it aside and out of the way.

4. Next, unbolt the toilet bowl from the floor.

5. Pick up the toilet bowl and set it aside out of the way. (It will probably be heavy, so you may need some help.)

6. Scrap away the old toilet gasket. This is often a wax-coated ring the shape of the bottom of the bowl.

7. Clean the entire surface where the bowl was sitting by scraping or scrubbing.

8. Push a new gasket ring down over where the old one was.

9. Now, reverse what you did in steps 3 and 4 above. Put toilet bowl down *carefully* over the protruding bolts and the new gasket.

10. Tighten the nuts on the bolts easily—EASILY. If you tighten too hard, you can crack the toilet bowl and then you have to buy a new one and do the whole thing all over again.

11. Put the toilet tank and lid back on and bolt them into place. Reconnect the incoming water line.

12. Turn the water back on and test flush to see if everything is sealed and working right.

CLEANING CLOGGED SINK DRAINS

Sometimes the chemicals we put down sink drains in the kitchen and bathrooms are not enough to clear out whatever is clogging the drain. That's when we have to get down and dirty. We have to get down under the sink and get dirty opening up the "trap." The trap is usually a U-shaped part of the drain pipe connecting from the straight pipe coming down from the basin above and going to the drain pipe thats goes into the back wall. It is U-shaped to trap some water in the pipe to keep unpleasant odors from seeping back into the room. Unfortunately, sometimes not only water is trapped in the U-shaped pipe, but also hair, dead skin, coagulated soap, and other guck.

Before beginning, lay down a towel or folded paper towels because you're going to spill some water in the process. You will need a wide mouth wrench or a pipe wrench to undo the coupling nuts at both ends of the U-shaped pipe. They are supposed to unscrew in a counterclockwise direction but that may be confusing to figure out. Try it gently in what seems to be the correct counterclockwise direction and, if that doesn't work, go in the other direction.

Before you start, notice if the pipes are metal or plastic. Some builders use plastic piping and, if that's the case with your drainpipes, be extra careful. Too much muscle and you could end up with a cracked pipe and the need for a replacement. The same could be true even if the pipe is metal and it is very old and rusty. If this U-shaped pipe is in delicate or bad condition, you may want to take it to the store and get a replacement.

In any case, when you have the U-shaped trap pipe off, check it out. And see if there is anything stuck in it or if that dreaded guck has formed. It's a good idea to run a wire coat hanger or other flexible device through the entire U-shaped trap pipe to clean out whatever may be lurking in there. Remember that this will often produce material coming out of the end of the pipe so hold it over paper towels or a bucket or something to catch it instead of making a mess.

Once the U-shaped trap pipe is cleaned out, reassemble the pipe drain unit carefully and run some water down it to see if you have solved the problem. If water doesn't drain freely, the problem is someplace further down the system of pipes and it may require a plumber and a plumber's snake to clean it out.

Check the U-shaped pipe a couple times over the next few days to make sure your connections are holding tight and not leaking. This is particularly important where you have plastic pipes since they will sometimes loosen up after you first tighten them.

There are various tricks you can use to keep hair from going down the drain in the bathroom. A good temporary screen can be made by covering the drain with a used hair net. You might also want to put in a filter or screen to permanently keep hair out of your drains.

Another time you may have to open that U-shaped trap pipe is when a piece of valuable jewelry accidentally goes down the drain. When that happens, you should immediately turn off the faucets so the running water doesn't wash the jewelry beyond the U-shaped trap to where you can never retrieve it. Then, quickly open up the U-shaped trap with a bucket or pan under it so the jewelry can drop into a receptacle where you can retrieve it.

BUILDING AND REMODELING

Ideas for changing things around and rebuilding a better place to live

Since both my father and grandfather were building contractors all their lives, I learned a lot about home repair and remodeling from them. It's an honor to share my legacy of handy ideas and techniques with you.

BATHROOMS BOOMING

In the year 2000, Americans spent over $100 billion on remodeling their homes and the boom room is the bath. It used to be the kitchen, but now it's the bathroom with a significant rise in prices and vocabulary. We are accustomed, for example, to "sinks" but those are being replaced by "ceramic vessels in mahogany vanities" at many thousands of dollars a pop. Faucets, showers, baths, and everything else is following the trend. The hardware in a shower can run in the thousand-dollar range for faucet, showerheads, body sprays, and wall bar even before it is installed. Even many faucets are now in the $100-plus category. The number-one luxury upgrade for bathrooms is now a luxury bathtub, even if you have to steal space from the bedroom to make room for it. Ironically, many people still prefer taking showers but love the idea of a huge, luxurious air-jet bath and, in fact, such a bath can enhance a home's resale value later on. Whirlpool baths and soaking tubs in the $3,500-plus price range are getting more attention, and redoing a bathroom is still cheaper than redoing a kitchen.

I remember being impressed with the Kohler plumbing fixture factory that I visited while we were still doing the *Home Improvement* show. It was amazing what a variety of bathroom fixtures they were producing as part of their "Bold Look of Kohler" slogan, and apparently they still are. I am sure others in the field like Moen are doing the same thing.

In spite of the fact that 80 percent of bathroom appliances are white, one of the surprising trends in bathroom equipment is color and design. We are now seeing leopard spots, dragonflies, sculpted animals, and fish plus dragons and zebra stripes all appearing on toilets and bathroom sinks. Design bathroom appliances come in the range of $1,500 to $4,000 with a custom, made-to-order seat going for $350 or so. The impact of the design invasion of the bathroom is, among other things, becoming a "bathroom celebrity" among your friends. Expect people you know to come over to take photos.

IMPROVEMENT SAFETY

No matter what home improvement job you tackle, you want to make sure the home-improvement job doesn't tackle you and send you to the hospital instead of the hardware store. Here are some basic tips on home-improvement job safety no matter what the job is. Some of it seems simple and obvious, but a lot a people ignore safety rules and end up hurt.

- First and most important, are YOU in condition to do the job? If you are aggravated, tired, or ill, forget the job until a later, more serene time.
- Always wear protective clothing, such as sturdy work boots or shoes and heavy clothing. Be sure to wear goggles or a facemask along with work gloves and a dust mask if necessary. This is particularly important when using any kind of power tool. In addition to always wearing protective clothing, remove all other extraneous articles from

your person. For example, never wear necklaces, wristbands or any dangling or loose jewelry or clothing that can get caught up in a whirling power saw or comparable tool. Keep hair out of the way— yours or anyone else's. Pull back long hair to be sure a tool doesn't catch it.

- Sharpen all your cutting tools before you start to work. You'll want your chisels, power drills, and saws all sharp and easy to work with. If you have a dull tool and you have to press too hard on it to make it do what it should, it might slip and severely cut you.
- Naturally, if you are working on electrical jobs, cut off the electric power. The same advice applies to water, natural gas, or heating oil projects. Turn every thing off until you're done with the job.
- Obviously, when working with power tools, keep away from the moving parts. Keep anyone not actively working with you away from the work, particularly children who often don't have a sense of respect for the danger of power tools.
- Never leave a power tool on or plugged in while you leave the job site—even for a moment. Don't leave tools of any kind lying where children can get them while you're not watching.

REMOVING WALLPAPER

Mix equal parts vinegar and hot water. Use a paint roller to wet the paper thoroughly with the mixture. Repeat. Paper should peal off in sheets.

CLEAN RUST FROM TOOLS, BOLTS, AND SPIGOTS

Soak the rusted tool, bolt, or spigot in undiluted white vinegar overnight.

STUCK BOLTS

When you are faced with tough bolts that just won't move when you try them with a wrench or pliers, soak the bolts in a cola drink for a short time. Then, try again with a wrench or pliers. Slipping a short piece of metal pipe over the end will help to lengthen the handle of the wrench. The longer the handle, the more leverage you'll have. See, you should have taken physics after all.

PUTTING IN TINY SCREWS AND NAILS

One thing that can drive you nuts when you are trying to screw in tiny screws (such as the itty-bitty ones that hold your glasses together), to hammer in tiny nails, or to deal with any very small part is the frustration of holding it in place while you use the screwdriver or hammer. Some helpful tricks include pushing it through a piece of heavy wrapping paper, a thin sliced vegetable (carrot, for example), or putting a drop of glue on you finger tip or the tip of a pencil eraser or something like that. This will hold the piece in place while you do what has to be done.

PAINTING TIP

When you are painting doors, shutters, window, furniture—anything—there are often places you don't want painted such as hinges, latches, numbers, and other hardware. So, either cover those parts with masking tape or coat them with petroleum jelly. This keeps paint from adhering to those parts. It wipes off with a paper towel after the paint is dry.

AFTER-PAINTING TIP

Keep leftover paint for later touch-ups. In addition, you should keep a record of the exact paint name, manufacturer, and batch code number. Put this information where you can find it later. Some suggested spots include the bottom of the paint can (the sides will probably have paint splashes covering up anything you wrote earlier), on the inside of an electrical switch plate in the room you painted, or taped inside a drawer or cabinet.

FILLING TINY HOLES

You can fill small nail holes when you don't have any spackle compound handy by rubbing them with a bar of white soap or toothpaste—don't use multicolored toothpaste or mint flavored.

RICHARD'S RULES FOR REMODELING

Here are my cardinal rules for saving your money, temper and aggravation level:

- **You will make mistakes.** Just accept as a given that you will get the wrong size, wrong color, wrong make, wrong something at some time with a do-it-yourself job. It is a given, and it's why so many do-it-yourself (DIY) jobs that should take ten minutes actually take half a day and three trips to the store. Here are my tips on easing the pain with your next DIY job.
- **Always measure and remeasure.** The professional carpenter's rule is "measure twice before you cut once." It's an excellent rule but too often DIYers ignore it. So, you go to the store and come back with something the wrong size and you have to go back again. The easiest way to avoid this aggravation is to have a tape measure or yardstick. Measure everything carefully—even get someone else to double-check the measurement for you—and write it down before you make the trip to the store.
- **Get a store buddy:** Become friendly with a particular clerk at the store and deal with him or her every time on a first-name basis. This one tip is worth ten times the cost of this book!
- **Take a picture or a part.** If you are replacing a part, take it out and bring it to the store with you to show to the clerk. If you can't take the part, try to take a photograph of the part and show that to the

clerk. This is particularly important if color is involved. If you can't bring a color sample to the paint clerk, try to bring a photograph. One reason this is important is that the color under your lighting at home may look different than the exact same color looks under the lights in the store. This happened when my wife, Tudi, and I were choosing colors for the last dining room we decorated. The recessed ceiling lights we had in the dining room made the colors appear different than they looked at the paint store.

- **Break the batch code.** It is no surprise that the manufacturers of most products such as paints, tiles, and electrical and plumbing parts have as much trouble keeping everything straight as we do. So, they cheat by assigning their various products code numbers or "batch numbers" to help keep things straight. Whenever you use any of these materials, be sure to get the manufacturer's name and the batch number. Write this down in a place you can find easily such as in your address book or on a note taped to the inside of a cabinet door. Next time you need it, you'll know just what to order.

- **Note what's left- and right-handed.** We all understand that there are left-handed and right-handed people but did you know there are other left-handed and right-handed things such as doors? To tell which is which with a door, face the closed door and see which side the knob is on. Right-handed doors have the knob on the right and left-handed doors have the knob on the left. Why is this important? Because changing the door from one side to the other can make it more convenient for you. In fact, most modern refrigerators are designed to allow switching the door from one side to the other depending on what works best for your kitchen.

  When we remodeled our house, we installed a new toilet in our son's bathroom only to find that we couldn't open the shower door. We puzzled over that for a day or so and suddenly realized we could switch the shower door from a right- to a left-side door. That solved the problem.

- **Sort out puzzling plumbing fixtures.** There seem to be a zillion different kinds of sinks, tubs, and toilets on the market. This was brought home to me a couple of years ago when I was given a tour of the Kohler factory and saw all the variations they manufacture. So, as with most plumbing fixtures, you have to check carefully if you are replacing any of these. Be sure to check how many holes your fixtures have for pipes and drains, what size and where they are. Here is another case where measuring is important. Some people even take a piece of heavyweight paper and cut out a template to match the holes and shapes. This makes it much easier to get the correct replacement piece of plumbing at the store. Beyond that, you should know that toilets are unusual because they are also different heights from the floor. You might not discover that until you arrive back home. Not only that, but frequently toilet seats are not sold with the toilet as a unit. You have to buy the seat separately and, worse than that, the store usually will not accept it back after you have taken it home.

· **Prepare yourself for happy returns.** The biggest irritation of buying the wrong thing is not just that you have made a mistake; it is that the store may not take it back and refund your money. So, check with the store before you buy anything on what their rules are about bringing back your mistakes.

As I have cautioned before, don't rip open the package with the new part until you are positive it is the right one. Instead, first read brand names, serial numbers, sizes, et cetera, through the plastic covering to make sure you've got the part you need. If you do open it, use a razor blade to slit the package very carefully and ease the part out. This way you can reseal it if you have to return it to the store—and more times than not you will have to return it.

Never—that word is NEVER—toss the old part away until the new part is in place and working properly.

THE TOOLS YOU NEED—RICHARD'S COMPLETE
BASIC TOOLBOX

My father and grandfather, both of whom were builders, as you know, agreed that having the right tool is having the job half done. The right tool will save you time, aggravation, money, and loss of temper. It will also make you look like a hero—the go-to guy for most of what needs doing around the house. Here is my list of a complete set of tools. You may want to start with some basics like a hammer, two kinds of screwdrivers, pliers, work gloves, and safety mask and add more as you go along. Ultimately, you will find great satisfaction in a complete set of tools. Here is what we think a complete set of tools would include:

Pipe wrenches (large and small, or if only one, a medium-sized one)
Claw hammer (you know, the one with those claws on one side)
Screwdrivers—an assortment of both Phillips head and slot
Jacob's wrench—If you have an electric drill
Measure—either tape or yardstick
Good, tough work gloves—one of the two most important things
Ordinary pliers but with some adjustment in the jaws
Needle-nosed pliers (you probably won't need these at first)
Flashlight or battery-operated light that stands up by itself
Snake or drain opener (a manual snake, electric snakes can do damage)
Plumber's putty—a good basic for a lot of things besides plumbing
Tape—you'll want various kinds such as masking, electrical, and duct
Small saw—for wood and metal
Variety of nails, screws, nuts, and bolts
Power-grip pliers that will lock in place and hold things for you
Some kinds of glue such as super glue and maybe some wood glue
An extension cord or two about 25 feet long each
Hand power $1/4$ inch drill—handy for drilling holes, screwing screws, et cetera.
Cutting tool like a razor with a retractable blade

Safety goggles or face mask—extremely important
A carpenter's level so you can judge when things are even
Machine oil for lubricating
Something to kneel on: piece of carpet, pillow, foam rubber
Several wood and metal files

One of the things you want to do to protect your tools is to keep them from rusting. This essentially means protecting them from moisture and air. Some workers coat their tools with a light coating of machine oil gently sprayed on the metal surfaces of the tools. This seals them off from moisture and air. Of course, if done too generously, it could make them slippery or hard to handle. So, you need to use some judgment. For garden tools and some other tools, we have known workers to have a sand box and to stick the metal parts of their tools in the sand. Another way is to keep tools locked in a tight box with something in the toolbox that will absorb moisture such as rice, mothballs, or dry cereal.

RICHARD'S DO-IT-YOURSELF REPAIR TIPS

- General twist rule: Clockwise to tighten. Counterclockwise to loosen. Or, twist right for tight. Twist left for loose.
- Mothballs, carpenter's chalk, or rice loose in tool box prevents rusting.
- Slip a piece of old garden hose over tool handles for a better grip.
- Store tapes in zip-locking bags to keep fresh and clean.
- Unclog aerosol spray heads by soaking in solvent.
- Mark drawer sides with heavy color line at the point where they might fall out.
- Rub lotion over hands and face before painting. Splatters will clean off easier.
- Write name and color on the *bottom* of the paint can where it won't get covered.

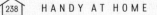

- To avoid skipping while drilling, put piece of tape over the spot and drill through it.
- To hold a screw or nail where you need one hand for the screwdriver or hammer and can't get your other hand in to position the screw or nail, use a shirt cardboard or other thin cardboard. Push screw or nail through the cardboard and, reaching with the extension of the cardboard, hold it in place.
- Placing a curtain rod at the back of a shelf creates nonspill area for bottles and cans.
- Sharpen utility-knife blades by honing on metal ladder step.
- Slip piece of pipe over wrench handle. A longer handle gives you more leverage and means more power.
- Avoid a banged thumb. Hold that nail with a paper clip, bobby pin, or slit card.
- With pliers or a wrench spanning both nuts, you should be able to undo them together.
- Tape a penlight flashlight to side of electric drill to see your work better.
- You mask surfaces with tape when you paint. Do it when you glue.
- Loop your belt through a small bucket to carry tools.
- Rub your pencil tip on keys. This will lubricate stiff locks.
- Cut used tennis or other small ball in half to make a mitt for holding steel wool.
- Remove steel wool residue left after use with a magnetic.
- Try using a wax paper cutter or windshield wiper good for spreading glue.
- A drop of clear nail polish on tiny eyeglass screws after tightening helps keep them that way.
- Clean files by pressing on and removing masking tape.
- Your belt through two slits in a paper cup equals a temporary nail holder.
- Take the rubber tips of an old crutch and tape it over the head of your hammer to avoid denting soft surfaces such as white pine wood when you hammer. Prevents denting of soft surfaces.

- Glue a small magnet to hammer handle; it will help you pick up nails.
- Soak wooden tool handles in linseed oil. Handle will swell and fit more tightly.
- Don't wear rings or other jewelry when using power tools—very dangerous!
- Tape a rag on a stubborn nut and soak it with penetrating oil to loosen.
- When you chew up a screw slot, cut new one at right angles with hacksaw.
- Lube a screw with wax or soap before screwing in.
- Penetrating oil substitutes include vinegar, cola, ammonia, lemon juice, peroxide.

THE LADDER TO HAPPINESS

Unless you're eight feet tall, a ladder is a very handy thing to have around the house. It seems to be simple in construction, but there are things about it everyone should—but doesn't—know.

What's not a Ladder: a chair, a box, a bucket, a trash barrel, and so on. All of these are NOT ladders. What they are is an invitation to the Emergency Room at the local hospital. You never know how sturdy any of these ladder substitutes is. Even if you're just going to use them for a quick job, the ambulance taking you to the hospital will be even quicker. Buy a ladder. Use a ladder, but use it correctly.

- Make sure the ladder's feet are firmly on the ground.
- Make sure the ladder's braces are locked if it's a stepladder.
- Use a wooden or plastic ladder for electric jobs unless you want to be lit up.
- Make sure everyone, particularly tiny tots, stay out from under the ladder.

- Never step on the top or the highest rung of the ladder.
- That cute little shelf near the top that folds out is not for you. It's for parts and paint.

GLUE GUIDE

The first thing that comes to our minds when we visit a hardware store or home-improvement center's glue section is "Wow! Where did all of these glues come from and which one is right for what I need today?" When that happens to you, or even before you go to the store, we hope you'll scan our glue guide so it will make it easier for you to stick (as in glue) with the right one. Here are some of our suggestions:

PVA GLUE (POLYVINYL ACETATE)

This is good as a general glue for projects around the house, including sticking together glass, china work, wood, metal, and plastic. Apply directly, clamp pieces together, wipe off excess, and let dry for several hours up to a day.

CARPENTER'S GLUE (ALIPHATIC RESIN GLUE)

This is usually yellow and is used for gluing together wood. Clamp pieces together for a few hours to a full day. Do not wipe away excess glue while it is wet. Let it dry and scrape excess away later.

EPOXY GLUE

This is good for joining metal, glass, and other materials that are different from each other. It is also good when you need a strong waterproof seal on wood.

It is really a two-part glue consisting of a liquid and of a hardening agent that makes the liquid solidify and hold materials together. It will hold materials together that don't even match perfectly, and it doesn't require clamping because it bonds so fast (usually five minutes or a little more). If you change your mind immediately, you may be able to undo epoxy glue with acetone or nail polish remover, but if you wait too long, it is stuck together for good—or bad.

CELLULOSE CEMENT

Clear cellulose cement works well for many smaller and lighter things made of wood, china, some fabrics, and some plastic. Apply the cement and tape the pieces together for a few hours.

SUPER GLUE

Super glue (cyanoacrylate) has become popular because it is strong and it is fast—sometimes too fast. There are really two super glues. One is a gel that is good for wood and cloth that is porous and lets the glue seep through. The other is for plastics, rubber, and metals that aren't porous.

Cautions you should know. It sets very fast. Usually in a few seconds and hardens as a clear, very strong binder. Keep it off your skin. You may be able to remove it if you instantly apply nail polish remover or acetone but, in a few seconds, it's all over.

GLUE, PREVENTING DRY OUT

To keep glue from drying out, store it in surplus bottles or zip-locking plastic containers. If your glue gets dried out anyhow, give it a touch of vinegar and it should become soft again. To keep the screw caps on tubes of glue from sealing themselves shut, smear a little petroleum jelly or other lubricant on the threads.

RECESSED BULBS

Recessed lightbulbs and spotlights are very chic in some modern homes except when you have to remove one that is burned out and then there isn't enough room between the bulb and the socket to slip your fingers around it to unscrew the darn thing. Some possible solutions include leave the burned-out bulb alone and forget about it. Or you can try this—AFTER YOU TURN OFF THE POWER. Take a length of duct tape and ball it up in the middle of the tape strip leaving both ends free and unattached. Then, stick the loose, sticky ends of the tape strip on the burned-out bulb. Grab the bunched up middle and gradually unscrew the bulb. Caution: The chances are very good that you will be below the bulb looking up into the socket as you are doing this—WEAR SAFETY GOGGLES in case the bulb shatters while you are unscrewing it. DON'T TAKE A CHANCE OF SERIOUS EYE INJURY.

KNOBS, LOOSE

We all get loose knobs on drawers, cabinets, and doors. These are easy to fix if you understand that there is a screw going into a hole. When the hole starts to get too big for the screw holding the knob in, the knob begins to wiggle. So, we need to make the hole smaller by stuffing in a wooden matchstick or toothpick, or inserting a plastic plug you can buy at the hardware store to do just that. On the flip side, you can make the screw bigger by wrapping it with fabric or steel wool threads or something like that. One last tip, paint the tips of the screw with glue or nail polish just before you screw it back in. This, obviously, will help the screw stay in place.

DRAWERS THAT STICK

Obviously, you want the runners of the drawers to slide smoothly. So, do what we suggested for sticking sliding doors, rub them with slippery stuff like a wax candle, soap, or furniture wax.

DUCKY DUCT TAPE

Be the first person on your block to know that the name of this handyman's standby is DUCT tape—not DUCK tape. This wide, strong tape originally was created to seal air ducts but has now become the universal adhesive tape around the house and the shop. Always keep a roll handy. If you are fashion conscious you will be pleased to know it now comes in colors besides its traditional silver-gray. Available in patriotic red, white, or blue plus orange and black.

NAIL REMOVAL TIPS

When faced with removing a rusty nail, give it a tap to drive it in a tiny bit more. This often will loosen it, shake the grip of the rust, and make pulling it out easier. You can also loosen it by letting a drop of oil or lubricant seep in for a few minutes at the nail shaft.

SCREW AND BOLT REMOVAL TIPS

To make it easier to remove a rusty bolt, give it a tap or screw it in a tiny bit more. This often will loosen it, shake the hold of rust, and make unscrewing it easier. You can also loosen it by letting a drop of penetrating oil or lubricant seep in for a few minutes at the screw or bolt shaft. Besides these lubricant helpers you can use cola, club soda, kerosene, ammonia, or brush on vinegar or wrap vinegar-soaked cloth around the screw or bolt. Also, applying heat to the screw, bolt, or nut with a hair dryer, soldering iron, or even a candle will cause it to expand and break loose more easily.

A mechanical way of removing stubborn bolts is to tighten a wrench on the bolt and then slip a short length of pipe over the wrench handle so as to make it longer. As I have noted elsewhere, the longer the handle, the more the mechanical power of your arm is multiplied.

BATTERIES

When dry cell batteries for your flashlights or radio run low, scrape the two ends of the battery with something like an emery board and it should give you some more electric power for a while. Another battery trick is to store extra batteries in the freezer until they are needed.

WORK IN PROGRESS

Whenever you are installing things on walls around your house, you wish you could tell exactly where each stud, conduit wire, pipe, and drain was located behind that outer covering. This is why it's a good idea to photograph construction work or remodeling work in progress before the drywall or plaster goes up. Keep the photos in a drawer in that room, and you can always check where all the hidden units are before you later put up shelves, hang something, or break in to insert something. Another trick is to put a tiny mark at the bottom of the wall or on the floor, marking exactly where every stud is located for future reference.

WINDOW BLIND CORDS, REPLACING

When you decide your old blind cords are getting tattered and should be replaced, cut off one end and sew (yes, sew) the beginning of the new cord to the end of the old cord. Then, you can, if you are careful and steady, pull the new cord into place.

BULB, BROKEN

TURN OFF THE POWER FIRST! We recommend you turn it off, not just at the plug or wall switch but also at the fuse or circuit box.

With an oven mitt, half a raw potato, wad of newspaper, or bar of soap, push down slightly—not too hard or you'll slip and cut your fingers—and turn counterclockwise. If you only break off more glass and you don't get the metal screw base, use a pair of pliers to grip and unscrew that. Wear goggles or a facemask to protect yourself from broken glass if the light is over your head.

DRAINS

Our plumbing drains are very important to most households and we don't pay much attention to them. But when they don't work, we pay lots of attention and lots of money to get them flowing again. Save aggravation and money by regularly cleaning them out by pouring one of these solutions down them:

- A cup of vinegar. Let it stand for half an hour and flush out with hot water.
- A cup of bleach (don't mix with anything else) followed by water rinse.

- One half cup baking soda and 3 cups boiling water. Let it bubble, then rinse.
- One half cup salt followed by hot water rinse.

RICHARD'S GUIDE TO EASY PAINTING

Painting is one of the messiest jobs there is around the house. The final result can be pleasing, but there can be aggravation along the way. As my building contractor father says, I hate to paint but I love to have painted. Here are some handy ideas that will make it a little easier and not so messy. The first has to do with painting and paper plates.

- Use a large paper plate in two ways while painting. Tape or glue a large paper plate to the bottom of the paint can. Instantly, you can see what it does. It catches paint dripping down the side of the can that would ordinarily go places you don't want it to go. Use a second paper plate as a shield for your paintbrush. Poke a hole in the middle of the plate and stick your paintbrush handle through it. Singer B. J. Thomas sings about raindrops that keep falling on his head. If you don't want paint drops falling on your head, this paper plate shield will help prevent that—especially when you're painting the ceiling or a wall higher than your head.
- If you look at the top of most paint cans, you will see a groove all around the edge into which the lid fits. If paint gets into that groove when you are wiping your brush on the edge of the can, it will harden after you put the lid on and be more difficult to open up again. One solution is to wrap a strip of aluminum foil around those exposed edges to prevent paint getting into the groove.
- One of the least lovely things that can happen while you're up on that ladder painting away enthusiastically is to have a fly or some other big bug plop down into your bucket of paint. So, now what do you do? If you leave him in there, you are liable to scoop him up in your brush and paint him on the wall or ceiling. Then, you have

to decide if you want that bug as part of your permanent interior decoration or if you are going to pick, poke, or scoop him off. This is not a major issue, but it certainly is an annoyance. We suggest a shot of insect repellent squirted into your paint when you first start the job. This can prevent the problem entirely.

• When you're painting a room, you actually don't want to paint everything. Hardware, for example, you will probably cover with masking tape, or as we have suggested elsewhere, petroleum jelly. Some other tricks include wrapping lighting fixtures with a plastic bag and pressing wet newspaper sheets against the glass parts of windows. The wet newspaper will usually stick to the glass while you are carefully painting the frame. When you're done, just leave the newspaper alone. In a little while, it will dry out and probably fall off by itself or you can remove it easily. Or when painting around windows, hold a shirt cardboard against the glass panes to shield them as you paint the frame. Another approach is to coat the glass with soap where it abuts the frame. This should keep most of the paint from adhering to the glass and should wash off without much trouble.

• When you're done painting, try plunging your rollers or brushes into a bucket of hot vinegar. Then take them out and wash in lukewarm soapy water and rinse in clear water. This should remove the paint and keep the roller or brushes in good condition for the next time you use them.

• There are a variety of odor removers to take the smell of the paint out of the room when you're done. Obviously, you can simply open the windows and air the place out. The problem with this is you might be inviting flying bugs and critters to come track through, and maybe get stuck, in the fresh paint. There are two other alternatives commonly used: 1) cover up the smell with another smell as with a deodorizing spray; or 2) absorb the paint smell by putting a pan of cut-up onions or charcoal briquettes or baking soda in the room.

One thing most homeowners eventually ask themselves is how they can cut down the cost of keeping the homestead warm, particularly since the cost of coal, heating oil, natural gas, and electricity keeps going up.

A good way to keep you and the family warm at minimum cost is to keep cold air from invading your living space. There are at least two basic ways to do this. One, keep cold air from seeping in directly by weather-stripping around your doors and windows and, two, keep cold from radiating through your walls and attic.

When you weather strip, of course, do all the obvious places such as the doors and windows, but also do the less obvious places. If your garage is attached to your home, do the garage doors. Check all your outside walls for holes and cracks and seal those up, too. Remember that you have some holes and vents in your outside walls that are there on purpose such as the vents from your bathroom, your laundry room (clothes dryer), hot-water heater, and chimney. Even though you don't want to seal this last group of vents, you do want them closed when they are not in use. To achieve that, install hinged vent covers that open to let exhaust out and close when that process is finished.

The second way, insulating walls and attic, is tougher. It is hard to insulate your exterior walls after the home is built. It is probably best done by a professional who can blow insulation material into the wall through small holes rather than opening up the whole wall. Another development in building design and construction is the insulating and weather stripping of interior walls and doors. This sounds silly until you think about it. If you have a room in your home that is not frequently used or a room with a door to the outside that is constantly opened and closed, you may want to isolate it with an insulated wall and closed, weather-stripped door. That way you are not paying to heat a lot of unused space or, worse yet, trying to heat the whole outside world.

Your attic is probably much easier. Here, as with the walls, the insulation can be blown in by a professional or it can installed in the form of rolls of insulation that a professional installs or you do yourself. In either case, there are various kinds of insulation graded by how efficiently they insulate according to what is called an "R" rating. For homes in areas with fairly normal climates, an R-30 rating should work well enough, but in very cold areas you probably should go for a higher rating such as an R-38 or more. Your local home supply store can probably clue you in on what is the best rating for your area.

If you are going to install insulation yourself, the first thing is to carefully inspect the attic. You want to check for all electrical outlets, wires and connections, and vents that may open into the attic. Check wires and make sure they are fully insulated—it's probably best to attach them high up, clear of where the insulation will be installed. Don't cover any electrical outlets or fan vents. In fact, fan vents should be rerouted if possible so they do not exhaust into the attic.

At the same time you can be measuring the area of the attic so you'll know how much insulation to buy. Fiberglass or other types of insulation in rolls is probably the easiest form to install. Avoid asbestos because of its pollution aspects or any insulation containing asbestos.

Some rolls of fiberglass insulation have what is called a vapor-barrier covering layer and you should not see this after you install it. It should be placed facedown toward the house below, or if against a wall, toward the outside of the house. However, some experts recommend you use roll insulation without a vapor-barrier layer. (A vapor barrier is a sheet of plastic that prevents moisture from passing through.)

There are two tricks to unrolling insulation rolls. Lay them at right angles to the ceiling joists or 2 × 4's and lay them loosely. Don't jam-pack the material. Just be sure to cover the total area.

Danger! Warning! The bottom or "floor" of the attic in which you are working consists of a framework of joints or 2 × 4's to which the thin ceiling of the house below is attached. *Do not step on this thin ceiling because you will fall right through to the floor below you.* This means you have to stay on the joints or 2 × 4 framework all the time or put a wide board down across the joints and keep moving it as you work. So, start by laying the insulation on the farthest side and work backward toward the attic exit. You will be covering up the joist framework as you unroll the insulation and won't be able to see where the joist framework is, so move backward on the joist framework and repeat the process. Lay the rolls of insulation perpendicular to the ceiling joists. This covers any air gaps in the original insulating material. As we said, be very careful that you don't step through the ceiling. Once you roll out the new insulation, the ceiling joists will be covered, and you won't know where to walk. Use walk boards, but remove them as you go so that they don't mash down the new insulation. Do not stuff the insulation too tightly against the roof decking at the eaves of the attic. Leave a 2-inch air gap for proper ventilation.

The insulation can be an irritation to your skin and eyes so wear a long-sleeved shirt and long pants along with a hat and face mask. Of course, you should be wearing work gloves as always and, perhaps, knee pads. To install the insulation, you'll need a knife or large shears to cut it to size. Another handy helper is a long-handled broom, mop, or just a pole to poke the insulation into corners and under edges without your having to crawl back over it with the danger of crashing through the ceiling below.

DAMP OR WET BASEMENTS

Damp or wet basements can be uncomfortable and also invite mildew, mold, and other growing things you don't want in your basement. The basic solution is to absorb the moisture in the basement air with something that you replace regularly. For example, make a mixture of several pounds of kitty litter and baking soda at a 2-to-1 ratio and either set it out in bowls, pans, or trays or sprinkle it on the floor. Empty, sweep, or vacuum and replace every week. Another absorbent is salt. Set out pans or trays of salt to soak up the moisture. One extra plus in using salt is you don't have to throw it away after. Dry it out in the sun and use it over and over again.

WATER IN THE BASEMENT

In *The Rime of the Ancient Mariner,* Samuel Taylor Coleridge writes, "Water, water, every where, Nor any drop to drink." It may be great literature, but it's a pain in the basement when that lower space gets wet and flooded.

The standard answer to finding water in your basement, after first pumping or bailing it out and waiting until everything is dry again, is to waterproof the place. You can get waterproofing sealant or coating at any home-improvement or hardware store in your area, but it won't do much good if you don't put it on correctly.

The first step is to carefully inspect the walls of your basement (and, windows, too, if you have them). They are probably concrete or stone, and you want to make sure they are solid with no cracks or breaks. A good way to inspect these walls is to scrub them with a dry, stiff bristle brush. This will dislodge loose mortar and chips to reveal breaks. Seal these up with a good-quality quick-drying cement.

When all the walls are inspected and sealed tight, apply a good coat of waterproofing sealer.

However, before you apply the sealer, you should understand at least two important things about such a project. First, be sure to apply the coat according to the instructions on the can. If you brush it on too thin, it won't keep water out. Brush it on in the proportions that the instructions call for, namely, so much sealant per square foot. Also, don't just "brush" it on. Dab it into all the nooks, cracks, and crannies of the wall so little drops of outside water cannot sneak through.

Second, make sure you know what you are applying. There are actually two kinds of coatings for concrete and masonry walls. One is called a "water-repellent" coating and the other is a "waterproof" coating. Just to make things hard on all of us do-it-ourselfers, some manufacturers use these names interchangeably. Here is the difference: Water repellent is designed for use outside on walls exposed to the weather where you want to temporarily repel (hence the name *repellent*) water. Typically, you might use this on the outside of a concrete foundation wall that extends above the soil line and is exposed to the weather. Waterproofing, in contrast, is for keeping water under pressure from coming through the wall. It is for preventing more than temporary water (such as rain) from seeping through the wall. This water is usually under pressure and might be from your water table or long-standing water of some kind or a stream of water flowing against the house or something of that nature. It is a longer lasting and often a bigger problem so your answer is probably to apply a good coat of waterproofing.

BASEMENT DANGER

We all remember those scary spook movies and plays about terrible things lurking in the basement. There was always a ghost or goblin or body buried in the basement. Well, that concern may be, to coin a phrase, alive even today if your basement gets flooded.

Obviously, a flooded basement is a giant annoyance for many reasons including that many things you have stored in the basement might get ruined. To avoid this kind of problem, don't store important files or expensive belongings in the basement. Or if you must store them in the basement, be sure they are up and out of reach, on tables or shelves. More important, however, a flooded basement can be a serious danger to you and your family because of that lethal combination of electricity and water. Remember, that water carries electrical currents and, just as you don't want electric appliances in the bathroom where they can fall into the tub and kill someone, you must avoid flooded basements where there might be contact with electricity.

The bad part is that many homes have their fuse box or circuit breaker box in the basement. So, you have to go down in the flooded basement and stand in the water to turn off the electric power—right? Wrong.

Before you go into the flooded basement, turn off the electric power!

If the fuse box or circuit breaker is in the flooded basement, you have several choices. One, call the electric power company and have them turn off the power to your house until you can bail or pump the water out of the basement. This seems like the most extreme course of action but it might save your life, which suddenly doesn't make it seem so extreme, does it? Two, ignore the water in the basement, lock the doors, and move out temporarily until the water dries up—another extreme solution and probably not too practical, particularly if you don't know why your basement is flooded. If, for example, it is from a broken water pipe, the water might keep rising and rising until it is coming into the upper floors and then you have a really serious problem, not only because of the water but also the wild electric current it brings with it. The power company is sounding better all the time, isn't it?

Finally, there are some home repair and improvement guides that recommend the macho approach. Don't let water and electricity scare you. Are you a man or a mouse? Put on rubber boots and rubber gloves and march down into that old basement armed with a long stick. When you get near the fuse box or the circuit breaker box, use the long stick to flip the master control level and turn off the power. This, of course, will leave you standing in the dark in the water. No, we recommend you bring in the experts. Call the power company and get it to turn off the electricity to your house and then call a plumber who has the equipment and experience to pump all the darn water out of the house and, if it is due to a broken pipe, to fix it.

PERSONAL CARE

Hints on all aspects of caring for your family and yourself

Our focus has been on caring for your home and your possessions. But you and your family need attention too. The following tips will help you look after your loved ones and yourself.

MEDICINE CABINET

OVER-THE-COUNTER MEDICINES

- 325 mg chewable aspirin tablets (Some doctors recommend one of these every other day to prevent heart attack. In the case of a heart attack, call for help and take two aspirin immediately.)
- A 1 percent hydrocortisone cream for rashes.
- Antibacterial salve to put on cuts, scrapes, and wounds
- Antacid for heartburn
- Ibuprofen or acetaminophen to reduce fevers and relieve pain
- Some form of antihistamine to treat allergies
- A nasal decongestant

> **Important:** Many of us try to keep our kitchen cabinet well stocked and, while that's nice, the most important cabinet to keep properly stocked is our medicine cabinet. That's the first place you turn to get help in case of an accident or trouble. Here is our suggested list of basics for every home medicine cabinet, based on information from one of the leading medical schools in the country.

- Sunscreen to wear when outside, with a minimum safety rating of 15
- A saline spray for the noses and eyes
- A dextramethorpham-based cough medicine

For internal problems:

- An oral rehydration solution (Take for diarrhea or vomiting.)
- Ipecac for inducing vomiting if someone accidentally swallows something poisonous. However, contact a doctor immediately in case of poisoning and read the following:

    IMPORTANT: Even though Syrup of Ipecac can be purchased over the counter, never give to anyone *except* under instructions from a doctor or your local poison prevention center.

    Give it to induce vomiting (it takes about 20 minutes to work) only when a doctor or poison prevention center directs. Don't give salt water or stick fingers down the throat to induce vomiting.

    Syrup of Ipecac must NOT be given to a person who has swallowed a caustic acid or alkaline such as lye, drain cleaner, or drain-unclogging product. These burn the victim's throat going down and they burn it coming up. Also, don't use Ipecac if the victim has swallowed gasoline, turpentine, or lighter fluid.

    Do not give Ipecac to victims who seem to be suddenly falling asleep, going unconscious, or having a seizure of some kind. You should be able to tell by the time you reach poison control or a doctor. These victims might choke to death if they were forced to vomit.

EQUIPMENT

Tweezers
Scissors
Gauze and adhesive bandages
Thermometer

PRESCRIPTION MEDICINES

Keep in sealed containers.

Store in a cool, dry location. This MAY NOT be the medicine cabinet. Often exposure to heat, air, and light can adversely affect prescription medicines.

Discard when you are done using. Preferably flush down the toilet so they don't accidentally fall into the hands of children or the paws of pets.

When you first get the prescription, tape over the label with clear tape to preserve the readability of the instructions.

If you can't read the small print, have someone make a label with large printed letters and tape that onto the bottle.

BEE WARY

One of the most painful insect attacks is the bee sting and many people don't know the basics of avoiding it. In fact, bee stings can be fatal to a few people, so it is always best to avoid bee stings if possible or to act quickly if stung.

One thing that may attract the sting of bees is wearing bright, flowery clothing. Another tip is to avoid going outside where insects may be right after a rain. When the rain has washed pollen off the flowers, there is less of it for searching bees, wasps, and other pollen-loving insects to eat. This means the insects out looking for pollen become more aggressive and are likely to sting anybody who thwarts them. You don't want to get in the way of a pushy bee!

The most important thing to know about a bee sting is that the stinger remains in your skin and continues to pump venom into you. This could go on for a quarter of an hour or more. So you want to locate the stinger and get it out immediately!

Examine the area where you were stung. It should be a painful, raised reddish area on your body. The stinger is that tiny, dark splinterlike thing sticking in the middle. Using your fingernails like tweezers, grab hold of the stinger and pull it straight out. Resist the temptation to run off looking for some tweezers in the house, the car, or even on your Swiss Army knife. Get that stinger out and get it out quickly with your fingernails. Every second you delay, more poison is going into your body.

Next, use soap and water on the string or, if you have some handy, alcohol. Some recommend an ice pack to reduce the swelling and smearing toothpaste (yes, ordinary toothpaste) or a paste of baking soda and water.

Be alert for headaches, cramps, or breathing problems. If these occur, get to a doctor as soon as possible because they are signs you may be more allergic to bee venom than you knew.

PERSONAL HYGIENE TIPS

Most of us have some kind of habit in which we indulge without thinking about it and which might not be good for our health. In fact, most of us probably have some such habit or belief for much of our lives. Now some medical researchers are pointing out these habits may not only be annoying to other people, or silly, but unhealthy as well.

For example, a great many people, particularly woman, cross their legs a lot when they sit down. Many women do this because it is what their mothers taught them was ladylike. So you can imagine that recent medical studies of what happens from crossing your legs a lot are not popular. According to the researchers, continual leg crossing with one knee lapping over the other knee tends to squeeze the leg veins and cut down on the free flow of blood. At the very least, this can stretch and damage the leg veins. At the worse, it may cause varicose veins. Recommended solution, crossing legs at the ankle.

Even adults can have the habit of biting his or her nails. One medical researcher says this can open the area around the nails to infection and, ultimately, change the shape of the nails permanently. It is recommended that nail biters substitute some other tension-relieving habit in place of nail gnawing. Maybe get a set of worry beads or buy a squeeze ball at a sporting goods store to let out the pressure and to build up your wrist muscles at the same time.

Another habit that can go wrong is spitting on your contact lens so you can polish them. Sounds like a reasonable idea except your saliva is loaded with bacteria. It may not be harmful to your mouth, but it can cause trouble for your eyes and even an infection. A Canadian contact lens expert, Robin Searle, warns that a worst-case scenario would be transferring cold-sore bacteria from your mouth to your eye where it could develop into an ulcer on your cornea with serious consequences. It's recommended that you carry contact lens solution with you in a small bottle or, in the case of hard lenses, just use water or put them in dry and let your tears lubricate them.

Ear picking is another common habit with some people where they are always sticking something in their ear, supposedly, to clean out earwax. Ear specialist Dr. Andrea Garland says that, instead of removing wax, this frequently pushes it farther into the ear canal. If something is stuck into the ear too vigorously, there is a danger of punching a hole in the sensitive eardrum. Dr. Garland suggests a drop of olive oil once a week in each ear.

This should help bring the earwax to the surface of the ear where you can wipe it out with a tissue or damp cloth.

Bad, smelly breath that some people have is one of the favorite subjects of TV commercial writers. But in spite of their extravagant claims for this solution or that mouthwash, most people are largely uninformed about the sources of bad breath, or as one TV commercial christened it, "Halitosis."

Bad breath simply is the smell of bacteria in our mouths working to process some bits of lunch or dinner still in there. It might also be due to an abscess or decaying tooth that is a problem to be solved by your dentist, not your TV set.

But for the ordinary bacteria-at-work bad breath, nothing will drive it away better than regular tooth brushing and flossing. Also, here is a pointer you've never heard on TV: Don't just brush you teeth. Brush your tongue, too! Yes, brush or scrape your tongue as thoroughly as you can.

Finally, remember that the natural saliva in your mouth will carry those bacteria away if you take drinks of water. In addition, the experts say that munching on some fresh fruit will handle your bad breath problem even better than that expensive mouthwash.

It's amazing but true: your feet have 250,000 sweat glands, all of which attract bacteria that have a smelly way of announcing their presence even in those cozy, dark shoes. Here are some tips to avoiding or getting rid of foot smells. First, wear dry socks that "breathe." That is, they are porous enough for air to move through them. Then, wear clean, dry socks every day and wash your feet thoroughly with soap and water. Dry them carefully including between the toes. Ideally, you should have more than one pair of shoes and trade off, wearing a different pair each day. Of course, don't wear wet shoes. Finally, if the foot odor hangs on, try soaking your bare feet in a strong immersion of tea every few days.

There is an interesting—some say "alarming"—trend in medicine these days. Namely, while we are making enormous progress against major diseases of the past, the incidence of childhood sickness is rising. Such maladies as children's allergies and immune-connected skin illnesses are becoming more frequent. The surprising reason given by many medical experts? Too much cleanliness. Amazing.

SURPRISING NEWS ABOUT PERSONAL CLEANLINESS FOR KIDS

The experts are saying that overzealous, clean-crazy parents are keeping our kids too clean! The constant washing and bathing is killing off the good bacteria in children's bodies that help build up their immune systems. For example, some parents rush to clean up their drooling baby, but a baby's drool is rich in natural antibodies that will protect the child from germs that may be on his or her toys or on playground equipment.

Studies show that children's allergies, eczema, and diabetes are more frequent than in previous times. Graham Rook, immunologist at University College in London, reports that studies of 14,000 English school children revealed that those who washed their hands and faces the most were most likely to contract allergies.

So what kind of kid cleaning regime do the experts now recommend? For one thing, they suggest not bathing the child every day. Young children and infants probably should be bathed daily—not more than ten minutes at a time—but as they grow older every other or every third day is satisfactory, say the experts. (It may be hard to convince a lot of mothers of this, but it's what the doctors say.)

Don't clean up every bit of slobber, says Dr. Suzanne Dixon of the University of California at San Diego. A little saliva, which is loaded with natural antibodies anyhow, is all right. Substitute a warm, moistened washcloth for the commercially sold diaper-wipe products that often contain perfumes and other chemicals to make them appealing to the mother. Since these wipes are frequently used in very sensitive areas of the baby's body, the perfumes and impregnated chemicals may irritate the baby's skin unnecessarily. The same thing is sometimes true of bubble bath in that it is sold as a "fun" product to make baby and mother think they're having a good time in the tub. In fact, the chemicals in the bubble bath may irritate the baby's genitals and urinary tracts.

The ritual of the daily shampoo is also not recommended for all young children. Ironically, many parents shampoo the baby's head as a way of getting rid of dandruff or what is sometimes call "cradle cap." Dr. Anthony J. Mancini, assistant professor of pediatrics and dermatology at Northwestern University Medical School in Chicago, is of the view that shampooing actually makes baby dandruff worse! He recommends rubbing mineral oil into the scalp and, then, brushing out the dandruff with a small hairbrush or old toothbrush.

So, there are some surprising new medical views on keeping baby safe and clean. Generally, the view seems to be that the three things most important to keep clean on young children are the mouth, hands, and bottom. Their other parts may benefit from some benign neglect. In a way, it reminds me of a story my grandmother used to tell about raising children. She claimed that when the first child swallowed a dime, they rushed him to the hospital for emergency care and to have his stomach pumped out. When the third one swallowed a dime, Grandma said, "That comes out of your allowance!"

PREVENTING FALLS

One of the biggest dangers for seniors in their daily life is falling. The U.S. Center for Disease Control reports that one out of every three seniors falls down and has a serious injury. Because of medication or heart conditions or hip troubles, among other things, most seniors are not as surefooted as they once were. What makes this worse is that seniors' bones are more likely to be brittle, so a fall that would be a minor annoyance to a younger person might mean a serious injury for a senior, often requiring expensive hospitalization and possibly leading to death. *Senior Health Newsletter* says 300,000 seniors fall and fracture a hip every year and one-third of these seniors die within a year from this accident.

Of course, other younger members of the household fall down, too, which makes it even more important to check your home for uneven floors, poor lighting, throw rugs, unstable furniture, and toys on the floor.

Here is what you can do to prevent falls in your home:

- Have a light by everybody's bed that they can turn on before getting up during the night. If there is no lamp, have a flashlight by the bed.
- Mark and illuminate rooms and hallways with night-lights. Have a night-light in the bathroom and by every exit door. By exit halls and doors, plug in the kind of battery night-light that automatically turns on when the household electricity goes off. These battery-operated lights are usually good for 15 minutes and can prevent serious injury or even save a life.
- Install strong grab bars and railings in crucial areas such as stairs and the bathroom.
- Have suction-cup rubber bath mats in every shower and bathtub. In some cases, you may want to put a small plastic stool or chair in the shower.
- Secure all area rugs, throw rugs, and doormats so they won't slide. Tape them down or use double-sided tape to hold them. You can now also get strips of Velcro at the office-supply store to hold them in place.
- Keep the floor clear of toys and clutter as well as electrical and telephone cords. For long cords, shorten them by doubling them together in the middle and holding them tight with tape or rubber bands.
- Make sure no floor covering such as carpets or tiles are curling up. Glue or tape all floor coverings down flush and tight.
- Get rid of wobbly stepladders and store frequently used things in lower cabinets.

- Light or paint the edges of stairs so they can be clearly seen.
- Outside, keep steps and walkways free of slippery material such as water, ice, snow, wet leaves, papers, and so on.
- Check the medicine used by everyone in the house. Some medicines induce dizziness as a side effect. Be especially careful walking with seniors who take such medicine.

THE HERBAL MEDICINE CABINET

One of the many chic trends these days is alternative medicine, alternative religion, and alternative drugs for illness. This last is called "Naturopathic Medicine" by some and is based on using natural herbs and roots to cure whatever ails you. The practitioners and believers rely on practices going back hundreds of years to other civilizations. It is similar to going back to grandmother's day and the pioneers for some of the things that worked for them and still work today. Many traditional Western doctors are adopting some of these approaches, too. Here are some of the more popular ones.

Garlic is a mainstay of Mediterranean cooking and used in soups, sauces, and other foods to help the immune system and to ward off a cold. Some jokesters say the reason eating garlic keeps you from getting a cold is that no one will come near to kiss you and, therefore, cold germs are not transmitted. Interestingly, some people use garlic plantings in the garden as a way to ward off various insects.

Sage, besides being part of a Simon and Garfunkel hit song, is related to mint and is popular in various food dishes. Some older women swear by it when mixed with peppermint in a tea for soothing hot flashes that come with menopause (which is something they swear at). Such a tea is also supposed to be good for the heart and liver and is thought to be a good antioxidant in the diet.

Echinacea is something we have used with success and can say it is easier to use than it is to pronounce. Basically, it is used to fight off infections such as the onset of a cold. As with many of these remedies, it can be used as a tea or you can purchase tablets at the drugstore, which is how we use it.

Rosemary is also in a Simon and Garfunkel song but is better known for soothing jangled nerves and gets rid of gas problems.

Mint makes a lovely tea and it is also supposed to help your digestion. We are told it also gets rid of gas problems. So it might be a good way to end a meal.

Chamomile has been a favorite of mothers and grandmothers for centuries and, like mint, is used to make a hot tea that is soothing to the stomach and to jittery nerves.

Lavender is pleasing for both its taste and its aroma. It is edible and is used in some baking recipes as well as in the form of a tea to soothe your insides. Lavender is also recommended for its soothing fragrance, in a potpourri or in a soaking, relaxing bath. Some people even put a lavender potpourri near themselves at night as a cure for insomnia.

Oregano is a widely used cooking herb, particularly in Mediterranean dishes, and is also suggested as a gargle (in solution, obviously) for treating a sore throat.

Calendula is, unlike some of these, used for external healing to be applied to cuts, burns, rashes, bruises, and scrapes.

A lesser-known herb is *feverfew,* which you can chew or use to make a tea. Either way, it is said to relieve migraines.

St. John's Wort is highly thought of in Europe and among some people in the United States as a relaxant and help in soothing hypertension.

Finally, *blueberry* is supposed to make veins and arteries stronger and to aid in the treatment of varicose veins, hemorrhoids, and urinary problems.

COOLING OFF

Sliced veggies have other uses, as my grandmother taught me growing up in Seattle. When you're really hot on a scorching day and there are no cool spots around, slice the end of a cucumber off and rub your head and neck with it. Why do you think they talk about being "cool as a cucumber"?

If you are stung by a bee or other insect, you want to get the stinger and the poison out as quickly as possible. That's another job a sliced veggie can do. Applying the cut side of a sliced potato, onion, or cucumber to the sting will often draw out the stinger and the poison. You may have to apply a freshly sliced veggie surface several times to pull out all of the poison.

RELIEVE A COUGH

Mix 1/2 cup apple cider vinegar, 1/2 cup water, 1/2 teaspoon cayenne pepper, and 4 teaspoons honey. Take 1 tablespoon when the cough acts up. Take another tablespoon at bedtime.

RELIEVE A COLD

Mix one-quarter cup apple cider vinegar with one-quarter cup honey. Take one tablespoon six to eight times daily.

CONDITION DRY HAIR

Shampoo then rinse hair with a mixture of one cup apple cider vinegar and two cups water. Vinegar adds highlights to brunette hair, restores the acid mantel, and removes soap film and sebum oil.

CURE THE HICCUPS

Mix one teaspoon apple cider vinegar in one cup of warm water and drink.

CLEANING DENTURES

Soak dentures overnight in white vinegar, then brush away tartar with a toothbrush.

PREVENT YEAST INFECTIONS

Douche with one tablespoon white vinegar to one-quart warm water to adjust the pH balance in the vagina.

RELIEVE ITCHING

Use a cotton ball to dab mosquito and other bug bites with vinegar straight from the bottle.

RELIEVE A SORE THROAT

Put two teaspoons of vinegar in your humidifier.

Or stir 1/2 teaspoon salt and 1/2 teaspoon baking soda in an 8-ounce glass of warm water for use as a gargle.

SOOTHE SUNBURN PAIN

Apply undiluted vinegar to the burn.

REMOVE CORNS

Make a poultice of one crumbled piece of bread soaked in 1/4 cup vinegar. Let poultice sit for half an hour, then apply to the corn and tape in place overnight. If corn does not peel off by morning, reapply the poultice for several consecutive nights.

CURE AN UPSET STOMACH

Drink two teaspoons apple cider vinegar in one cup water to soothe an upset stomach.

RELIEVE ARTHRITIS

Before each meal, drink a glass of water containing two teaspoons apple cider vinegar. Give this folk remedy at least three weeks to start working.

CLEANING TEETH

Mix one part salt to two parts baking soda after pulverizing the salt in a blender or rolling it on at kitchen board with a tumbler before mixing. It whitens teeth, helps remove plaque, and is healthy for the gums.

BATHING EYES

Mix 1/2 teaspoon salt in a pint of water and use the solution to bath tired eyes.

TREATING POISON IVY

Soaking the exposed body part in hot saltwater helps hasten the end to poison ivy irritation.

STRENGTHEN YOUR GRIP

Squeeze a tennis ball repeatedly in each hand as a regular exercise.

CARING OF KIDS AND SENIORS WITH USED TENNIS BALLS

To childproof the sharp corners of furniture, cut tennis balls in half or quarters and use Scotch Packaging Tape to tape the sections over sharp corners of coffeetables, end tables, cabinets, dining room tables, and other pieces of furniture that might be dangerous to a small child.

BABY BOTTLE ID

When you are out with your baby, you probably will have a bottle or two handy. To make sure that you don't bring home someone else's bottle from the park, it's good to have identification on them. You can use stick-on labels, but these come off when you wash the bottle or it gets wet. A better way is to slightly rough up a spot on the plastic bottle with an emery board or sandpaper and write the baby's name on it with a marking pen. You may want to seal it with clear nail polish so it won't wash off later.

SAFETY TIPS FOR CHILDREN

The most important thing to realize about your kid's room is that it is more important to them than your room is to you! For you, the entire house is your domain. For your kids, their room is their domain. It is their sanctuary from the world and, yes, from you and the rest of the family. They spend much more time in their room playing, studying, relaxing, thinking, wondering, and sleeping than you do in yours.

Safety is probably the most important single factor in the design and furnishing of your kid's room. Things can happen to small people in that room that you can't imagine. For example, small, crib-bound children whose cribs are too close to the drapes or window blinds have gotten their necks tangled in drapery or blind cords and strangled—or pushed their heads between the bars of the crib and choked to death. Older, more active children in upper-floor rooms playing and bouncing around on beds have propelled themselves to their death out the window. When the glass window is open, all that keeps a kid inside is a flimsy screen held in place by even flimsier latches.

Pick furniture that does not have sharp edges or corners. Make sure all drawers have automatic stops that keep drawers from falling out. If they don't, you can make one. Tilt the drawer out and screw a wood screw part way into the top of the back so it extends up beyond the top of the drawer opening. Tilt the drawer back into place and that extended screw should prevent little kiddy hands from pulling the drawer too far out. Make sure all the surfaces are smooth and sturdy for kids who climb on tables and desktops and that everything is painted or finished with nontoxic lacquers or enamels. Check that there are no places for fingers and other body parts to get pinched or wedged.

The room should reflect your child's interests. Obviously, a bed and a dresser are basic furnishings. A comfortable reading chair and lamp is a good idea if space allows. If he does homework, draws, or writes, the room should have a good work table or desk and chair, even a big table for art or science projects. An older student will need a computer stand. Extra cabinets or shelves will hold books, toys, and mementos. He or she may want a bunk bed for sleepovers.

Many manufacturers are making children's furniture modules that can be expanded and adjusted as the child grows. This is something that may be helpful, but make sure what you choose is all basically sound and sturdy construction, built to last and to prevent injuries. It is a good idea to have your child participate in making the room layout and furnishing it even if there is a danger of his initially wanting items that are too expensive or impractical. Even so, it helps create a good mood and atmosphere if the child is part of the process.

CHILDREN'S LIGHTS

Sometimes children awaken in the night and are frightened of the dark. Initially, you may want to get one of those battery-operated stick-on lights that is turned on by simply pushing the top of the light. You can mount that on your child's bed so he can turn it on by himself anytime he is frightened. As he grows older and more competent, you may leave a flashlight handy in his or her room, in case of a major emergency at night when he or she may need to find the way out of the house.

FALLING OUT OF BED

Sometimes as kids get older and graduate from a crib to a child's bed, they miss the safety of the crib sides and may accidentally fall out of bed. You can start by putting pillows along the top of the mattress to block the child rolling out. Or, if that doesn't work you may want to put his or her old crib mattress or a set of pillows on the floor by the bed to ease the shock of falling.

PRESERVING FUTURE MEMORIES

Ask your own mother or grandmother, and we'll bet they will agree this is true. The drawings, writings, and art work that kids do when they are young become heirlooms the parents want to preserve for enjoyment in the years to come. But how do you keep and preserve them? One suggestion is to go to an art supplies store and buy a large artist's folder or envelope and a can of clear acrylic spray. Lightly coat the material with the clear spray, which will preserve it for future years, then file it in the folder or envelope. You may want to note the date and place on the pack. Keep the folder or envelope in a safe storage place and add to it from time to time. It is a way of enjoying lovely memories for years to come.

DOWNSIZING THE WORLD

It is easier to teach kids to be neat if you put up hooks and hanger rods that are their size and easy for them to reach like on the inside of their closet doors and the ends of their beds.

SHOES

When you're teaching your child how to put on shoes, the first lesson he or she has to learn is right from left. One way of helping is to put a small mark on one of the shoes. It could be a dot with a marker pen on the back of the heel or a paste-on star or decal. You child will quickly learn, for example, that the marked shoe is the right one and it will soon be easier to put them both on.

PRECOCIOUS WANDERERS

Some children can be precocious wanderers or even sleep walkers who leave their room when they are not supposed to in order to go places they aren't supposed to go. Here are some of the ways to thwart that, depending on the age and ingenuity of the child. You could tie a bell to the door so it would ring when opened or leave a stack of empty cans against the outside of the door that will crash if the door is opened. Some people suggest various ways of making it impossible for the child to open the door from the inside. This can be frightening for a child because it imprisons him or her in the room and, in case of a fire or accident or panic attack, could hurt the child both physically and emotionally.

IMPORTANT THINGS TO LEARN

Of course, it is important for your child to learn his or her full name and phone number as early as possible. It is also important for the child to learn the name and phone number of a family friend or relative not living with you. If the child gets lost and knows his name and phone number, it isn't much good if nobody is home or if you are all out looking for the child. An alterative emergency contact person and number are important.

SAFETY TIPS FOR SENIORS IN YOUR FAMILY

All of us go through life changes, and we all have to adjust. We all were or will be babies, teens, middle-aged, and seniors at some point. We also often have to care for other people of a different generation with different living problems. Here are some tips about senior life—for those who are seniors—and for those who have to help someone who is.

MEDICINE

Medicine is common for most seniors and, also common, is forgetting what medicine has to be taken when. Devise some system that works for you to divide up medicines in clearly marked containers according to when the particular medicine is to be taken. For example, birth control pills often come in a reminder container showing what to take and when, so if you forget whether you've taken the medication or not, you can check the container to see. Here are some examples of the sort of systems I'm talking about. Take an empty egg box and mark each egg hole with the day of the week. Put a day's supply of pills in each hole. Some people will also put a strip of transparent adhesive tape over the holes to keep the medicine from getting jumbled up in case the egg box is dropped. Peel back or clip open one egg hole each day to get the needed medicine. Or get a bunch of small medicine vials from the druggist, label each one with a day of the week, and divide up a week's medicine. Put them all together in a box or a drawer. Because labels on medicine vials can get smeared or blurred from handling, cover them with a piece of transparent tape.

HOME EMERGENCIES

When a kid or senior is at home during an emergency (earthquake, fire, tornado, et cetera), he or she may need extra care. We have said this before and we're going to say it again—post information about children and older residents in the home where emergency people can quickly find it. Label it in big letters something like "PEOPLE IN THIS HOUSE" or "FIRE AND POLICE INFORMATION." Then clearly list the names, ages, and locations of each person such as "Father, Ralph Jones, 72, back bedroom on the left."

Also list any medicine the person needs and any disabling condition or illness. In addition, list names and phone numbers of other family members or friends *not* living in this house so they can be called. We suggest this information be on an easy-to-read, nonwhite sheet so it stands out. Red is probably not good since it is often hard to read. Perhaps yellow would be workable. Slip it into a plastic sleeve so it doesn't fade or get smeared and hard to read, then tape it up where it can be found by a fireman or policeman coming into the house under emergency conditions. Where is that? You may want to post duplicates in various places. One should definitely go on the refrigerator door. You may want to post one on both the front and back doors, *but not* outside where every snoop can see it or where it can be stolen or defaced. We suggest posting a copy on the inside of both front and back doors. Then on the outside of those doors simply post a notice saying something like "EMERGENCY INFORMATION ON OTHER SIDE OF THIS DOOR."

Another place you want to have emergency information is on your senior citizen him or herself. They should have an identification bracelet or plastic card with emergency information about address, phone, emergency contacts, medical information, and medicine.

HELPING SENIORS READ

Many seniors have trouble reading small print. A good idea is to print important phone numbers of friends, family, doctors, and other services on a card in large letters and post the card or duplicates of it by every telephone.

MAKE A WALKER GLIDE MORE EASILY

Cut a hole in two tennis balls and fit them on the back feet of the walker.

SENIOR'S EMERGENCY KIT

You should create an emergency kit for each senior in your home. It should be small enough to grasp easily and kept by the bedside or attached to the wheelchair or both. Such a kit can save that senior's life. It should contain a police whistle for summoning help and for letting emergency personnel know where the senior is in the house in case of fire or earthquake or other catastrophe. It should also have a small flashlight, small battery-operated radio, and bottle of water. Both inside and outside of this little kit should be the senior's name, address, and family names and phone numbers.

GETTING A GRIP FOR SENIORS

Often seniors have trouble gripping things tight enough to use them. You can fix that by creating more traction where seniors hold on to the objects they use most. For example, wrap rubber bands around handles, put a shower curtain ring or large paper clip on anything that has to be pulled, and use double-sided Velcro (available at many stationery stores) on other things. You might also consider removing shoelaces from senior's shoes and replacing them with Velcro strips to make it easier to get shoes on and off.

PURSE GUARD FOR SENIORS

If your senior is a lady who carries purses with a shoulder strap, make it easy for her not to lose it or to have it snatched by a robber. Do this by attaching it to some other article of clothing such as her skirt, top, jacket or slacks. Either sew a button onto the purse strap that can be buttoned into a button hole in her top or sew loop or shower curtain ring onto her skirt or slacks and thread the purse strap through that.

OUCH-LESS BANDAGE REMOVAL

Sometimes taking off an adhesive bandage hurts almost as much as the original injury. One way to ease the *ouch!* is to apply some oil—baby, vegetable, or cooking—on to the adhesive parts of the bandage. Let that soak in for 10 or 15 minutes, and the bandage should pull off easily.

CHRISTMAS STAMPS

If you have ever faced a pile of Christmas cards that had to have postage stamps and perhaps also seals affixed, you know you're in for glue tongue. Of course, you could be lucky enough to have some self-adhesive stamps. But if you are faced with a lot of stamps to be licked, try using a sliced potato. It is usually moist enough to wet the stamp glue and you can save your tongue from curling up.

PIONEER FIRST AID

There are so many wonder medicines and miracle cures on the market today that it is unbelievable. Still, these medical blessings all have one great shortcoming: They aren't where you are when you need them. They are at the drugstore and sometimes the drugstore is too far or it's closed. So what are some of the things you normally just have around the house that can help in time of discomfort and pain? This is the same dilemma our pioneer forefathers and foremothers faced. What do we have around the wagon or the log cabin that can help right now?

Earlier we noted that Grandma Karn would hold a piece of bread in her mouth to ward off the tear-producing mist of cut onions. Well, she also might use bread for an earache as funny as that sounds. You can often ease the pain of an earache with some locally applied heat, and one way of doing that is to warm up some bread and hold that against you painful ear. Another painful ache in the head is a toothache and grandma would go into the kitchen spices to help that by getting a clove and holding it against the spot on your tooth that ached or where the nerve was exposed.

GRANDMA KARN'S HEADACHE REMEDY

Got a throbbing headache that's driving you crazy? Slice a lime and rub on your forehead. She claims it stops the pain right away. We don't know why, but she's right.

MOTION SICKNESS REMEDY

If you get motion sickness on airplanes, whale-watching boat trips, roller-coaster rides in theme parks, you may want to trying an old pioneer preventative: ginger. Take a couple of ginger capsules an hour ahead of time and take two more every two hours after that. It is a herbal method that works for many people.

SPLINTER REMOVAL

Taping over a splinter with some adhesive tape and then pulling the tape off will sometimes easily remove the splinter.

ODDS AT THE END

A variety of hints and tidbits to make your life better
with some nifty ideas that just defy categorization

UNWANTED CALLERS

Practically all of us have had unwanted telephone callers at times, be they telemarketers calling at dinnertime to sell you swamp land in Florida or ex-boy friends who haven't learned to accept "no" for an answer. A dramatic and effective way of rid yourself of them is to have an ordinary police whistle by the phone. Warn them to hang up immediately—it's the courteous thing to do—but if they don't, one blast on the whistle into the phone will terminate the call instantly.

ODOR CHASERS

Chase odors out of the room by leaving an open can or jar of vanilla beans. This, of course, assumes you like the smell of vanilla. Kitchen odors can be chased by baking fragrant citrus-fruit peels (orange, lemon, lime) in the oven with the oven door open. Chase smells from lunch boxes, plastic containers, and other enclosed food containers by soaking a slice of bread in white vinegar and leaving it in the container for a day or two.

Add a lovely aroma to your bathroom or other places in the houses by daubing a tiny bit of your favorite cologne on a light bulb. When you turn the bulb on, the heat will radiate the aroma and give the area an appealing but subtle scent.

RICHARD'S ELECTRICAL TIPS

The electrical system in your home is much like the water system in many ways. We think and talk of the electrical power in some of the same language and context as we do with water, starting with calling the electricity "flow" and "current," which goes through wires instead of pipes. One of these wires carries the electric power and is often called the "hot" wire that, just as with your water system, lets electricity flow into your home, and into your lightbulbs and appliances. This "in" wire is traditionally black. Balancing that is the wire that allows the electricity to flow out of your appliances, lights, and house. This "out" wire is traditionally white and usually called the "neutral" wire, which doesn't make particular sense, but don't worry about that—just accept it. In addition, starting after World War II and having nothing to do with that war, electricians began using a third wire for use in emergencies to carry excess power out of your system and into the earth on which we spin around in space. This wire is called "the ground" and it is often green or just bare.

Just as with water into your home, the flow of electricity has emergency cut-offs, which you can use when you need them. For example, elsewhere in this book, we alerted you to the need to shut down all utilities coming into your home in case of emergencies such as floods, tornadoes, earthquakes, explosions, and so on. The two emergency shut-offs you should attend to immediately are water and electricity. The third is gas, if your home is serviced by gas.

However, the flow of electricity has a feature that the flow of water and gas do not normally have. That is an automatic shut-off. This is good because it can prevent electrical shocks and fires. Here is how the automatic electrical shut-off works: All electricity coming into your home passes through a choke point or constriction spot. One of two systems control this electrical flow-restriction point. In older homes, the electricity flows through a piece of soft metal that will only accept a certain level of power. When the power is greater than that level, the metal melts or "fuses," breaking the electrical circuit and stopping any more power from coming in. As the name implies, this soft metal is housed in screw plugs cleverly called "fuses." When you want to restore power, you go to the fuse box (usually in the basement or garage or some place like that out of the weather). There, you unscrew the "blown" fuses with fresh fuses which, if you are organized, you have a supply of sitting at the fuse box.

In more modern homes, the fuse box has been replaced by a group of switches for different electrical circuits in your home. When there is a surge of unwanted power above a certain level, the switches automatically turn off until you come and flick them back on. This is called a circuit-breaker panel. In addition to the switches for individual circuits, it also has a big master switch that turns everything off.

Whichever system you have, a fuse box or a circuit-breaker panel, it is very important that you trace which fuse or circuit breaker feeds electricity to what part of your home. You should have labels by each fuse and each circuit-breaker switch identifying it. One way to do this is turn on everything in the house and then unscrew a fuse or flip a circuit switch to off and go see what was turned off. Then, paste a label there or mark the panel with a marker pen.

FINDING YOUR WAY IN THE DARK

One of the biggest problems when the power goes out is that the power is out. If you are going to grope your way to the fuse box or circuit-breaker panel, you may have to do it in the dark, and take the chance of falling down and hurting yourself. There is a solution to this problem of no lights. At the hardware or home-improvement store you can buy a battery-powered light that goes on when the power goes off! It plugs into ordinary sockets and its battery is charging all the while. When the power goes off, the little socket light comes on. We recommend that you have a set of such emergency lights that illuminate where you live from your bedroom to the exit and, also, to the fuse box or circuit-breaker panel. At the fuse box or circuit-breaker panel, you should have a regular flashlight so you can see what went wrong and where.

QUICK HOW-TOS

PREVENT DECK CHAIRS SLIPPING
Slit four tennis balls and fit them on the feet of the deck chair.

GET RID OF CIGARETTE SMOKE
Place a small bowl of white vinegar in the room.

DEODORIZE A STALE LUNCH BOX
Soak a paper napkin in vinegar and leave it inside the closed lunch box overnight.

RICHARD'S STAND-INS

As actors, both my wife, Tudi, and I know about stand-ins in the theater and on TV. We also know about stand-ins to use around the house when what you need isn't available there, and you don't want to disrupt things with a drive to the store. Here are some handy substitutes for the real thing.

Fireplace Matches	If you're out of those long fireplace matches and don't want to singe your hand with short matches, use a piece of dry spaghetti.
Toothpicks for Snacks	When baking pasta or rolled snacks, use dry spaghetti in place of toothpicks.
Freezer Ice Supply	Use a plastic egg carton or put water in sealed zip-locking bags.

Corkscrew	In place of a corkscrew, hold the neck of a room-temperature wine bottle under hot water from the tap. This expands the glass neck and makes prying the cork out easier.
Jar and Bottle Openers	If you don't have a bottle-cap opener for jars with metal lids, hold the metal lid under hot water from the tap as you would do for a missing corkscrew. This time, however, it's the metal lid that will expand faster than the glass jar, and it should open easily.
Snail Poison	A great stand-in for poison when your yard is infested with snails is ordinary salt. Ring the yard with a line of salt and, when snails touch the salt, they dissolve to snail heaven.
Ant Repellent	The safest and most effective way to repel ants without using poisons is to draw a thick chalk line. Ants will not walk across the chalk.
Stuck Sliding Doors	The sticking is usually from dirt and crud that builds up, so, first clean the track with a vacuum and brush. Then, coat with a non-oil-based lubricant such as graphite. Haven't got that? Then, rub the track with a wet bar of soap.
Kiddie Safety Latches	When kids are brought into a household without kids, there usually are no safety latches on cabinet doors to keep them from getting into mischief. Using rubber bands around cabinet door pulls acts as a temporary and effective stand-in when kids are visiting homes that are not child-proofed.

Shoe Polish Cloths	Old panty hose are great for polishing shoes.
Dusting Gloves	Once your sweat socks develop one hole too many, use them for dusting.

RICHARD'S RECYCLE, REUSE HINTS

We often throw away the plastic containers for butter, margarine, cottage cheese, yogurt, vinegar, and the like, but these plastic containers have multiple reuses. They can be reused as they are for Jell-O or pudding molds, containers for jewelry, office supplies, nails and screws, keys and so on around the house. They are also good for packing things in your luggage or car. In addition, you can take the large plastic containers such as the gallon jugs in which juice or water is packaged, and cut them in half about one-third to one-half way down. When you do this, you end up with two handy things: a funnel (top half turned upside down) and a good-sized pot in which to store larger items or a planter (punch a hole in the bottom for drainage) or a pot for holding charcoal briquettes that you set in various closets or the refrigerator for deodorizing purposes. Used plastic jugs are handy for holding washing-up water along with paper towels when you have kids in the car (and, let's face it, some messy adults, too). It's a good idea to label the jug *do not drink* and to warn children who can't read that it is only for washing.

There are a lot of uses you can make of plastic squeeze bottles and other containers when you have used up the mustard, detergent, vinegar, catsup, or whatever was originally in them.

Reused condiment squeeze bottles can be used for dispensing glue, grease for lubricating joints, spackle for plaster touch-ups, and grout for squeezing into joints. You are only limited by your imagination. For most of these second uses, you should choose a squeeze bottle with a top that will be airtight when not in use. Otherwise, the new contents (glue, grout, spackle might harden and become useless).

Another use for glass jars with lids such as baby food, jam, peanut butter, sauce, and other product containers is to hold items you use regularly in particular areas of the home. Nail or screw the lids onto the bottom of a shelf or cabinet, fill the jar with what you need at that location and screw the jar into the secured lid. This is a convenient, space-saving method of storing nails, screws, nuts, and bolts at your garage work bench or craft material in your den or sewing materials such as buttons and thread in the sewing room, and so on and on. (We resisted the temptation of saying, ". . . and sew on and on.")

Used plastic jugs have many uses. For example, if you live near the ocean or a lake, you can screw the lid tight on the empty jug so it will float and act as a buoy. You can string several together to mark areas in the water such as boat channels or even in your swimming pool you can use them to mark off areas where children shouldn't go. With the bottom cut off, the remainder with the handle is a handy scoop, dustpan, seed or fertilizer spreader. If you unscrew the cap, it becomes a perfect funnel for motor oil, water, chemicals, paints, or any other liquid. If you want to slowly drip water or chemicals into a garden bed or a tree root or a gofer hole or dispense almost any liquid gradually almost anywhere, punch a small hole that will let the liquid out a little at a time and set it where you want the drip to go.

When you've gotten a gift in a decorative box or tin, you can reuse it for many things, such as filling it with hard candy or cookies as a gift or to have around when children come visiting, or to store sewing and knitting things, ornaments, and jewelry.

GIFT BOXES OR BASKETS

Have a gift basket or box into which you put small items as you accumulate them. For example, sample shampoos and lotion bottles from hotels, hard candies, and miscellaneous items you collect along the way from parties, visits, and gifts to you. This then becomes a treasure trove from which you can create a new gift basket.

PRICE TAG REMOVAL

When you're giving a gift and you don't want the recipient to know the price, put some tape over the price tag and then rip it off. It may not always take off the price tag, but it usually pulls off the price printed on the tag.

EMPTY TISSUE BOXES

Empty tissue boxes are handy for use as trash containers where a big trash basket would be inconvenient, such as in your car or boat or other small place. When you have a cold, keep the empty box next to the new one by your bedside to alleviate the need to get up and toss the used tissues out.

RECYCLING TIPS

Here is how to prepare materials for the recycler.

Cans: Wash, remove labels, and smash flat.

Glass: Wash and remove any metal from necks. Sort into green, clear, and brown or yellow.

RICHARD'S GUIDE TO HOME IMPROVEMENT BOOKS

Abram, Norm, ed. *This Old House Essential Hand Tools: 26 Essential Tools to Renovate and Repair Your Home*. Des Moines, IA: This Old House Books, 1998.

Advanced Masonry (Home Repair and Improvement). Updated Series, Vol. 29. Alexandria, VA: Time Life Books, 1998.

Advanced Wiring (Home Repair and Improvement). Updated Series. Alexandria, VA: Time Life Books, 1998.

Advanced Woodworking (Home Repair and Improvement). Updated Series. Alexandria, VA: Time Life Books, 1998.

Algozzine, Robert. *Handyman's Little Book of Wisdom*. Merrillville, IN: ICS Books, 1996.

Bathroom Makeovers (Home Repair and Improvement). Vol 35. Alexandria, VA: Time Life Books, 1998.

Bennett, Allegra. *Renovating Woman: A Guide to Home Repair, Maintenance and Real Men*. New York: Pocket Books, 1997.

Best, Don. *The Do-It-Yourself Guide to Home Emergencies: From Breakdowns and Leaks to Cracks and Critters: Step-by-Step Solutions to the Toughest Problems*. Emmaus, PA: Rodale Press, 1996.

The Big Book of Easy Home Fix-Ups. Alexandria, VA: Time Life Books, 1997.

Brenhouse, Barbara, and Ellen Laird. *The Network of Home Repair & Decorating Services (Lairhouse Guides)*. Vernon, NJ: Lairhouse Publications, 1998.

Buracree, Tom, and Andy Pargh. *The Gadget Guru's Make-It-Easy Guide to Home Repair*. New York: Warner Books, 1997.

Carey, Morris, and James Carey. *Home Remodeling for Dummies*. St. Paul, MN: Hungry Minds Inc., 1998.

Carrell, Al. *Super Handyman: Al Carrell's 1000 Questions About Home Repair & Maintenance*. Indianapolis, IN: Summit Publications, 1997.

Cleaning (Home Repair and Improvement). Updated Series. Alexandria, VA: Time Life Books, 1997.

Closets, Space, and Storage (Home Repair and Improvement). Vol 33. Alexandria, VA: Time Life Books, 1998.

The Complete Book of Kitchen & Bathroom Renovation. Alexandria, VA: Time Life Books, 1998.

The Complete Book of Old House Repair & Renovation. Alexandria, VA: Time Life Books, 1998.

The Complete Guide to Home Wiring: A Comprehensive Manual, from Basic Repairs to Advanced Projects. Minnetonka, MN: Creative Publishing International, 1998.

Complete Kitchen & Bathroom Manual. Alexandria, VA: Time Life Books, 1997.

Dadd, Debra Lynn. *Home Safe Home: Protecting Yourself and Your Family from Everyday Toxics and Harmful Household Products in the Home*. New York: J. P. Tarcher, Inc., 1997.

Davidson, Homer L. *Troubleshooting and Repairing Microwave Ovens (Tab Electronics Technician Library)*. New York: McGraw-Hill Professional Publications, 1996.

Everyday Home Repairs Software: Black and Decker Home Improvement Library: How Things Get Done. Minnetonka, MN: Creative Publishing International, 1996.

The Family Handyman Power Tool Techniques & Tips. New York: Reader's Digest Adult, 1997.

The Family Handyman Updating Your Home: Easy Ways to Make Your Home Look and Work Better. New York: Reader's Digest Adult, 1996.

Finish Carpentry (Home Repair and Improvement). Updated Series, Vol. 31. Alexandria, VA: Time Life, 1998.

Fireplaces and Wood Stoves (Home Repair and Improvement). Alexandria, VA: Time-Life Books, 1997.

Fisher, Charles E. *Caring for Your Historic House: Heritage Preservation*. New York: Harry N. Abrams, 1998.

Get House Smart: The Easy Quick-Start Guide to the Workings of Your Home (Reader's Digest Smart Series). New York: Reader's Digest Adult, 1997.

Goldstein, Carolyn M. *Do It Yourself: Home Improvement in 20th-Century America*. New York: Princeton Architectural Press, 1998.

Greguire, Helen. *Collector's Guide to Toasters & Accessories: Identification & Values*. Paducah, KY: Collector Books, 1997.

Guide to Fixing over 200 Annoying Breakdowns. Emmaus, PA: Rodale Press, 1996.

Hamilton, Gene, and Katie Hamilton. *Home Improvement for Dummies*. St. Paul, MN: Hungry Minds, Inc., 1998.

―――. *Rules of Thumb for Home Building, Improvement and Repair*. New York: John Wiley and Sons, Inc., 1997.

Hamilton, Katie. *Do It Yourself. . . or Not?* New York: Berkeley Publishing Group, 1996.

Haege, Glenn, Kathy Stief, and Jerry Baker. *Fix It Fast & Easy! America's Master Handyman Answers the Most Asked "How To" Questions*. Southfield, MI: Master Handyman Press, Inc., 1996.

Handyman Home Storage Projects: A Room-by-Room Guide to Practical Storage Solutions (Family Handyman). New York: Readers Digest Adult, 1997.

Heldmann, Carl. *Be Your Own Home Renovation Contractor: Save 30% Without Lifting a Hammer*, revised and updated edition. Pownal, VT: Storey Books, 1998.

Herrick, Lynn. *The Woman's Hands-On Home Repair Guide*. Pownal, VT: Storey Books, 1997.

Hingley, Brian D. *Furniture Repair & Refinishing*. Saddle River, NJ: Creative Homeowner Press, 1998.

Home Do-It-Yourself Projects. New York: Reader's Digest Adult, 1996.

Home Improvements & Projects Index, 1990–1993. Ft. Atkinson, WI: Highsmith Press, 1996.

Home Masonry Repairs & Projects (Black and Decker Home Improvement Library). Minnetonka, MN: Creative Publishing Int., 1996.

Home Offices (Home Repair & Improvement). Alexandria, VA: Time Life Books, 1997.

The Home Workshop (Home Repair and Improvement). Updated Series. *Security (Home Repair and Improvement).* Vol. 13. Alexandria, VA: Time Life Books, 1996.

The Home Workshop (Home Repair and Improvement). Updated Series. Alexandria, VA: Time Life Books, 1997.

Insulating and Weatherproofing (Home Repair and Improvement). Updated Series. Alexandria, VA: Time Life Books, 1996.

Jones, Jack Payne. *Builder's Guide to Room Additions.* Carlsbad, CA: Craftsman Book Co., 1996.

Kennelly, Brett P., and Eddy Hall, contributor. *The Homeowners' Guide to Hiring Contractor's: How to Save Time, Money and Headaches by Hiring the Right Contractor for Your Job.* West Lafayette, IN: Information Services Group, 1997.

Kent, Cassandra. *Household Hints & Tips.* New York: DK Publishing, Inc., 1996.

King, June. *Helpful Household Hints: The Ultimate 90s Guide to Housekeeping.* Santa Monica, CA: Santa Monica Press, 1996.

Kitchen, Judith L. *Caring for Your Old House: A Guide for Owners and Residents.* Washington, D.C.: Preservation Press, 1996.

Kitchen Renovations (Home Repair and Improvement). Updated Series, Vol 32. Alexandria, VA: Time Life Books, 2000.

Krigger, John T. *Your Mobile Home: Energy and Repair Guide for Manufactured Housing.* Helena, MT: Saturn Resource Management, 1998.

Long, Charles. *Cottage Projects.* Toronto, ON: Warwick Publishing Inc., 1997.

MacLeod, Jean B. *If I'd Only Listened to My Mom, I'd Know How to Do This: Hundreds of Households Remedies.* New York: St. Martin's Press, 1997.

Maguire, Jack. *500 Terrific Ideas for Home Maintenance and Repair.* Reissue ed. New York: Budget Book Service, 1997.

Masonry (Home Repair and Improvement). Updated Series. Alexandria, VA: Time Life Books, 1997.

Meany, Terry, and Henry Tragert. *The Lazy Way to Care for Your Home (The Lazy Way Series).* New York: Macmillan General Reference, 1998.

Munn, Jeni E., and Joan Sittenfield. *The Modern Woman's Guide to Home Repair.* New York: Perigee, 1997.

New Fix-It-Yourself Manual. New York: Reader's Digest Adult, 1996.

New Living Spaces (Home Repair and Improvement). Alexandria, VA: Time Life Books, 1996.

O'Connor, Raymond. *The Healthy Home Environment Guide.* New York: Berkeley Publishing Group, 1996.

Outdoor Structures (Home Repair and Improvement). Updated Series. Alexandria, VA: Time Life Books, 1997.

Owen, David. *Around the House: Reflections on Life Under a Roof.* New York: Villard Books, 1998.

Peterson, Franklin. *How to Fix Damn Near Everything.* San Antonio, TX: Wings Press, 1996.

Philbin, Tom. *How to Hire a Home Improvement Contractor Without Getting Chiseled.* New York: St. Martin's Press, 1997.

————. *The Everything Home Improvement Book: Everything You Need to Know to Keep Your Home Looking—and Working—Better Than Ever (The Everything Series).* Holbrook, MA: Adams Media Corp., 1997.

Phillips, Bill ed. *This Old House Sourcebook: Where to Find and How to Use Tools and Materials to Fix and Improve Your Home.* Des Moines, IA: This Old House Books, 1997.

Powers, Chase M. *Builder's Guide to Cosmetic Remodeling (Builder's Guide Series).* New York: McGraw-Hill Professional Publishing, 1997.

Ramsey, Dan. *52 Easy Weekend Home Improvements: A Year's Worth of Money-Saving Projects,* 1998.

————. *Century 21 Guide to Remodeling Your Home.* Chicago, IL: Dearborn Trade, 1997.

Reeder, Curt. *The In-Home VCR Mechanical Repair & Cleaning Guide.* Indianapolis, IN: PROMPT Publications, 1996.

Repairing Furniture (Home Repair and Improvement). Updated Series. Alexandria, VA: Time-Life Books, 1997.

Schnaser, Gene L. *The Home Repair Emergency Handbook.* New York: Budget Book Service, 1996.

Shepherd, James M. *Be Your Own Contractor and Save Thousands,* 2nd ed.. Chicago, IL: Dearborn Publishing, 1996.

Smith, Terry. *Advanced Home Plumbing (Black & Decker Home Improvement Library)*. Minnetonka, MN: Creative Publishing International, 1997.

Taylor, Jeff, and Thomas Carpenter. *The Basement Book: Upstairs Downstairs: Reclaiming the Wasted Space in Your Basement*. Boston, MA: Houghton Mifflin Co., 1996.

Tenenbaum, David J. *The Complete Idiot's Guide to Trouble-Free Home Repair (Complete Idiot's Guides)*. Rickreall, OR: Alpha Books, 1996.

———. *The Pocket Idiot's Guide to Home Repair (Pocket Idiot's Guides)*. Malibu, CA: Alpha Books, Inc., 1998.

This Old House Essential Power Tools: 19 Essential Tools to Renovate and Repair Your Home. Des Moines, IA: This Old House Books, 1998.

Traister, John E., preface. *Home Inspection Handbook*. Carlsbad, CA: Craftsman House Book Co., 1997.

Ultimate Decks (Home Repair and Improvement). Updated. Alexandria, VA: Time Life Books, 1998.

Vandervort, Don. Home *Magazine's How Your House Works*. New York: Ballantine Books, 1997.

Walls and Ceilings (Home Repair and Improvement). Alexandria, VA: Time Life Books, 1996.

Windows and Doors (Home Repair and Improvement). Alexandria, VA: Time Life Books, 1997.

Wing, Charles. *The Big Book of Small Household Repairs: Your Goof-Proof Guide to Fixing Over 200 Annoying Breakdowns*. Emmaus, PA: Rodale Press, 1996.

Working With Wood (Home Repair and Improvement). Updated Series. Alexandria VA: Time-Life Books, 1997.

Worthington, Julian. *The New Encyclopedia of Home Repair*. Toronto, ON: Key Porter Books, 1996.

Yapp, Bob, and Rich Binsacca. *About Your House*. San Francisco, CA: Bay Books, 1997.

Ziegner, Richard, ed. *Walls, Floors & Ceilings*. Saddle River, NJ: Creative Homeowners Press, 1997.

INDEX

aluminum siding, cleaning, 118
animal first aid, 186
antique furniture, cleaning, 125
ants
  controlling, 128
  repelling, 5, 279
appliances
  in the bathroom, 49
  cleaning, 110
  packing for storage, 161–62
  unplugging before cleaning, 110
  repairing, 14–15
  and safety, 49
arthritis
  relieving with home remedies,
    266
artificial flowers, refreshing, 136
auto maintenance, 171–79
  battery care, 171
  brake fluid, 175
  bumper stickers, 172
  cats sleeping on parked cars, 172
  chrome care, 172

auto mechanics, 78–82
  attitude, 79
  Automotive Service Excellence, 79–80
  background check, 81–82
  evaluating the problem, 80
  post-car repair tips, 81
  price, 80–81
  specialty shops vs. general repair shops,
    80
  written estimates, 80
azaleas, caring for, 148

baby-sitters, 82–86
  basic instructions, 83–84
  before arrival, 82–83
  daytime baby-sitters, 86
  emergency information, 84
  house rules, 84–85
  upon return, 85
bacteria in water, 66
bad slats, keeping from slipping, 15
baking soda
  as a cleaning tool, 100

baking soda (*continued*)
  drains, opening with, 5
  garbage disposal odors, eliminating, *x*
barbecues, 206–8
  beach barbecue safety, 208–9
  cleanup, 208
  cooking, 206
  fire, putting out, 207–8
  fire, starting the, 207
  insect repellent, 208
  serving tips, 207
basements, 250–53
  danger, 252–53
  flooded, 250–52
bathroom fixtures
  storing heavy items, 5
  jamming the drain, 5
  lid down rule, 5
bathroom safety tips, 49–50
bathroom tiles, cleaning, 109
bathrooms, remodeling, 230–31
batteries
  extending life of, 244
  recharging, 22–23
  recycling, 23
battery care, 171
bedroom storage space, 154–58
bee stings, treatment for, 256–57
bleach, laundry tips for, 193
blenders, cleaning, 110
blood stains, removing, 133
blueberry, medicinal use for, 264
bolt removal, 232, 244
books, cleaning and repairing, 136
Booth, Cecil Hubert, 104
bottle opener, stand-ins for, 279
bottled water, 64–65
brake fluid, 175
bras, laundry tips for, 194
brass, cleaning, 136
breakables, packing for storage, 162
broiler pans, cleaning, 110–11
broken glass, picking up, 56
brooms, storage of, 100–10
brown sugar, keeping fresh, 93

brushes, as cleaning tools, 100
bug bites, relieving with vinegar, 265
building and remodeling, 230–53
  after-painting tip, 233–34
  basements, 250–53
  basic toolbox, 237–38
  bathrooms, 230–31
  batteries, 244
  do-it-yourself repair tips, 238–40
  drains, 245–46
  DUCT tape, 243
  glue, 241–42
  improvement safety, 231–32, 233
  knobs, loose, 243
  ladders, 240–41
  lightbulbs, broken, 245
  lightbulbs, removing recessed, 242–43
  nail removal, 244
  painting tips, 233, 233–34, 246–50
  remodeling, rules for, 234–36
  screw and bolt removal, 244
  sticking drawers, 243
  stuck bolts, 232
bulk buying, 42
bumper stickers, 172
burn marks, removing, 133
buttons, sewing and replacing, 199–200

cabinets
  cleaning, 111
  cleaning-out, 153–54
  as storage space, 152–53
calendula, medicinal use for, 264
can openers, 97
candle droppings
  carpets, getting out of, *x*
candlesticks, cleaning wax from, 136
canine care, 188–89
  chewing, 187
canned goods, keeping fresh, 93
car dealers, 27–28
  used cars, 32–33
car insurance, savings, 33–35
car jacking, safety tips, 181–82

car maintenance, 171–79
  battery care, 171
  brake fluid, 175
  bumper stickers, 172
  cats, 172
  chrome care, 172
  cold engine, 172
  dog hair, 172
  gas, 175–76
  locked out, 176–77
  oil, 173–74
  See also cars (buying)
car mechanics, 78–82
  attitude, 79
  Automotive Service Excellence, 79–80
  background check, 81–82
  evaluating the problem, 80
  post-car repair tips, 81
  price, 80–81
  specialty shops vs. general repair shops, 80
  written estimates, 80
carbon monoxide gas
  checking venting pipes, 2
  preventing poisoning from, 50–51
carpenter's glue, 241
carpet cleaners (professional), 86–87
  precleaning preparations, 87
  price, 86–87
  references and contract, 87
carpets
  candle droppings, getting out of, x
  cleaning, 118–20
  static, removing, 5
cars (buying)
  car dealers, 27–28
  closing the deal, 30–31
  refurbishing, 31–32
  shopping for, 23–27
  trade-ins, 28–30
  used cars, 32–33
cast-iron pots and pans
  cleaning, 115
cats sleeping on parked cars, 172

caulking, 11–14
  how to, 13–14
  kinds of, 11–13
  large cracks, repairing, 14
caustic products, danger of, 105
ceiling fans, cleaning, 137
celery, keeping fresh, 93
cell phones
  and travel emergencies, 181
cellulose cement, 242
ceramic floor tiles
  cleaning, 120
  repairing loose, 15–16
chamomile, medicinal use for, 264
chemical combinations, danger of, 105
chemical safety, 101
chewing gum, removing, 133
children (safety tips for), 267–70
  baby bottle ID, 267
  and cleaning products, 105
  falling out of bed, 269
  furniture corners, 267
  hooks and hanger rods, making accessible, 269
  important things for children to learn, 270
  memories, preserving, 269
  night lights, 268–69
  precocious wanders, 270
  shoes, 269–70
children
  personal cleanliness for, 260–61
  safety tips for, 267–70
chocolate
  and pets, 189
  removing stains, 134
Christmas trees, and safety, 51
chrome
  and car maintenance, 172
  polishing, 137
cigarette smoke, getting rid of, 278
circuit breakers, checking, 2–3
citrus fruit
  peeling and juicing tips, 90

cleaning, 98–141
  anti-Martha Stewart approach, 99–100
  the appointment system, 98–99
  assigning chores, 99
  bathroom, 106–8
  cleaners and tools, 100–104
  dangers, 105–6
  floors and walls, 118–24
  furniture, 124–28
  kitchens, 110–18
  miscellaneous, 134–41
  odors and unwanted smells, 131–32
  pest control, 128–31
  stains and marks, 133–35
  systematic, 98–100
  time management and, 99
  toilets, 108–9
cleaning chemicals safety, 101
cleaning dangers
  caustic products, 105
  chemical combinations, 105
  child protection, 105
  rags, 105–6
  solvents and painting products, 106
  ventilation, 105
  vinegar, 106
cleaning products, saving on, 42
closet chaos, eliminating, 156–58
clothes dryers
  cleaning and maintaining, 200–201
clothes hampers
  cleaning and maintaining, 200
clothing, removing ink from, x
club soda, as cleaning tool, 101–2
cobwebs, dusting, 137
cockroaches, controlling, x, 129
cocoa stains, removing, 134
coffee, saving on, 42
coffee filters, 97
coffee grinder, cleaning, 111
coffee makers and pots
  cleaning, 89, 111
coffee stains, removing, 134
cold engine, 172
colds, relieving with home remedies, 265

colored paper, burning in fireplace, 51
computer keyboards, cleaning, 137
contact lenses, cleaning, 137
contractors, 87–88
cooking and kitchen tips, 89–97
  clean kitchen, 89–90
  cooking tips, 90–93
  keeping food fresh, 93–96
  kitchen freshness, 96
  tools and supplies, 96–97
copper, cleaning, 137–38
copper-bottomed pots and pans
  cleaning, 115
corkscrew, stand-ins for, 279
corn, cooking tips, 90–91
corns, removing, 266
cough, relieving with home remedies, 265
countertops, cleaning, 112
coupon saving, 43
cracks, sealing, 10–11
crayon marks, cleaning off walls, x
credit card security, 68
crystal, cleaning, 112
Culinary Parts Unlimited, 15
cut flower care, 150
cutting boards, cleaning, 112

dated foods, 43
deck chairs, preventing slipping, 278
decorating, 163–70
  child's bedroom, 170
  entryway, 163–65
  feng shui, 165–66
  walls, 166–70
dentures, cleaning, 265
dish towels and cloths, 102
  cleaning, 90, 102
dishwashers, cleaning, 113
dogs
  care of, 188–89
  chewing damage, 43
dog hair, and car maintenance, 172
door security, 51
doorbell, repairing broken, 16–18
doors, sticking, 279

doorstops, 165
downspouts, checking, 3
drains, 245–46
   avoiding jamming, 5
   baking soda, opening with, 5
   cleaning, 117
drawers, sticking, 243
dry hair
   conditioning with home remedies, 265
dryers, 200–201
   ironing, 200
   irons and ironing, 201
   laundry tips, 193–96
DUCT tape, 243
dust cloths, cleaning, 90, 102

earthquakes, responding to, 73–74
echinacea, medicinal use for, 263–64
egg cartons, dated, 43
eggs
   cooking tips, 91
   keeping fresh, 93
electric pots, cleaning, 113
electrical appliances
   in the bathroom, 49
   and safety, 49
electrical tips, 276–77
electricity, 35–39
   energy savings, 36–38
   lightbulbs, saving on, 38–39
electrolysis, 218
emergencies
   clothing, 77
   emergency workers, assisting, 77
   responding to, 73–74
emergency kits, 73, 74, 182–83
   emergency phone cards, 179–80
   escape tool, 183–84
   evacuation survival kit, 76
   extra key, 180
   for your car, 182–83
   home survival kit, 74–76
   personal documents, 179
   personal survival kit, 76
   reflective safety jacket, 183

   for seniors, 272
   vigilance, 180
emergency lights, 277–78
energy savings, 36–38
entertaining, 203–13
   barbecue, 206–8
   creating a mood, 204
   dining rooms, 209–10
   fireplace fires, 210–13
   food and drink, 204–5
   food and drink safety, 205–6
   holiday book, 206
   theme parties, 205
epoxy glue, 241–42
evacuation survival kit, 76
eyeglass frames, repairing broken, 18
eyes, bathing with home remedies,
   266

fabric, measuring twice, 44
falls, preventing, 49–50, 261–63
faucets
   dripping, 219–21
   slow flow, 223–24
feng shui, 165–66
fertilizers, 145–46
feverfew, medicinal use for, 264
fiberglas, cleaning, 138
filter systems (water), 66–67
fire extinguishers, 51–52
fireplace fires, 210–13
   building a good fire, 210–11
   burning colored paper in, 51
   firewood, 211–13
   potpourri, 211
   safety, 211
fireplace matches, stand-ins for, 278
first aid, 273–74
   headache remedy, 274
   motion sickness, 274
   splinter removal, 274
flashlights, locating in the dark, 53
flatware, cleaning, 113
fleas, controlling, 191
flies, controlling, 129

floor tiles (repairing)
  curling, 19
  loose, 15–16
floors (cleaning)
  carpeting, 118–20
  ceramic tile and grout, 120
  linoleum, 121
  vacuuming, 120
  vinyl, 121
  wood, 122
food
  and entertaining, 204–5
  excessive salt in, 92
  freezing, 46–47
  refrigerating, 95
  safety, 60–61, 205–6
  storage, 95
food stains, removing from hands, 90
forced-air furnace, checking filter, 2
freezer ice supply, 278
freezer safety, 63–64
  disposal of, 63–64
  usage, 63
freezers, cleaning, 116
front door
  individualizing light, 151
  security, 51
frozen pipes, 218
fruit, keeping fresh, 94
fruit flies, controlling, 129
furniture
  refinishing, 167
  repairing loose legs, 20
  packing for storage, 162
furniture (cleaning), 124–28
  antique furniture, 125
  leather furniture, 125
  mattresses, 125
  patio furniture, 126
  plastic furniture, 126
  upholstery, 126–27
  wicker furniture, 127
  wood furniture, 127–28
furniture scratching, 192
fuses, locating in the dark, 53

garage, parking in, 173
garage doors, 53–56
  trimming with weather stripping, 6
garage floors, dealing with oily, 18–19
garbage disposals
  cleaning, 113
  jammed, 221–23
  odors, eliminating, x
gardening, 142–51
  garden lights, 149
  ground covers, 143–45
  garden tools, 147–49
  potted plants, 150–51
  yard, planning, 142–43
  yard care, 145–49
garlic, medicinal use for, 263
gas, 175–76
gift boxes or baskets, recycling, 281
gift wrap, making your own, 43
glass, picking up broken, 56
glass tabletops, cleaning, 138
glassware
  pouring hot liquid into, 6
  unsticking nested glasses, 6
glues, 241–42
  carpenter's glue, 241
  cellulose cement, 242
  epoxy glue, 241–42
  preventing dry out, 242
  PVA glue (polyvinyl acetate), 241
  super glue, 242
gophers, eliminating, 131
grains, keeping fresh, 94
grass stains, removing, 134
grease stains, removing, 134
greens (salad), keeping fresh, 94
grip, strengthening, 267
grocery stores
  and bargain brands, 44
ground covers, 143–45
grout, cleaning, 109, 120

hairbrushes, cleaning, 138
ham, cooking tips, 91
hand brushes, as cleaning tools, 100

hand washables, laundry tips for, 194
headache, home remedy for, 274
herbal medicine cabinet, 263–67
 blueberry, 264
 calendula, 264
 chamomile, 264
 echinacea, 263–64
 feverfew, 264
 garlic, 263
 lavender, 264
 mint, 264
 oregano, 264
 rosemary, 264
 sage, 263
 St. John's Wort, 264
hiccups
 relieving with home remedies, 265
hiring help, 78–88
 auto mechanics, 78–82
 baby-sitters, 82–86
 carpet cleaners, 86–87
 contractors, 87–88
home improvement books, 283–88
home improvement safety, 231–32, 233
home improvement scams, 39–41
home security tips, 57–59
home survival kit, 74–76
hot water heater
 checking for leaks, 2
 flushing sediment, 3
 maintenance, 202
house keys, hiding, 56–57
house training lapses, 191–92

improvement safety, 231–32, 233
ink stains, removing, x, 134
insect repellents, 69–72
 mosquito bite prevention, 71
 pesticides, 71–72
 tick bite prevention, 70
inspection checklist, 1–4
Insurance Institute for Highway Safety,
 34
ironing, 200
 ironing board covers, 201

irons, 201
 steam irons, 201
ivy-covered walls, 146

jar opener, stand-ins for, 279
jeans, laundry tips for, 194
jewelry, cleaning, 138
juice stains, removing, 134

keyboards, cleaning, 137
keys, hiding, 56–57
kiddie safety latches, 279
kidnaping, safety tips, 181–82
kitchen
 cabinets, cleaning, 111
 childproofing, 59–60
 countertops, cleaning, 112
 deodorizing, 96
 food safety, 60–61
 safety, 59–62
kitchen storage space
 creating new, 154
 cubbyholes, 158–59
 pantry, creating a, 159–60
 sink as counter, 159
knobs, loose, 243

label removal, and laundry, 195
ladders, 240–41
lampshades, cleaning, 138–39
laundry tips, 193–96
 bleach, 193
 bras, 194
 brights, 194
 energy saver, 194
 hand washables, 194
 jeans, 194
 label removal, 195
 lint prevention, 195
 loading washing machine, 195
 socks, 195
 sorting, 196
 whites, 196
 wool sweaters, 196
 wrinkle prevention, 196

lavender, medicinal use for, 264
lawn maintenance
    fertilizing, 145
    mowing, 144–45
    seeding, 146
lead in water, 65
leather furniture, cleaning, 125
leftovers, keeping fresh, 94
lid handles, replacing missing, 19
lightbulbs
    broken, 245
    changing, 62
    removing recessed, 242–43
    saving money on, 38–39
linoleum floors, cleaning, 121
lint prevention, 195
lipstick marks, removing, 135
locked out of car, 176–77
locks, repairing sticking, 19
luggage identification, 73
lumber, measuring twice, 44
lunch box, deodorizing, 278

marks and stains, 133–35
    blood, 133
    burn marks, 133
    chewing gum, 133
    chocolate and cocoa, 134
    coffee and tea, 134
    grass, 134
    grease, 134
    ink, 134
    juice stains, 134
    and the laundry, 196–98
    lipstick, 135
    nail polish, 135
    pet hair, 135
    smudge marks, 134
master valve, 218
mattresses, cleaning, 125
meat, keeping fresh, 94
mechanics (auto), 78–82
    attitude, 79
    Automotive Service Excellence, 79–80

background check, 81–82
evaluating the problem, 80
post-car repair tips, 81
price, 80–81
specialty shops vs. general repair shops, 80
written estimates, 80
medicine cabinet (herbal), 263–67
    blueberry, 264
    calendula, 264
    chamomile, 264
    echinacea, 263–64
    feverfew, 264
    garlic, 263
    lavender, 264
    mint, 264
    oregano, 264
    rosemary, 264
    sage, 263
    St. John's Wort, 264
medicine cabinet equipment, 256
mice, controlling, 129–30
microwave
    boiling water in, 62
    cleaning, 113–14
    using round bowls, 97
mildew, removing, 135
milk cartons, dated, 43
mint, medicinal use for, 264
mirrors
    packing for storage, 162
    un-fogging, 109
moles, eliminating, 131
mosquito bite prevention, 71
motion sickness, home remedy for, 274
mud in water, 66

nail polish stains, removing, 135
nail removal, 244
non-stick pots and pans
    cleaning, 115

odors and smells
    eliminating and/or covering, 131–32
    garbage disposal odors, eliminating, x

litter box, 192
  odor chasers, 275–76
oil, 173–74
onions, peeling and slicing tips, 91
oregano, medicinal use for, 264
orphan socks, 198
  sewing supplies, 200
  used for dusting, 280
outdoor party lights, 44
oven
  cleaning, 114
over-the-counter medicines, 254–56

packing tips (rented storage space), 161–62
  appliances, 161–62
  furniture, 162
  mirrors and breakables, 162
paintbrushes, cleaning, 45
painting
  extra paint, 8
  masking hardware, 7
  picking color, 7
  picking type of paint, 7
  preparatory work, 6–7
  taking breaks, 8
  using drop cloths, 7–8
  where to begin, 8
painting products, danger of, 106
painting tips, 233
  after-painting tip, 233–34
  guide to, 246–50
paintings (artwork), cleaning, 139
pans (cleaning), 114–15
  cast-iron, 115
  copper-bottomed, 115
  non-stick, 115
  stainless steel, 115
pantyhose
  keeping in freezer, 45
  as polishers, 45
  uses for, 102
parasites in water, 66
parking in garage, 173

patio furniture, cleaning, 126
personal care, 254–74
  bee stings, treatment for, 256–57
  children, safety tips for, 267–70
  children, personal cleanliness for, 260–61
  falls, preventing, 261–63
  herbal medicine cabinet, 263–67
  over-the-counter medicines, 254–57
  personal hygiene tips, 257–59
  pioneer first aid, 273–74
  prescription medicines, 256
  seniors, safety tips for, 270–73
personal documents
  and travel emergencies, 179
personal hygiene tips, 257–59
personal survival kit, 76
pest control
  ants, 128
  cockroaches, controlling, x, 129
  flies, 129
  fruit flies, 129
  mice, rats, and other rodents, 129–30
  silverfish, 130–31
  spiders, 131
  spider mites, 131
pesticides, 71–72
pet collars, reflective tape on, 188
pet food attracting insects, 190
pet hair
  on upholstery, 191
  removing, 135
pets, 185–92
  animal first aid, 186
  chewing damage, 43
  fleas, 191
  furniture scratching, 192
  hair on upholstery, 191
  house training lapses, 191–92
  litter box odors, 192
  pet food attracting insects, 190
  reflective tape on collars, 188
  stray cats, 192
  vacations and, 186–87
  veterinarians, 185–86

pewter, cleaning, 139
phone cards, 45
  and travel emergencies, 179–80
photo albums, maintaining, 45
piano keys, cleaning, 139
pickpockets, deterring, 73
pictures, cleaning, 139
pioneer first aid, 273–74
  headache remedy, 274
  motion sickness, 274
  splinter removal, 274
pipes
  frozen pipes, 9
  winterizing, 8
plants, poisonous, 62
plastic bags, storing, 155
plastic containers
  cleaning, 115–16
  saving, 45–46
plastic furniture, cleaning, 126
plumbing, 216–29
  basic facts, 218–19
  electrolysis, 218
  faucets, slow flow, 223–24
  faucets, dripping, 219–21
  frozen pipes, 218
  garbage disposal, jammed, 221–23
  master valve, 218
  showerhead, unclogging, 216–17
  sink drains, clogged, 227–29
  toilet clogs, preventing, 217–18
  toilet overflow, 217
  toilet repair, 224–27
poison ivy
  treating with home remedies, 266
poisonous plants, 62
possessions, proving ownership, 46
potatoes
  baking tips, 91
  keeping fresh, 95
  preventing boiling over, 92
pots (cleaning), 114–15
  cast-iron, 115
  copper-bottomed, 115

  non-stick, 115
  stainless steel, 115
potted plants, 150–51
power bill, managing, 35–36
power steering fluid, 175
prescription medicines, 256
price tag removal, 282
PVA glue (polyvinyl acetate), 241

radiator coolant, 174
rags, combustibility of, 105–6
rats, controlling, 129–30
Rechargeable Battery Recycling
  Corporation (RBRC), 22
recycling, 280–81, 282
  gift boxes or baskets, 281
  price tag removal, 282
  tissues boxes, 282
reflective safety jacket, 183
refrigerator safety, 63–64
  disposal, 63–64
  usage, 63
refrigerators
  cleaning, 116
  deodorizing, 96
remodeling, rules for, 234–36
repair jobs, 46
  tips, 238–40
roaches, controlling, x, 129
rodents, controlling, 129–30
roof, checking, 4
roof gutters, checking, 3
rosemary, medicinal use for, 264
rust
  cleaning from tools, 232
  shaving cream can rings, preventing, 139–40
  in water, 66

safety, 48–77
  disaster, dealing with, 73–77
  in-house precautions, 48–68
  outside the home, 68–73
sage, medicinal use for, 263
St. John's Wort, medicinal use for, 264

salad greens, keeping fresh, 94
salt
    dealing with excessive in food, 92
Savings in Your Pocket, 43
scalding water, 67–68
scissors, sharpening, 46
screen doors, 147
screw removal, 244
scrub brushes
    as cleaning tools, 100
seniors (safety tips for), 270–73
    bandage removal, 273
    emergency kit, 272
    furniture corners, 267
    gripping things, 272–73
    home emergencies, 271–72
    important phone numbers, posting,
        272
    medicine, 271
    purse guard, 273
    stamps, licking, 273
    walkers, 272
sewing supplies, 200
shakers, personalized, 97
shaving cream can rings, preventing, 139–
        40
shoe care, 197
shoe polish cloths, 280
shopping and saving money, 21–47
    electricity, 35–41
    major savings, 22–35
    miscellaneous, 41–47
    organizing, 44
shower
    car wax, 107
    cleaning, 106–7
    chips and scratches, 107
    decals and stickers, removing, 107
    drain, 108
    showers heads, 108
    sliding doors, lubricating, 107
    soap scum, 107
showerhead, unclogging, 216–17
silver, cleaning, 140
silverfish, controlling, 130–31

sinks
    cleaning, 117
    clogged drains, 227–29
skunk odor, eliminating, 132
"sleep tight," 126
sling doors, dealing with sticking, 19
smells and odors
    eliminating and/or covering, 131–32
    garbage disposal odors, eliminating, x
    litter box, 192
    odor chasers, 275–76
smoke detectors, checking, 2
smudge marks, removing, 134
snail poison, 279
socks, 195
    orphan socks, 198
    sorting, 196
    used for dusting, 280
solvents, danger of, 105
soup
    freezing, 46–47
    oversalted, 92
sore throat
    relieving with home remedies, 266
spider mites, controlling, 131
spiders, controlling, 131
spills, preventing, 90
spinach, cleaning, 95
splinter removal, 274
sponge mops
    cleaning, 103
    keeping damp, 103
sponges, sanitizing, 103
stainless steel pots and pans
    cleaning, 115
stains and marks, 133–35
    blood, 133
    burn marks, 133
    chewing gum, 133
    chocolate and cocoa, 134
    coffee and tea, 134
    grass, 134
    grease, 134
    ink, 134
    juice stains, 134

stains and marks (*continued*)
   and the laundry, 196–98
   lipstick, 135
   nail polish, 135
   pet hair, 135
   smudge marks, 134
stamps, unsticking, 47
steel wool, 103
stickers, removing, 140
storage boxes, hanging, 156
storage rentals, 160–62
   agreement, 160–61
   insurance, 161
   packing tips, 161–62
   routine check-ups, 161
storage space, 152–62
   expanding, 152–58
   new, 158–60
   storage rentals, 160–62
stray cats, 192
stucco, cleaning, 121
stuffed toys, cleaning, 140
sunburn pain, soothing, 266
super glue, 242
sweat socks, used for dusting, 280

tablecloths, removing spots from, 140
tea kettles, cleaning, 117
tea stains, removing, 134
teas, saving on, 42
teeth, cleaning, 266
telephone, disinfecting, 140
telephone calls, unwanted, 275
television screen, cleaning, 141
thermoses, cleaning, 117
throw rugs, 64
tick bite prevention, 70
tiles
   cleaning, 109
   repairing loose, 15–16
   repairing curling, 19
tiny holes, filling, 234
tiny screws and nails, putting in, 233
tires, 177–79
tissues boxes, uses for empty, 282

toilets
   avoiding jamming the drain, 5
   cleaning, 42, 108–9
   clogs, preventing, 217–18
   lid down rule, 5
   overflow, 217
   repair, 224–27
   storing heavy items on lid, 5
toolbox (basic), 237–38
tools
   cleaning rust from, 232
   maintaining, 47
toothbrushes
   as cleaning tool, 100
toothpicks for snacks
   stand-ins for, 278
transmission fluid, 174–75
trash barrels
   keeping animals out of, 9
travel tips, 179–84
   car jacking, theft and kidnaping, 181–82
   cell phones, 181
tub
   cleaning, 106–7
   chips and scratches, 107
   decals and stickers, removing, 107
   drain, 108
   soap scum, 107

unwanted telephone calls, 275
upholstery
   cleaning, 126–27
   pet hair on, 191
upset stomach
   relieving with home remedies, 266

vacations and pets, 186–87
   veterinarians, 185–86
vases, cleaning, 141
vacuum cleaners, 103
vacuuming, 120
vegetable bin, lining with paper, 95
vegetable gardens, 147
   watering, 147
vegetables, cooking tips, 91

Venetian blinds, cleaning, 141
ventilation, danger of, 105
veterinarians, 185–86
vigilance
    and travel emergencies, 180
vinegar
    danger of, 106
    shower walls, cleaning, 107
    uses for, 104
vinyl floors
    cleaning, 121
    tiles, repairing curling, 19

wallpaper, cleaning, 123
walls (cleaning), 122–2
    aluminum siding, 118
    crayon marks, x
    stucco, 121
    wallpaper, 123
    wood paneling, 123
wardrobe (maintaining), 193–202
    buttons, 199–200
    clothes hampers, 200
washing machines
    cleaning and maintaining, 201–2
    loading, 195
wastebasket liners, 104
wasted food, preventing, 92
water safety, 64–66
    bacteria and parasites, 66
    bottled water, 64–65
    chemicals, 65
    filter systems, 66–67
    lead, 65
    rust and mud, 66
    scalding water, 67–68
wax cereal box liners, use for, 47, 95
wax drippings, removing, 141

weather stripping, 11
whipping cream, cooking tip, 93
wicker furniture, cleaning, 127
window blind cords, replacing, 245
window screens, cleaning, 123–24
window shades, that won't roll up,
    19
windows
    cleaning, 42, 123–24
    sticking, dealing with, 19
wine, freezing leftover, 96
wine bottles, opening, 97
wood floors, cleaning, 122
wood paneling, cleaning, 123
wooden bowls, cleaning, 117
wooden furniture
    cleaning, 127–28
    refinishing, 167
    repairing loose legs, 20
wool sweaters, laundry tips for, 196
working at home, 213–15
    comfort, 214
    cubbyhole syndrome, 214
    decorate, 214–15
    L-shape work area, 213
    mobility, 214
    privacy, 215
    telephone tips, 215
wrinkle prevention, 196

yards
    care, 145–49
    lawn maintenance, 144–45
    planning, 142–43
    seeding, 146
yeast infections, preventing, 265

zipper lubrication, 199